D1438760

NEWS FROM A NEW REPUBLIC

Ireland in the 1950s

NEWS FROM A
NEW REPUBLIC

Ireland in the 1950s

TOM GARVIN ∾

Gill & Macmillan

Gill & Macmillan Ltd
Hume Avenue, Park West, Dublin 12
with associated companies throughout the world
www.gillmacmillan.ie

© Tom Garvin 2010
978 07171 4659 8

Index compiled by Helen Litton
Typography design by Make Communication
Print origination by Carole Lynch
Printed and bound by MPG Books, Cornwall

This book is typeset in Linotype Minion and
Neue Helvetica.

The paper used in this book comes from the wood pulp
of managed forests. For every tree felled, at least one
tree is planted, thereby renewing natural resources.

A CIP catalogue record for this book is available
from the British Library.

5 4 3 2 1

In memory of Michael Mills, great journalist,
old friend

CONTENTS

ACKNOWLEDGEMENTS

I wish to acknowledge the advice, assistance and information of many people: at Boston College, the encouragement and assistance of Thomas Hachey, Kevin Kenny, Joseph Nugent, Robert O'Neill, Robert Savage, James Smith and Liz Sullivan in the Irish Studies Program (*semper floreat!*) at 300 Hammond Street, Chestnut Hill; David Horne in Archives at BC and the staff at the O'Neill Library, in particular Howard Martin, good at asking interesting if occasionally unanswerable questions.

In University College, Dublin, my intellectual debts are, as usual, legion. Bryan Fanning supplied a lively, well-informed and often funny sounding-board and Andreas Hess an energetic, if occasionally frenetic, microclimate of methodological criticism. Nicholas Williams gave unexpected perspectives, as usual. John Horgan of Dublin City University has been my mentor and kindred spirit on the politics of Irish journalism and on Seán Lemass for many years; as he says himself, *aithníonn ciaróg ciaróg eile.* His extraordinary generosity in sharing his own research notes has been unprecedented in this writer's experience. Tomás Finn generously gave me access to his PhD thesis on Tuairim. Maire Garvin put up with me, as usual, in both America and Ireland. Thanks are due to UCD for giving me leave of absence during the year 2006/7 to work in Boston College at an early stage of this project and to Attracta Ingram, head of the School of Politics and International Relations at UCD, for her unstinting loyalty and support for this particular old-stager. John Coakley gave me house room during the gestation of this project and another one as well. I wish also to thank Dr Kieran Allen of UCD and Prof. Peadar Kirby of the University of Limerick for providing me with intellectual reassurance of a quite original if apparently unintentional kind.

Elsewhere I have benefited from conversations with many persons living or departed. Among the quick, Dermot Humphreys, Frank Litton, John O'Dowd, Fergal Tobin and Ken Whitaker. Fergal, the prince of Irish editors and an old friend, has been his usual encouraging self and a tower of strength. Among the departed, Todd Andrews, Michael Mills, Desmond Roche, Tom Barrington, Bob Briscoe, James Deeny, Willie Philbin and John Garvin unintentionally introduced me to their world, and I suppose I have never quite escaped from it.

Chapter 1

INTRODUCTION

ANOTHER COUNTRY

Some time in the late fifties, going home in mid-afternoon from school in Dublin, I was standing on the steps outside what was then Harcourt Street railway station, waiting for a number 14 bus to get me back home to Dartry. A priest came out of the station, evidently in a hurry, cut through the bus queue, and jumped into his Morris Minor, which was parked outside. (In the Dublin of fifty years ago there was no parking problem.) The street was two-way and almost empty. He executed a rapid U-turn, apparently intending to drive to the city centre. Simultaneously a motorcyclist came round the corner from Harcourt Road and struck the Morris broadside on. The motorbike had the right of way. The unfortunate rider flew over the car, landed with a dull thud on the roadway, and lay very still. A small crowd gathered round his body. The priest got out of the car and called out to no-one in particular, 'Is he all right?' He then got back hurriedly into his car and fled down Harcourt Street. I was so nonplussed I didn't have the wit to take his number. I have no idea what happened to the rider. Eventually an ambulance came along and picked him up, alive and injured or, perhaps, dead. Possibly the priest phoned for help; even now I still hope he did.

This is one of my abiding memories of the fifties in Ireland; it somehow summarises the way things were often done at that time. Things happened to people, and explanations were not given, or even sought. A girl I knew fairly well was raped while going home along the banks of the River Dodder, and everyone knew about it. No-one, however, talked about it out loud, few even in whispers.

There were Protestants and Jews as well as Catholics in Dartry. I thought Jews were an exotic kind of Protestant; but religious issues were never discussed, or rather the relationships between religions were not spoken of by adults. When I was about eleven I was playing toy soldiers with two other boys, one a Protestant and one a Jew, from around the corner. We kids sorted it out amicably among ourselves: Jews had it cushy, because they only had to believe in God; Protestants had a tougher row to hoe, because they had to believe in Jesus as well; while we Catholics were burdened with Our Lady on top of the other two. Having concluded this much, we all lost interest in the knotty problems of theology, a word we had never heard of, and went back to the far more interesting topic of Tommies and Nazis or Japs and Yanks.

Protestant kids stopped playing with you when they reached twelve years of age, an unexplained and much-resented mystery. Authority was commonly seen as capricious and possibly dangerous: you never knew who might get annoyed by something you did or said. Nor did you know why. All kinds of topics of everyday concern seemed to be under some kind of unspoken taboo. Secrecy and obscure systems of responsibility, or irres-ponsibility, prevailed. Admittedly this was a child's view of things in any time and in any place, but the perspectives of childhood seemed to persist sometimes into adulthood in the other country that the Ireland of that time was.

A fascinating example of an adult version of my little uncom-pleted tale of Harcourt Street is furnished by Gerard Whelan and Carolyn Swift in their joint study of the bizarre and unexplained illegal attempt by the Gardaí to stop an allegedly obscene play, *The Rose Tattoo* by Tennessee Williams, in a Dublin fringe theatre in

1957. Swift, with her husband, Alan Simpson, had founded and run the tiny Pike Theatre for some time without comment or molestation. The policemen had not even seen the play in question, and Simpson refused, as was his legal right, to take the play off. He spent a night in the cells, and the shamefaced Gardaí released him the following morning. The play finished its run unmolested, the police evidently knowing that they were out of order. Simpson, an army officer, was given an informal guard by men of his unit, presumably in case the Special Branch tried something. The soldiers in fact had built the theatre in their spare time, at Simpson's instigation.

Simpson was ruined by the costs of his defence, though he was found innocent even by the standards of that time. The state's case was thrown out by the court, but no costs were given against it, in what seems like a characteristic piece of mean-mindedness. The marriage broke up, Simpson sold his house to pay the legal bills and subsequently went to make a new life in Britain, while Swift went to work in television. It took Carolyn Swift *fifty years* to find out what probably drove elements in the Government to behave in such a strange, bullying and incoherent way. It seems that the Gardaí were ordered by the Minister for Justice, Oscar Traynor, to close down an allegedly obscene performance that was actually nothing of the sort. This was apparently to ensure that the minister and the Fianna Fáil Government of Éamon de Valera, administering a literary censorship that was extreme even by the standards of that strange time, could appear to be more censorious and Catholic than the Knights of Columbanus.[1]

Traynor had been put up to it by Fianna Fáil backbenchers and others who imagined all kinds of thrilling and immoral goings-on among the secularised and free-thinking literati of Dublin. Two years previously he had defied the Catholic authorities by attending a soccer match between 'communist Yugoslavia' and Ireland, and he may have been trying to mend a fence. For years it was assumed by the general public that the legendary John Charles McQuaid, autocratic Catholic Archbishop of Dublin, had vetoed the play. In reality he had nothing to do with it, other than being such a power in the land that even senior politicians, many of them anti-clericals and tough revolutionary gunmen in their youth of thirty-five years earlier, were somewhat afraid of him. For years afterwards Irish soldiers in basic training were taught to ignore orders that were prefaced by 'Traynor says.' Oscar's final achievement was to replace the mythical O'Grady as the figure to be disobeyed.

The Republic of Ireland was the product of a revolution that, like most revolutions, removed a ruling class and replaced it with another. British Ireland was replaced by an Irish Ireland that was uncertain of itself and of its class and status divisions. As revolutions go, the Irish one had been a reasonably civilised affair, the remains of the old Anglo-Irish, mainly Protestant, upper class remaining more or less unmolested. One of them, in Anglo-Irish Malahide, reminisced fondly many years later:

The fact that an Irish Free State did exist was hardly noticeable. If the Paddies and Bridies who had been the servants of the old Ireland—gardeners and kitchenmaids, errand boys and shop girls—were aware that they had won their political independence, they showed no sign of it. They made little attempt to exploit it to secure better pay or conditions; they too carried on as though the Treaty had made no difference . . . If a few of the younger ones grew 'bolshy', there always seemed to be an unlimited supply of their elders to fall back on; characters who might have stepped out of the pages of Somerville and Ross. These, we would point out to visiting English friends as really Irish—Murphy the gardener, Christie the postman, Vincie the ferryman—with their fine flow of language, their gift for casual repartee, and their instinctive ability to put a stranger at his ease by making him feel intelligent and perceptive and popular. We loved them as a landowner in the deep south loves his negro servants, because they knew their place and stayed in it; but we did not think of them as people; pets, rather.[2]

However, the greater, mainly Catholic, society did not know its place. As late as the nineteen-fifties the society itself, in the absence of the old aristocracy, was presided over by a rather populist democracy and a popular Catholic Church. Irish society was divided over who had responsibility for governing the country, and an underground and rather confused struggle was going on between secular and ecclesiastical authorities, neither being quite sure who was in control, or even who ought to be in control. All this was going on behind closed doors, and the general public merely heard incoherent noises and shouts and were not consulted about issues that did, after all, concern their own collective future.

This situation even affected economic policy, the Government vacillating between reflecting the interests of agriculture and the few existing protected industries on the one hand and preparing the country for a free-trade era, an era that pretty well everyone saw coming, on the other. Similarly censorship, the issue of Northern Ireland and the growth of demand for education were all the subjects of a deep ambivalence and an almost pathological irresolution. Eventually various Gordian knots were cut, but it took time; some would say that indecision and vacillation, combined with a tendency to make daft decisions rather than make none, have become traditional and ineradicable traits of Irish government.

This book is in part an investigation into why things happened the way they did and, as in some earlier work of mine, why things didn't happen—an even trickier exercise in investigation.[3] The public record of expressed public opinion of the time constitutes the principal data. The methodological starting point is the proposition that the opinions of intelligent observers of the time are to be canvassed and respected unless they are very obviously prejudiced, incompetent or extreme. The main body of evidence used is an informal and unsystematic, but complete, survey of the three Dublin daily newspapers of the time: the *Irish Independent, Irish Press* and *Irish Times,* between 1948 and 1962. This has been supplemented by an extensive, but less complete, examination of other Irish journalism of the time, in particular of papers that appeared to express views associated with significant sections of opinion, whether Catholic, nationalist, republican, liberal, unionist or socialist in general tenor. Dublin journalism is assumed, somewhat heroically, to be the main conduit of thinking about public policy to government.

The approach is empiricist, even of the barefoot variety, and it cannot claim the rigorous and measurable, if unimaginative, accuracy of a classic social science quantitative content analysis. However, it can be claimed that a serious attempt was made to assess accurately and sympathetically the main strands of public opinion expressed by journalists and other commentators at the time. As already suggested, there is always the problem of the lies of silence: the things they were not permitted to say, would not say, or were not in them to say. The solution here has to be the old, inevitable and dodgy one of reading, or pretending to read, the minds of dead people. It must further be remembered that what is written in the papers does not reflect the opinions of the mainstream of the population. Writers are sometimes statistically atypical or even mildly peculiar people, and their opinions tend generally—with some exceptions—to be to the left and among the more liberal of the general population. However, there is presumably some relationship between what is written in the newspapers and the opinions of those who buy them. Furthermore, broadsheet newspapers tend to be read by those who are fairly literate and commonly of higher educational level than average, and they were therefore likely to be the opinion-formers and leaders of the society before the explosion of the electronic mass media in the following decades.

COMING OF AGE

The fifties are the last decade in which a pre-television Ireland can be observed at work and play. It was in many ways a very different country from its successor of the early twenty-first century. It could be argued that the country was not only pre-television but also in some ways pre-radio, as radio broadcasting was on a far more modest scale than it would be later. The state-controlled station, Radio Éireann, for example, went off the air during the working hours between ten and one o'clock, and again from half-two to five o'clock in the afternoon. Despite these restrictions it got in some rather good children's programmes, an irreverent comedy series ('Living with Lynch'), several family soaps and entertaining quiz programmes. Traditional music began its revival on Radio Éireann, particularly through 'The Ballad Maker's Saturday Night' series with Donagh MacDonagh and Ciarán Mac Mathúna in the mid-fifties. Radio Éireann also had a feature that became known throughout the world: tap-dancing on radio. (I have not made that one up.)

BBC stations broadcast no recorded popular music, because of union restrictions, and had a resident orchestra to play inferior versions of current hits instead. If you wanted to hear Elvis Presley or Cliff Richard you listened to Radio Éireann sponsored programmes at lunch hour or, in the evenings, to Radio Luxembourg, a uniquely commercial station in a world of state-controlled broadcasting. For what were called negro spirituals and for rather good classical jazz you went to AFN, the American Forces Network, broadcasting from Germany. AFN was the ultimate in cool. We young commies also listened occasionally to

Radio Moscow, and found it boring; it gave you long lectures on the superiority of something called Soviet man.

The country was poor and, more worryingly, was getting relatively poorer in a western Europe that was bouncing back from wartime conditions in an extraordinary burst of economic growth. In some ways it was archaic. Flocks of sheep and herds of cattle walked through the streets of Dublin on their way to the cattle boats for Britain. Equally bucolic scenes could be seen elsewhere. Children commonly went barefoot in summer. Educational levels were low, with most children leaving school at the age of twelve.

Terence Brown has made the argument that the period of isolation caused by the Second World War began not exactly to make a nation out of the twenty-six counties of independent Ireland but at least to make that entity be perceived as the inevitable unit for collective political action. A slow realisation was dawning in the forties and fifties, despite much noisy denial both in rhetoric and in militant action on the part of the IRA, that partition was no temporary improvisation and that Northern Ireland was an entity that was not going to go away, mainly because the bulk of its population wanted it to continue to exist and to adhere to the union with Britain.[4]

The argument that partition itself was the root cause of Irish underdevelopment was one that was commonly made. Ulster, it was argued by many nationalists, was the only part of Ireland that had successfully industrialised in the nineteenth century, and a truncated republic, deprived of its industrial arm, would never be viable unless the injustice of partition was finally ended. However, this argument increasingly looked suspiciously like an excuse for failure. It also began to seem more and more irrelevant to the actual parlous circumstances of the Republic. Despite the stagnation of the country's mainly rural economy, Dublin by 1948 had become recognisably a modern city, with a large work force of increasingly skilled workers and a growing white-collar class of businessmen, civil servants, professional workers, journalists and academics; the older city of Olympian imperial officials and a huge population of unskilled labourers had almost evaporated. The notorious Georgian slums of old Dublin that featured in O'Casey's classic plays still survived but were gradually being demolished and replaced with somewhat soulless but recognisably modern and well-built council houses in suburban estates far from the old city.[5]

However, rural ways of familial and social organisation succeeded in transferring themselves to the city, and Dublin remained for a time an uneasy mixture of rural and urban styles of life. The city became, and remained, the main conduit through which outside ideas, standards, fashions and books penetrated the popular culture of the country. Its dominance, already established by 1950, was to become overwhelming by 1990.

Not least, Dublin was the centre of a national press, publishing daily and weekly newspapers that were read by most national and local opinion-formers, and there was also an increasingly lively flotilla of literary and political periodicals, which managed to survive in a city that could, just about, provide a sufficient market to keep a small magazine's body and soul together. Despite censorship and an extraordinarily aggressive anti-intellectualism, the forties and fifties saw the emergence of a new generation of young writers, able to see their own work in print in their own country for the first time in several decades.[6] A new wave of journalists emerged, expressing cautiously views that were more radical or, more subversively, more liberal than those of their predecessors. Times were about to change, and the fifties were to see a kind of underground struggle over culture and politics that was eventually to change the face of the country.

The period 1948–62 was, then, a crucial period of transition in the Republic, or so it has come to be seen in retrospect; so much so that commentators who have made that claim have occasionally been accused of engaging in hindsight wisdom—a wisdom that, as everyone thinks they know, is thought to be always accurate. It usually isn't. To anticipate the argument, or rather the observation, one of the more satisfactory conclusions this book is able to come to is that the commentators of the time, writing with premonitions but with no sure awareness of what the future might bring, would have agreed with that hindsight wisdom. Many of them sensed that transition was occurring, even though, of course, they could not engage in detailed prophecy. Furthermore, they were divided over the nature of the transition that was occurring. Some foresaw failure and national extinction, others predicted prosperity and cultural change.

Occasionally full-blown prophecy was actually attempted. In 1950 the Christian Brothers, perhaps the most important teaching order in Ireland and the former of much of the political mentality of the general male population of the time, made exactly such an attempt, in Irish-language comic-book form designed for children. A copy of it was proudly presented to Éamon de Valera, leader, in opposition, of the Fianna Fáil party. The island is presented in little pictures as having been colonised millennia ago by Neolithic farmers, with Newgrange being built later on by master craftsmen and with later legendary invasions culminating in the coming of the Milesian Celts, associated vaguely with *Mileadh Spáinne* or *Miles Hispaniae* (Soldier of Spain). Then along came St Patrick and a golden age of monasteries; piety and learning resulted from this happy marriage of Celtic culture and Christianity. All this was to be symbolised by the Ardagh Chalice and the Book of Kells. Then we had the Viking raids, brutal *Lochlannaigh* burning down the magnificent monastic settlements and generally wrecking the country. This was followed by the victory over the Vikings by Brian Bórú in 1014, then by a period of confused conflict, and finally by the Norman invasion of 1169. There followed the usual story of seven hundred years of slavery punctuated by gallant risings against English tyranny, capped eventually by the heroic Rising of 1916 and the War of Independence.

The bitter little civil war that followed the Treaty of 1921 and that was very much within living memory in 1950 was more or less skipped, and William T. Cosgrave, the first prime minister of an internationally recognised Irish state, was given honourable mention, first honours, however, going to his erstwhile colleague and later enemy Éamon de Valera. This republican ecumenism reflected the fact that the Brothers' market was not all derived from de Valera's mass political party, Fianna Fáil; Cosgrave's political heir, Fine Gael, also had quite a few kids enjoying, or at least experiencing, the educational process of attendance at the schools of the Christian Brothers.

The interesting thing about this confection was that the comic strip continued on into the future. In the future of the young boys at whom this production was aimed Ireland would somehow be reunited and Irish would be revived as the ordinary language of the people. Huge concrete churches would be built in the late twentieth century and filled with the growing millions of eager worshippers. That much was true enough in reality. In the comic book there followed pictures of these immense churches besieged by enormous crowds, vying with each other to get in, in ways reminiscent of queues in the fifties for cowboy or cops-and-robbers pictures outside Dublin cinemas in the real future of 1950.

In the comic strip, Ireland, led by its priests, nuns and brothers, attains great cultural and economic success, and foreigners fly in, the prosperous gentlemen wearing snap-brim hats and the glamorous ladies sporting large race-meeting headgear, landing at Dublin Airport in propeller-driven aeroplanes—all items suspiciously derived from already obsolescent 1940s styles—to contemplate the glorious cultural, geographical and demographic resuscitation of Éire in the latter part of an imagined twentieth century.[7] Partition would come to an end and an Irish-speaking 32-county Irish state, prosperous and led by its priests, would be a mirror for all observers. As the authors might have said, '*Beidh Éire fós ag Cáit Ní Dhuibhir*.'[8] Everyone would live happily ever after.

There were other attempts at prophecy. De Valera, in early 1957, predicted an 'entirely new era.' The Irish state had now outgrown its infancy, the old man claimed, had solved its problems of political legitimacy and could set to some hard thinking and to making important decisions on its economic future. He was electioneering, but he was also evidently following the lead given by his Minister for Industry and Commerce, Seán Lemass, who by this time was supplying his own familiar rhetorical magic to his leader's economistic progressivism in an effort to give it popular legitimation.[9]

Despite the almost comical contrast between the two as leaders, de Valera and Lemass made rather an effective team, particularly perhaps when Dev lost the whip hand, as he clearly did in the fifties. Sancho Panza got the better of Don Quixote in the long run; like Sancho, Lemass even got his island, or most of it. The notorious culture of pessimism of the mid-fifties was itself bad-mouthed by Lemass a few months later when, once the election had been decisively won by Fianna Fáil, he felt he could say, 'Those who are still pulling long faces and making gloomy forecasts about the future will look just as foolish, when the future arrives, as the Jeremiahs of the past.'[10] It was widely understood by the mid-fifties that the era of high tariffs was over and that the future was with a free-trade area embracing all of Europe.

Journalism could have a direct and even dramatic effect on public policy. T. K. Whitaker, the most important civil servant of the era, has famously reminisced that one of the things that impelled him to write his key document, *Economic Development*, was a piece of journalism of the kind this book addresses: a

cartoon in *Dublin Opinion*, a popular monthly humorous journal
of the time, created in 1922 by a coterie of civil servants. The
cartoon, in the issue of September 1957, portrayed Ireland as a
beautiful if slightly worried young woman asking a fortune-teller
to get to work, as people were saying she had no future.[11]

Actually the country was finally becoming healthily obsessed
by the future in the mid-fifties. It was facing a future of free trade,
dominated by 'America' and a new thing called 'Europe', while no-
one was really quite clear about what either of these words
represented. Civil servants commonly envisaged a north-
European common market consisting of Germany, the Benelux
countries and the Scandinavian countries and led by Britain and
France. Some few looked hopefully to an apparently progressive
alternative future offered by the victorious Eurasian superpower,
the Soviet Union. The horrific events in Hungary in 1956, when
the Soviet tyranny murdered the Hungarian nascent democracy,
effectually snuffed out that option in the minds of most western
Europeans.

The idea of a virtuous Ireland surrounded by economic and
ideational walls of tariffs and censorship was dying, but nothing
much had yet taken its place. Interestingly, waiting in the wings
was the rather novel proposition that the national project was to
be a technical one rather than one involving romantic and militant
heroism, and this was proffered by a curious and rather new-
fangled group of opinion-formers: civil servants, politicians,
journalists and academics.[12] Economics, technocracy, technical
education and 'scientific' rational administration were to be the
means of a new, non-heroic but dedicated Irish patriotism. Arthur
Griffith had prefigured this mood during the Treaty debate by
asking passionately whether Irish politics was always to be about
the dead generations or the unborn generations to come but
never about the present living generation, with all its practical
and everyday problems.

This project of non-romantic national reinvention was the joint product not only of the opinion-formers mentioned above but also of a remarkable group of political leaders in all the main political parties. Chief among them were Lemass, James Ryan and their juniors in Fianna Fáil, Patrick Hillery, Jack Lynch, Donogh O'Malley, Charles Haughey, and a following of younger would-be politicians, civil servants, labour leaders and business people. In Fine Gael, Daniel Morrissey and Gerard Sweetman, and in the Labour Party William Norton and James Larkin junior, were part of this invisible college or movement. Perhaps a better way of saying this would be that a 'collective mindset' was coming into existence among elites that was unprecedented in independent Ireland's history.

Kenneth Whitaker became recognised as the leader or informal spokesman for this inchoate but very real cross-party or even non-party movement or collective mood. In his eccentric way, Seán MacBride of Clann na Poblachta also belongs to this new modernising elite, not quite sure of what it should do but willing, in quite a new way, to experiment, improvise and ask empirical questions that cut across inherited orthodoxies in many unexpected and sometimes creative ways.

The key to their political leverage was the unconditional and monolithic support of the Fianna Fáil of Éamon de Valera, with its traditional rural support base supplemented by an extraordinary cross-class urban base built up over the years since independence. De Valera, a politician of genius, had put together an election-winning machine of unparalleled efficiency in the 1920s, with the assistance of Lemass, Seán MacEntee and the other leaders of that time. Fianna Fáil was substantially built on the ruins of the defeated anti-Treaty IRA of 1922–3, persuaded eventually to try to win by peaceful and legal means the political power that it had tried to usurp by force in mid-1922. The party was manned by the leaders and men of the IRA after they had been released from the prison camps of the Irish and British governments between 1923 and 1925. In effect, an organisation that had denied the right of Irish democracy to rule in 1922 because the voters had chosen the wrong people had come to rule the country ten years later in the name of that same democracy.

What was then termed the Irish Free State was taken over in the thirties by a highly organised political organisation led by de Valera, one derived from the rank and file of the old pre-1923 IRA and reflecting the upwardly mobile children of the small farmers, rural and urban skilled workers and lower middle class—'the men who had no arse to their trousers,' as the adage of the time had it. This electoral hegemony—echoing in part an earlier hegemony in the form of the agrarian anti-landlord Land League, later the Irish National League of Charles Stewart Parnell between 1879 and 1890—was challenged in the late forties and mid-fifties by the inter-party alliances. However, it was a traditional agrarian and populist national alliance that was eventually to reassert itself in the late fifties as a revamped version of Fianna Fáil and was to undergo a generational change.

Samuel Huntington documented a generation ago the common pattern experienced in relatively underdeveloped democratic countries that had begun to develop successfully. In effect, he argued, the upwardly mobile rural poor must engage in mass organisation for a determined and popular modernising elite to emerge. The regime is legitimated by being seen to represent the needs and aspirations of the rural poor; this legitimation is not necessarily seen as preserving that rural culture and the poverty that too often accompanies it but as giving the next generation the hope of an urban future. In the most benign of Huntington's 'democratic modernisation' scenarios, rural classes are organised by nationalist and modernising political parties to build an urbanising society and economy that is descended from and then replaces the slowly dying rural society and culture. The basic model was post-independence India, led as it was for a long time by Nehru's Congress Party. Huntington termed this phenomenon of a dying class giving rise to a new set of classes through political action the 'Green Uprising'.[13]

In the nineteen-fifties the national newspapers of this new nation reflected quite vividly the Irish version of this confrontation between older, mainly agrarian relative privilege and new urbanising popular and populist ambition very vividly, as this book illustrates. This confrontation was expressed through the newspapers and was mediated through the party system, in ways that the book attempts to illuminate and in ways that some readers may find somewhat unexpected and even surprising.

Chapter 2 ∼

POLITICS IN THE NEW REPUBLIC, 1949–60

AN UNEASY DECADE

The post-war period began with a mini-boom as independent Ireland experienced a recovery from wartime conditions, and by 1949 it had recovered economically to something like 1938 levels. Agriculture remained stagnant, more or less as it had been since the 1900s; but industry was doing fairly well, and services, that much-neglected future mainstay of the Irish economy, made good progress. There is a persistent stereotype of the Ireland of the forties and fifties as being under the sway of a puritan, repressive and authoritarian regime that illegalised divorce, made contraception virtually illegal, tortured little boys, banned anything worth reading and illegally imprisoned girls and young women for alleged immorality, being 'wild' or simply for being too pretty. It has been presented in journalism, academic work and popular culture as a society in which the thrashing of children, cruelty to animals and an essentially superstitious popular religious culture held sway. All this is close enough to reality, but the system did work for two-thirds of the population; for one-third it certainly didn't.

Despite repression and censorship there was a relatively lively intellectual and cultural life, documented by many contemporary and later writers. Furthermore, a very large minority enjoyed a somewhat bucolic but leisurely life-style. Another large minority enjoyed a more modest version of the same thing. Something like a tame version of the modern consumer society was anticipated in the Ireland of 1948. For example, the *Irish Independent* announced in tones of mild unease in May 1949 that the consumption of beer in 1948 had been one-third higher than it had been in 1938; the consumption of whiskey was up by 15 per cent and tobacco by one-third.

Thus in this happy country we are not only drinking more per man and woman than we did before Hitler broke out but we are paying more for our pleasures, with a falling population, and apparently can afford to do it. All of which goes to prove that we are not to be denied our pleasures.[1]

Irish people were the most eager cinema-goers in Europe, and sports and improvised entertainment flourished. No-one danced at crossroads, and that worthy if traffic-jamming activity is, incidentally, nowhere mentioned in de Valera's notorious and much-misquoted speech of St Patrick's Day, 1943. American films were particularly popular. One reason for the popularity of the cinema was the fact that it was one of the few places other than fields and parks where courting couples could be together in something like privacy, as cars scarcely existed, housing was chronically scarce, families were large and privacy was itself a scarce good.[2] Some years later the *Indo* commented sympathetically on worried comments in the bishops' Lenten Pastorals about the apparent growing wantonness and laziness of the general population.

The Pastorals indicate with authority some weaknesses in our way of life that we should do well to ponder over. The craze for pleasure-seeking in ways that are too often objectionable seems to have increased rather than diminished. Only some days ago a minister gave impressive details of the amount that is now spent each year on gambling and on dancing, drink and tobacco. There seems to have been a startling increase in these directions in the last decade. Some relaxation is useful if the work that is to be done is in fact done, but we have not to look far to see the evil results of preferring pleasure to work.

The task of building up the country demands a sustained effort from our people and a smaller degree of relaxation than may be possible for more developed peoples. We need too a greater sense of co-operation and responsibility. The Pastorals wisely point out that the damage done by strikes often outweighs the possible gains that may be secured. In material as in spiritual affairs the Pastorals provide guidance that we should be wise to accept.[3]

Dance styles changed during the forties, American popular dances such as swing and jitterbug replacing older ballroom dancing and Irish dancing alike, the main influence being the United States and, more directly, the loosened-up London of the wartime and post-war period. In England women had gone through an emancipation by being permitted to work in occupations previously reserved for men. In wartime Britain women drove lorries, flew fighter planes from factories to the airfields, shortened their skirts and became sexually more free than hitherto. The demonstration effect on Ireland was considerable, particularly in Dublin and Belfast.

During the fifties many young Irish women left for England, partly to get employment and partly to experience a more emancipated life-style than was offered them at home. It was obvious to many commentators that the dullness and patriarchal character of Irish rural life was itself a major 'push' factor. By the mid-fifties this emigration was to become a flood that in fact was to scare policy elites into a serious change in their thinking.

Motor cars were almost unknown to the majority of the population and would remain so for more than another decade.

Despite this evidence of modest means, the *Irish Independent*, essentially a Fine Gael paper but with a wider circulation than either the *Press* of Fianna Fáil or the ex-unionist *Times*, noted in January 1949 that Ireland, in common with the rest of Europe, was really living beyond its means on American charity.[4] Attitudes to poverty were fatalistic; 'the poor you always had with you' seems to have been the attitude, and the mainstream newspapers, catering for a relatively prosperous readership, discussed the problem very sporadically, if at all. In 1951 the *Irish Times*, in the wake of the Mother and Child affair, portrayed the views of the 'Catholic in the street.' This composite figure, apparently middle-class with rather conservative views, spoke of the 'submerged thirty per cent' of the population who did not get a living wage and were given subsidised housing and free health treatment but who remained poor—'a bad system.'[5]

The *Independent* was a staunch defender of the interests of the emergent professional middle class. In an editorial commentary on the national income of the Republic in 1951 it complained bitterly that there had been a redistribution of income since 1938 from the middle class to the working class and farmers.

This increased earning was not equally spread. Agricultural income rose from £36 millions in 1938 to £88 millions in 1944 and thence to £99.4 millions in 1949. Non-agricultural wages and salaries increased in the same years from £69 millions to £92 millions and thence to £157 millions. On the other hand, the income of the professional section of the community increased only from £20 millions to £26 millions and thence to £32 millions. It is easy to see, that without any deliberate Government policy, the circumstances of the time have led to a great redistribution of income. The point should be borne in mind in framing financial policy.[6]

The communist *Irish Democrat*, published in London, gave a rather different take on things, providing a vivid little picture of Irish poverty and the country's persistent material inequalities in early 1951.[7] In 1949 the national income was £140 per head, compared with a huge American figure of £484, Canada's super-rich £290, New Zealand's £282, Britain next door to Ireland at £258 and little Denmark at £229. Denmark, although occupied by Germany, had been fairly well treated by the Hitlerite regime, because it was seen as a reservoir of Aryan racial purity; the country had even been permitted to hold a general election in 1943, in which the voters had carefully demonstrated their genetic excellence by giving the local Nazis virtually no votes. Ireland's national income per head was a little lower than that of France, at £160, but higher than Portugal, at £84, and Italy, at £78.

However, France had been expertly looted by the Reich, which had fixed conquered France's currency at a low rate to the reichsmark so as to depress French prices and permit Germans to buy the country up. Italy had been fought over, and wrecked, first by a spectacularly incompetent dictatorship for twenty years and subsequently by a battle between three powers that went on for more than two years. In the memorable phrase of the unknown GI, 'we sure liberated the fuck out of that country.' Portugal was burdened with an immense and fundamentally useless overseas empire and was still in the grip of a semi-feudal and archaic land-owning elite and ruled by an economist turned dictator. Peaceful, post-feudal, neutral and democratic Ireland had none of these excuses.[8]

The inter-party Government of John A. Costello was elected in early 1948, ousting de Valera's Fianna Fáil for the first time in sixteen years. It was a strange mixture of old pro-Treaty people, labour leaders, agrarians and 'new republicans' opposed to Fianna Fáil. Costello, a Dublin lawyer and Fine Gael stalwart, was a compromise Taoiseach, as several of his colleagues had been actively involved in the executions of republicans during the Civil War period. His greatest merits were that he had no blood on his hands and was well liked. His greatest strength and weakness was his reluctance to give up his leisurely and profitable law practice for the relatively ill-paid and highly demanding job of Taoiseach.

The new Government declared Ireland a republic in April 1949, the thirty-third anniversary of the Easter Rising. This was a cutting of the constitutional Gordian knot, and it was designed to term-inate finally the apparently interminable debate over whether the state was or was not a republic. The occasion was marked by a military parade, a *feu de joie* from the roof of the GPO—hallowed site of the declaration of the original Irish Republic in 1916—and a fireworks display. Subsequently, the *Leader* acknowledged the effectiveness of this decision.

> [De Valera] has always endeavoured to capture and mono-polise the legacy of Republicanism, and he has not as yet wholly failed. The Republic Act of 1949 has indeed changed the position, and the former issues that excited people on the eve of polls have now vanished from popular consciousness. A new era has commenced. Mr. De Valera was in office during sixteen of the most dangerous years of modern history and must indeed feel that he has improved in experience and policy during his tenure. Power has often been said to corrupt and Mr. De Valera's power was more absolute than that possessed by any other Irishman for a long time.[9]

It should be remembered that Éamon de Valera, a much-loved and much-hated politician, dominated Irish democratic politics in the early twentieth century. A tall and austere black-clad figure, he retained his native Limerick countryman's accent and priestly mien into old age. Presiding over a slowly urbanising and mod-ernising Ireland, he understood profoundly the uses of nostalgia in appealing to the common man and woman. 'I am one of you, reared among you and chosen to lead you only by your own collective will,' he seemed to be saying, while also seeming to be the aloof schoolmaster of the nation at the same time. He reiterated constantly that the Irish people had a long and illustrious history, were one of the founding nations of Europe and had no reason to be ashamed of themselves and should have pride in their tradition, culture, faith and heroic struggle for independence. Much of what he said was self-serving baloney, but he taught the voters self-respect, and they loved him for that.

Electorally, it did him no harm that he had been a hero of the 1916 Rising and had been condemned to death; at that time, to have been 'out' in 1916 was the golden key to political success. Unlike later political figures, people who were veterans of the liberation struggle, such as de Valera, Seán Lemass, William Cosgrave and Frank Aiken, could be elected possibly to any constituency in the country, as their national reputation would override local loyalties and interests. Even out of power, as first among these putative heroes, Dev overshadowed other political leaders of the time.

The fifties were to see the rise of Seán Lemass, Fianna Fáil Minister for Industry and Commerce, although still in the shadow of Dev. Like his boss, Lemass was a 1916 veteran, but he was, by seventeen years, a much younger man and a Dublinman, at a time when cultural differences between Dubliners ('Jackeens') and country people ('Culchies') were quite marked and sometimes generated mutual hostility. Lemass even looked the part of the smart Jackeen, with his sharp city suits and hats, Italianate features and sometimes sardonic disregard for rural affairs; he had a faint resemblance to Humphrey Bogart, a film star and fashion plate of the time. His belief that Ireland's future lay in non-agrarian economic development marked him out from many of his political peers.

The army got a lot of public airings in 1949. A month before the declaration of the republic, in what seems to have been a dress rehearsal for the declaration, a massive military parade was held in Dublin for St Patrick's Day, in a characteristic and wonderfully incongruent mixing of the sacred, the traditional, the nationalist and the militaristic. The *Irish Press*, although evidently smarting from Fianna Fáil's departure from power a year previously, was still able to celebrate the Emergency army, which still existed in remnant form, in an almost kinky front-page story. The paper appealed directly to the volunteer part-time soldiers who had formed the Local Defence Force (LDF) during the war, rechristened afterwards by patriotic translation An Fórsa Cosanta Áitiúil (FCA).

These militia soldiers echoed Fianna Fáil's own volunteer military tradition, inherited from the revolutionary Irish Volunteers and Old IRA. Many of the older soldiers were, very probably, voters for, and many of them active loyalists of, the party.

The term Fianna Fáil is in itself an interesting one. It was believed to have been the name of the warrior bands (Fianna) of ancient Ireland (Inis Fáil, or Isle of Destiny, a mediaeval poetic name for Ireland). It was proposed by Eoin MacNeill (joint founder with Douglas Hyde of the Gaelic League in 1893) as the Irish name of the insurrectionist Irish Volunteers of 1913, the immediate ancestors of the Irish Republican Army of 1919, but was rejected in favour of the literal translation Óglaigh na hÉireann. As a compromise, an FF monogram was incorporated in the Volunteers' badge (designed by MacNeill himself).

When founding the party as a split from the anti-Treaty fundamentalist Sinn Féin of 1926 de Valera was able to say with a smile that the essential untranslatability of the phrase was itself something of an advantage. Lemass had wanted the new party to be entitled the Republican Party, in English, and his suggestion became the official subtitle of Fianna Fáil. The contrast between de Valera and his brilliant lieutenant could scarcely be better symbolised. Cleverly enough, de Valera's pinching of the term as an ideological property has led to a permanent confusion in many people's minds over the distinction between Fianna Fáil and the democratic government of the entire country. De Valera was always adept at stealing other people's ideological clothing and even their symbol systems. Significantly, he always insisted that the organisation was a 'national movement' rather than a mere political party, thereby suggesting that Fianna Fáil represented the most patriotic, most energetic and most alert segment of the population—in other words, an Irish version of the Leninist vanguard idea. The original Irish Volunteers' badge continues to be used as the badge of the Defence Forces. Neither the Department of Defence nor the army ever pressed for any court decision concerning violation of copyright.

The *Irish Press* report of 17 March 1949 gushed:

A new kind of army paraded Dublin yesterday. They gave the city something of a surprise because for the most part they were part-time soldiers, obviously trained in the use of military mechanics of modern design.

No longer are the FCA volunteers simply an adjunct to the regulars. If yesterday's show is a pointer they are the Army. The fairly futuristic looking howitzer carriers and streamlined ack-ack affairs were manned by these civilian volunteers. They rode enigmatically beside the three-point-sevens that padded along steadily with smooth throats in their suavely vicious mouths.

The big crowds cordoned off by the Gardaí along Dame Street, College Green and the Westmoreland-O'Connell Street route saw a slick ensemble in light green. Every gun, wheel, bonnet and chassis, armoured plate and caterpillar chain had the same colouring that battleship grey has become to the Navy.

There was no other colour to the parade except the regimental flags and the single pride-of-place Tricolour. Those and the saffron [kilts] of the pipers. Simplicity is the keynote of the new rather frightening efficiency of the small weapon and the small vehicle.

The tommy-gun has come into its own here with its brief pneumatic-drill pattern menace sticking out under the elbows of men with whom we rub shoulders every day in shops and offices and buses and lorries and lifting bales and tilling cabbage plots. Men who say nothing about it but are automatically on parade at twenty-oh-oh hours when other fellows are going to the pictures or the dogs.

The LDF men of the old days have become successors to the Invisible Army and their brief public appearance on such an occasion as Saint Patrick's Day makes you doff a mental hat and salaam. To put it bluntly and in common parlance they look tough.

The Army Proper was there too, for the first two contingents, but they seemed to be presenting us with the LDF. (It's hard to get used to that FCA title). The 'Regulars' seemed to hint: 'We've trained these lads and see if you see the difference.'

That stoic grimness and immobility that seems to mark the trained-to-the-ounce soldier was evident in the Bren-carrier-men, the howitzer boys and the chaps with walkie-talkie aerials sticking out of the boxes on their belts.

Almost reluctantly, the paper subconsciously documented the fact that this beloved Irish citizens' army of the Fianna Fáil party (in the party's own collective mind) was not being reviewed by a Fianna Fáil Government.[10] In the mind of Fianna Fáil, the Soldiers of Ireland were no longer controlled by the Soldiers of the Isle of Destiny but by a strange coalition of renegades and amateurs, led by the traitors who signed the imperialists' Treaty of 1921–2.

During the Second World War, when the world was going through the greatest and most murderous convulsion the human race had ever been through, little neutral Ireland had forged a local national solidarity around the Catholic Church, the Fianna Fáil national-populist party of Éamon de Valera and Seán Lemass, the Gaelic Athletic Association and the Irish army. At the height of the 'Emergency' a little state of three millions had more than 80,000 men under arms. As the *Leader* correctly commented at the time, the Irish democracy gave de Valera enormous power to ride out the storm, including quite literally the power of life and death over the citizenry.[11]

With the ending of the war, the fear of invasion and the sense of being under siege weakened, and this solidarity was felt to be less necessary. The sense of national solidarity gradually began to evaporate because of the growing realisation that western Europe was to be protected against possible German revanchism and Soviet adventurism by the mighty American military shield. Symptoms of this evaporation occurred early on. One such was the entry into the political system of IRA leaders released from Irish prisons on the occasion of the surrender of Germany. A bitterness against the de Valera Government existed in the minds of these men, as he had imprisoned more than a thousand of them in the Curragh Camp, mostly without trial, and had stood over the ill-treatment of many, including the execution of several. A consequence of this mass release was the building of a new republican party on the ruins of the New IRA, much as Fianna Fáil had been built on the ruins of the Old IRA. It seems probable that the reason for de Valera's notorious sending of condolences to the German Legation on the death of the Führer in 1945 was his wish to outflank the Germanophile and pro-Nazi elements of the IRA and his own greener Fianna Fáil supporters. Being obsessed with winning elections and being an accomplished student of the Irish voter, he concentrated on his vulnerable, hyper-nationalist flank:

the more absolutist, anti-partitionist or more republican section of the voting public.

Another reason for Dev's undoubted gaffe was his legalistic determination to assert the absoluteness of Irish neutrality, even were the heavens to fall. And fall they undoubtedly did, in the form of a part-ostracism of the country from international society for some years after the war. It took ten years for Ireland to enter the United Nations, and the offer by the inter-party Government to cut a special alliance deal with the United States, analogous to that of Franco's Spain, rather than join the North Atlantic Treaty Organisation was cold-shouldered by the Americans.

The new republican party, Córas na Poblachta, later Clann na Poblachta (Children of the Republic), was led by Seán MacBride, son of Major John MacBride, Boer War hero, 1916 martyr and husband of Maud Gonne, lifelong love of William Butler Yeats. For a while MacBride seemed to possess a republican charisma similar to that of de Valera but less compromised by power and the necessary political opportunisms of government in dark times. He had a marked French accent, having spent his childhood in Normandy in the early years of the century, and he had been chief of staff of the IRA in the thirties. He was an elegant figure, very attractive to women and, rather like Lemass, seemed somehow a more modern figure than de Valera and his older lieutenants.

Again, the coming of Marshall Aid was seen, quite accurately, as a turning point in 1948, both by Irish observers and by its American progenitors.[12] However, the Irish people, still wedded to the idea that Ireland's future lay in farming rather than in non-agricultural economic activity, were to sink most of the American soft loans and grants into agriculture-related projects. Another symptom of the evaporation of the wartime solidarity was a discontent that showed itself in the voting into office in early 1948 of a 'Coalition of All the Talents.' C. Desmond Greaves, a well-known left-wing writer, writing for the *Irish Democrat*, wrote rhetorically:

Was there ever such a collection of glorified nonentities? At its worst, say what you will about it, Fianna Fáil had a certain rugged solidity, a dignity which arose from its huge mass backing, confused, misled, deceived as this might be.[13]

Even the *Irish Press*, however reluctantly, admitted that the inter-party Government had brought off something of a coup and had, for once, stolen something of Fianna Fáil's republican ideological thunder, while burying the old Free State versus Republic division between itself, the Labour Party and the New Republicans of MacBride. Its political correspondent commented rather sourly:

Reassembling for the longest Dáil session of the year, Fine Gael deputies are in somewhat higher spirits than usual. They believe that their political stock has been enhanced by the Easter celebrations which, they consider, served the dual purpose of throwing a veil round the party's rather trouble-some past and of distracting public attention from pressing material problems. Naturally, their new role of upholders of the [1937] Republican Constitution, the enactment of which their party opposed, has found most Fine Gael members a little self-conscious and even embarrassed when they contest those whose Republican faith is deep-rooted and long established. But they all believe that their party leaders handled the whole business skilfully, drawing from it the maximum political advantage. Whatever doubts exist in their minds stem from the apprehension that the advantage will not last long enough to affect the next General Election.[14]

Few made the obvious point that the declaration of a republic not only eliminated one of many sources of division within the inter-party Government but also copperfastened partition, by accepting the then-logical consequence of leaving the British Commonwealth. This move in turn increased the constitutional distance between the two parts of Ireland and provoked London to pass the Ireland Act (1949). This measure guaranteed to Northern Ireland continuing membership of the United Kingdom as long as it consented to such membership through its own provincial parliament in Belfast.[15]

The Republic, at the instigation in particular of Seán MacBride, refused invitations to join the newly forming NATO on the grounds that it involved accepting the existing frontiers of Europe, including the Irish border.[16] Irish neutrality became institutionalised in a quite extraordinarily permanent and extra-legal way, so much so that it began to act like an unwritten and therefore unamendable clause in the Constitution of 1937. Ironically, similar considerations did not inhibit the Irish from embracing the European Economic Community twenty years later with a massive, even overwhelming, 'yes' vote, despite a frantic 'no' campaign by nationalists, isolationist leftists and the Labour Party and Irish Congress of Trade Unions.[17]

Although something of a wounded giant, Dev's formidable political machine dominated even the uneasy years of the 1950s, undergoing a reorganisation and rejuvenation under Lemass after 1948. The party returned to power in mid-1951, forming an unstable alliance with a clutch of independent TDs; this was something of a surprise at the time, as the papers saw the election as having been clearly lost by Dev. Eventually Fianna Fáil lost power again in 1954 to a second inter-party Government, which in turn lost office in early 1957. Much of the instability and apparent indecisiveness of economic policy, the thinking about education and employer-labour relations were actually derived from the unusual electoral instability of the period, characterised by the rise and fall of two flash parties (the 'two Clanns'), the continuing divisions in the Labour movement and the revival of the IRA in the mid-fifties in the form of Operation Harvest. There was a general sense of unease and the widespread anticipation of an imminent coming of great changes in Irish society, combined with a sense of continuing stasis. There was also a general sense of gerontocratic and bureaucratic tendencies in the political ruling cohort. Between 1944 and 1961 the electorate returned no Government immediately to power.

Much of the innovation in economic policy in the fifties was associated as much with inter-party Governments as with Fianna Fáil Governments; after all, the Industrial Development Authority (IDA) was the initiative of Daniel Morrissey of Fine Gael, partly on the advice of a Czechoslovak businessman who had had experience of pre-war Czechoslovakia's economic success. The first inter-party Government brought in a capital budget for the first time, and Gerard Sweetman, the Fine Gael Minister for Finance, had begun introducing a tax holiday system for foreign investors just before the second inter-party Government fell in 1957.

Morrissey had been a Labour TD in the early years of the Free State. A Tipperary auctioneer, he was a very successful businessman and, like Lemass, a firm believer in industrialisation as being the future of the country. Sweetman was a lawyer and Trinity College graduate with a keen understanding of economics, and he elevated T. K. Whitaker to the post of Secretary of the Department of Finance and effectual head of the civil service in 1956. Whitaker, the most prominent public servant of his generation, was from Rostrevor, Co. Down, and was an interesting mixture of Celticist, mathematician and economist. A brilliant administrator with a wise and humorous personality, he injected a certain wisdom and sanity into public affairs at a time when it was most needed. Sweetman, a man of huge political potential, is now an almost forgotten figure, and this is so mainly because he was killed in a car crash in 1970. He had a patrician and somewhat off-putting personality, which was unhelpful in the populist politics of Ireland.

Lemass, partly on Whitaker's advice but also because he had independently come to similar conclusions about free trade many years earlier in the late twenties, subsequently introduced an intensified and expanded version of Sweetman's economic programme; it was to be very successful. One of the rules of the game seemed to be that only de Valera's party had the electoral staying power and brute political weight to push the more unpopular reforms through—or, more accurately, those reforms unpalatable to powerful interest groups.

Because of this essentially structural circumstance, in a strange way Seán Lemass, whether at his traditional seat as Minister for Industry and Commerce or in opposition and expressing his trenchant views about Fine Gael's alleged reactionary character and his obsession with industrial development, was the truly dominant figure in an uneasy time; his own noisy confidence was, particularly in opposition, mingled with unused energy, purpose and frustration. Much of the policy package he pushed through came from both sides of the party divide or from the civil service, the new business elites, trade union leaders and academia. Figures such as Whitaker, Charles Murray and Patrick Lynch have become almost legendary, but others, such as Morrissey, Sweetman, William Norton of Labour and other trade union leaders or well-known businessmen such as Kevin McCourt, should not be forgotten.

The fifties saw something like a broad consensual movement among the elites and even the general population in favour of wide-ranging change. This movement, partly cultural and partly generational, eventually and very slowly wore down an equally widespread and powerful institutional resistance from parts of the educational authorities, many farmers, parts of the civil service, some trade unionists and some protection-fed industrialists. A significant part of it was symbolised and articulated by Tuairim, a loosely organised federation of discussion groups that produced influential pamphlets on such topics as proportional representation, higher education, primary education and Northern Ireland. Very revealingly, Tuairim refused membership at one stage to anyone over the age of forty. This was the dusk of the era of the pamphleteer; inexpensive pamphlets had been a common way of publishing one's opinion for more than two centuries, and the institution did not die out until television and the television talk show established themselves in the sixties.

The passive and active resistance to change was very strong, and the reactionary role of popular opinion should not be underestimated either; change threatens the poor more directly than it does the prosperous, and many people saw their jobs and the prosperity of their neighbourhoods as being under threat from free trade. Sometimes they were, unfortunately, quite right.

Another sixteen-year period of Fianna Fáil dominance of the system was to come eventually, lasting from 1957 to 1973; but in the fifties its electoral dominance was seen by many as a thing of the past, given in particular the revival of Fine Gael's electoral fortunes after its nadir of 1948. To some, Clann na Poblachta, with its modern, stylish publicity and young profile, looked briefly like the wave of the future. The inter-party Government of 1948 admittedly looked a bit unlikely, putting together Fine Gael, the old pro-Treaty party that had executed republicans in the Civil War of 1922–3, with heirs to those extreme republicans in the form of MacBride's Clann na Poblachta, which brought together IRA and radical activists, two Labour Parties and a neo-agrarian western smallholders' party, Clann na Talmhan (Children of the Land).

Political scientists have seen the Irish party system and other analysts as eccentric, not following the usual European left-right alignments typically tempered by centre-periphery tensions and local ethnic-minority parties. Perhaps the most conspicuous peculiarity of this far-western European system was the absence of any large bloc of socialist, social democrat or communist voters in the electorate. The Labour Party and its breakaway National Labour Party, based on the Irish Transport and General Workers' Union, did indeed echo weakly an internationalist-nationalist division, but both parties were small; furthermore, they reunited in 1950. The absence of a classic European left-right distinction did have its defenders; some argued that it at least had the virtue of permitting two different sets of people to attempt to solve the nation's problems by different means through the same institutions and with basically the same ends in view. Sometimes the means were identical and occasionally filched from the other side.

In 1948 the established pattern was 'Dev versus the Rest,' the 'Rest' being a much-diminished Fine Gael, the two Labour Parties, Clann na Talmhan, Clann na Poblachta and some independents. Both blocs were left-to-right within a rather short ideological spectrum, but Fianna Fáil had the advantage of being all of a piece and glued together by a nationalist solidarity. To oversimplify, Fianna Fáil was the party of more of the have-nots in a country of many have-nots, and both ecological statistical analysis and the observations of contemporaries concur in this general picture. It was sometimes colloquially termed 'the party of the Joe Soaps.' It was particularly strong in its early years among small farmers and other groups, particularly in the west and south-west; there is a strong ecological correlation between distance from Dublin and support for Fianna Fáil, if the county and city of Dublin are taken out of the calculation. The western and south-western counties were also areas where the Tan War and the Civil War had been at their most intense, where many atrocities had occurred and had affected local political culture and loyalties.[18]

As we have seen, Fianna Fáil was built on the ruins of the defeated anti-Treaty IRA, and, having lost the war in 1923, it won the peace in the general election of 1932. De Valera was a charismatic figure to his own followers but a hate figure to the leaders of the pro-Treaty party: he was 'The Man They Could Never Forgive' because of his perceived divisive behaviour in the period leading up to the Civil War in 1921–2. Personal hatred as much as ideological differences distinguished the two post-Sinn Féin parties until the revolutionary generation died out.[19] This is not to say that there were no differences: as will be seen, Fianna Fáil was more clearly a modernising and industrialising party than was Fine Gael, with its strong agrarian bias. However, the latter party had its advocates of industrialisation too, and Fianna Fáil was not without agrarians.

Irish political culture had traditionally linked political sovereignty with cultural and economic recovery, and an obsession with the symbols and realities of sovereignty gripped the minds of nationalist leaders in the first generation after independence. This almost archaic style of thinking arguably had its roots in the seventeenth century and survived the linguistic transition from Irish to English that occurred in the period 1690–1800 to act powerfully on the minds of modern leaders during the revolutionary period 1890–1923.[20]

The defeat and replacement of one democratically elected government by another as in 1948 has commonly been seen as a coming of age, particularly when combined with the declaration of the Republic in 1949 by the new inter-party Government and the concomitant leaving of the British Commonwealth. Sovereignty, it seemed, had been achieved, at least for the twenty-six counties of independent Ireland. 'Civil War politics' were to be laid to rest, it was hoped, and ideological space was finally to be provided to permit the discussion of economic, social, educational and foreign policy issues in a way that was not wholly possible earlier. For many this symbolic event made a very real difference, and many ideological ghosts were finally laid to rest.[21]

Fianna Fáil had indeed had the support of the have-nots, but it also became the party of the able and energetic upwardly mobile, appealing to the new working and lower-middle classes that grew up in the protected economy of Seán Lemass as Minister for Industry and Commerce in the thirties and again after the war. In an adaptation of the phrase of C. S. (Todd) Andrews, they were the men of no property coming into their own.[22] Furthermore, even before 1948 it was becoming the party of a new business class, much of it coming originally from the public sector, civil service and state-sponsored companies that had proliferated behind tariff barriers. Thus, even though the party had been founded on classes that were dying slowly—the small farmers and landless labourers of a poor agrarian peripheral state—it was also the party of new urban working-class and upwardly mobile middle-class socio-economic groups that clearly were on the way up: the future belonged to them, and they sensed it.

The Fianna Fáil paper, the *Irish Press*, as we shall see, although rhetorically loyal to a rural nostalgia was very much focused on non-agrarian work and urban life. A significant source of inno-vative public opinion, it was very different from the other two main daily papers. De Valera's party was a modernising force, committed to state-led capitalist modernisation but with a traditionalist and old-fashioned small-farm base, anxious that its children would have lives off the farm and, preferably, within Ireland.[23] The *Press* contrasted particularly starkly with the two other Dublin dailies, the *Irish Independent* and the *Irish Times*, in its commitment to industrialisation, urban values and a strong sense that the future belonged to a world led by the United States rather than to a resurrected British Empire or even to Europe. The other two papers appeared almost pastoral by contrast, almost fatalistically content with a static and semi-rural society; and the

Times in particular was datedly Anglocentric. The *Independent* was, by contrast, quite alert to the rise of America.

There was a strong sense that great changes were coming, that the post-war world was a very different one. America and Russia dominated a wrecked Europe between them, and the world was a dangerous place, much as it had been in the thirties. A crucial difference, however, was the existence of atomic weapons. No-one had yet realised that the atomic threat was to create a balance of terror between the superpowers that made the possibility of a surprise knock-out attack by either side increasingly unlikely the more heavily armed the powers became. This was a historically unprecedented situation. The terrifying emergent German power of the thirties, with its genocidal ideology, had been definitively eliminated from the picture, although some still imagined an aggressive German resurgence which never happened. Many also expected a rapid return to the depression conditions of the thirties, and some feared a massive immigration from post-war Britain of thousands of Irish workers demobilised from the armed forces or from the closed-down factories, their heads filled with alien and un-Irish ideas such as atheism, social equality or even communism. Others feared a Third World War. Instead Ireland was to witness thirty years of unprecedented European prosperity, a prosperity it did not share and gradually became increasingly desperate to achieve.

Not only were Irish Governments unstable, weaker and more unsure of their own longevity than they had been in the previous two decades but it appeared superficially that the Catholic Church was more powerful than it had been, arrogating to itself even more of what elsewhere might have been regarded as part of the civic and secular order. In the thirties the bishops had prevented the Labour Party from announcing a set policy of establishing a workers' republic, 'founded on the principles of social justice sustained by democratic institutions and guaranteeing civil and religious liberty and equal opportunities to achieve happiness to all citizens who render service to the community.'[24]

However, elements of the church's leadership had been seen off by a Fianna Fáil Government, by Seán MacEntee as Minister for Local Government and the civil servants of the Department of Local Government when an attempt was made in 1944, led by a bishop, to take over the health service and have it run on 'vocational' principles by doctors, surgeons and ecclesiastics.[25] The picture seemed to change in 1951 when a dramatic clash occurred between Dr Noel Browne, the inter-party Government's rather glamorous and charismatic Minister for Health, and the bishops over a wide-ranging Mother and Child health scheme, which proposed giving hygiene and medical instruction to expectant mothers.[26] Browne was forced to resign by his party leader, Seán MacBride. On resignation, he did the unprecedented thing: he released the entire correspondence with MacBride to the press. This rocked the political system in an extraordinary fashion, because it documented the secret ways in which clerics routinely bypassed democratic channels in influencing Government policy.

Browne became a kind of martyr-hero after this episode. He had grown up in a family that had been devastated by tuberculosis, and he spent time in England, where he was treated very well. In 1948 he took over an emergent and very progressive Department of Health, with Dr James Deeny as Chief Medical Officer, but did so as an inexperienced minister, almost on his first day in the Dáil. His inexperience made him a brave innovator and also blinded him to certain political realities of Irish life at that time. When he ran into the hierarchy he assumed that an understanding had been reached between them and the Government, but apparently he was wrong. The bishops had been got at by the doctors, who were scared of socialised medicine.

Irish doctors seem to have been, as they certainly often are nowadays, rather crafty and often mischievous backstairs conspirators. The bishops had been persuaded that civil servants were going to get between the priests and the womenfolk of Ireland, mainly because of the proposed production by the department of a little free booklet about hygiene during and after pregnancy. Deeny and John Garvin, Secretary of the old Department of Local Government, had arranged for finance for the pamphlet as an afterthought to the Health Bill of 1947. William Philbin, later Bishop of Down and Connor, was also present when this addendum was agreed. The Mother and Child Scheme collapsed. The *Irish Times* famously editorialised after Browne had resigned at the instigation of his party leader rather than that of the Taoiseach, John A. Costello:

> This is a sad day for Ireland. It is not so important that the Mother and Child scheme has been withdrawn, to be replaced by an alternative project embodying a means test. What matters more is that an honest, far-sighted and energetic man has been driven out of active politics. The most serious revelation, however, is that the Roman Catholic Church would seem to be the effective government of this country.[27]

The use of the term 'Roman' immediately suggests that the editorial was not written by a Catholic; but it is clear that many Catholics agreed completely with it. Seán Ó Faoláin, Catholic and loyal in his way while a dissenter from the bishops' actions, wrote in the *Bell* in April 1951, using that imperial R-word:

> The issue is that no country can be ruled 'democratically' by two parliaments; or, at least as the world understands that word.
> Here in the Republic, as this crisis has revealed to us, we have two parliaments; a parliament at Maynooth and a parliament in Dublin . . . Nobody, so far as I have observed, has denied the

right of the catholic bishops to 'comment'; or to give 'advice' on proposed legislation; or to enunciate the official attitude of the Roman Catholic Church to proposed legislation . . . I doubt if anybody, north or south, could even object to the Hierarchy publicly condemning any proposed piece of legislation, provided that, in the end, it is the Parliament which freely decides . . . In practice, the Hierarchy does much more than 'comment' or 'advise.' It commands.

The Maynooth Parliament holds a weapon which none of the other institutions mentioned holds: the power of the Sacraments . . . when the Catholic Church, through its representatives, speaks, he realises, and the Roman Catholic public realises, that if they disobey they may draw on themselves this weapon whose touch means death.

. . . There is, therefore, no use in talking blandly about 'comment,' or 'advice.' The lightest word from this quarter is tantamount to the raising of the sword. That is why it is just to speak of two parliaments. The Dáil proposes; Maynooth disposes. The Dáil had, when up against the Second Parliament, only one right of decision: the right to surrender.

That is what made the Browne affair so interesting and so dramatic. It revealed to the people of the Republic that if this is a Democracy it is a form of Democracy unlike any other in the world. That is to say: the supreme power is not here, in practice—which is what matters—vested in the people's Parliament.[28]

All this was grist to the mill of anti-clericals, and the country was becoming gradually ready for a quiet and mainly undercover anti-clericalism among the younger generation. It could be argued that the Mother and Child affair damaged the power of the church quite seriously, although it took decades for this to become evident. Certainly its emotional echoes lasted for decades. There was a quiet undercurrent of agreement, or at least sympathy, with Ó Faoláin's line. People muttered quietly, 'The bishops have gone too far this time.'[29]

THE EAGLE AND THE BEAR

Another post-war development was the rise of a certain anti-Americanism of a rather new type, although it had been pre-figured in the work of left-wing writers in the pre-war period, most notably in the left-leaning comic novels of Eimar O'Duffy (*Asses in Clover, King Goshawk and the Birds, The Spacious Adventures of the Man in the Street*), a dentist from UCD and a predecessor of Ireland's best satirical writer of the twentieth century, Brian Ó Nualláin (alias Flann O'Brien and Myles na gCopaleen), also of UCD and the civil service.[30] During the Second World War the United States had sent various emissaries to Ireland to scout out the local political climate. Only one of these, Martin Quigley, escaped the attentions of Colonel Dan Bryan's very efficient Military Intelligence section, also known as G2. In June 1943 Quigley, a son of a senior figure in the firm, met the Taoiseach, Éamon de Valera, in his assumed identity as an agent of RKO Pictures and was struck by his pro-American stance. He noted that de Valera had the American Declaration of Independence and a framed portrait of Abraham Lincoln in the reception room beside his office in Merrion Street, Dublin. These were not there for Quigley's benefit but had hung there for many years.[31]

Quigley's view on Irish neutrality was quite sympathetic, reporting home to his Irish-American boss at the Office of Strategic Services (forerunner of the CIA), William (Wild Bill) Donovan, incidentally cutting across the anti-Dev assessment of the official American envoy to the Ireland of the period, David Gray. He argued that a neutral but covertly pro-Allied Ireland under de Valera was by far the best Irish situation the Allies could reasonably ask for. There was a pro-Nazi minority, but the vast majority of the population was quietly anti-Nazi. 'During World War Two, the most important, and, to many outsiders, the strangest action of the Irish was their neutrality.'[32]

Quigley ascribed the neutralism to the recent painful experience of internal war in a normally peaceful island. This sense was intensified by a general awareness of Ireland's puny military strength and its inability to defend itself against the neighbouring great powers of the time. A deeper reason, which he did not refer to, was the profound bitterness and hatred that had been generated by the Civil War of 1922–3. This was reinforced by the unspoken but very real fears of reigniting that conflict that haunted the minds of Irish leaders. Neutrality was a default position imposed on Irish leaders by the population and its collective mentality and by the very recent traumatic experience of mutual slaughter.

Quigley reported also on the popularity of American films in Ireland. Interestingly, Irish tastes in films echoed those of American viewers. He discovered also that the IRA, which had a habit of destroying British films that it thought glamorised the Allied cause rather too much, had no hostility to American films.

In endeavouring to uphold strict neutrality the Irish censorship during the war fell into most unreasonable varieties of censorship. For example, in September 1943, for the first time in Irish history, the government film censorship authority decided that the American flag should be cut from a motion picture. Except for the green, white and orange of the Irish flag, the American flag is held in highest esteem among the Irish. Censoring the American flag in Ireland is a strange act: Ireland owes a great deal to the United States, and virtually every family in Ireland has extremely close ties with America.[33]

Pro-American feeling at that time is easy to explain. It was the United States that became the haven for Irish rebels in the years after the failed risings of 1798, 1848 and 1867. The 1867 rising was planned in the United States with the toleration, if not direct encouragement, of the US government, at that time at odds with London over the British Empire's tilt toward the South during the American Civil War. American dollars, collected from the huge and increasingly prosperous Irish diaspora in America, were behind much of the republican or 'Fenian' separatist tradition in Ireland between 1865 and 1923.[34] Furthermore, the American struggle for independence had served quite specifically as a direct model for the Irish independence campaign of 1913–22. Again, even direct family relationships, reinforced by travel, correspondence and telephone, existed between Irish and Irish-American people, sometimes enduring for generations. None of this can explain the rise of a certain anti-Americanism in the years after the war.

As early as December 1946 the *Leader*, a Dublin nationalist paper, rebuked the United States for not backing a Russian proposal to force elections on the Franco regime in Spain, on the grounds that the Soviet Union was a dictatorship and was in no position to force elections on anybody. It argued that the Americans could not preach to others about democracy, as no 'coloured person' in Mississippi could vote. Spain was a small and unimportant country compared with America.

From the point of view of the peace and security of the world it is actually far more important to end the ill-treatment and brutal bullying of the coloured inhabitants of the United States than to end any elements of fascism which may exist in Spain ... The United States is quite the most advanced country in the world; and at the moment she is militarily the most powerful, though both Russia and China may have the potentiality of ultimately becoming more powerful still. She is obviously on the threshold of a career of imperial conquest.

Her establishment of a widespread system of naval and air bases may not necessarily prelude vast territorial acquisitions but it certainly does prelude the creation of spheres of influence and an effort to obtain unchallenged economic or commercial dominance over large areas of the earth's surface. In a word, America's twentieth century imperialism may differ in form from England's eighteenth and nineteenth century imperialism but that will not, of itself, lessen the suffering of those who may be bruised by the Yankee jackboot.

The thing that might make America's coming imperialism milder and more endurable than it now threatens to be would be the triumph, within the United States, of true democracy and of an honest regard for the human rights of every individual. If all categories of citizens within the Union are treated with equal consideration and equal justice, then it may be taken that American imperialism will have some regard for the rights of foreigners who fall directly or indirectly within its power. But if the bullying and ostracism of the Negro and the shameless denial in practice of the rights theoretically granted to him by the Constitution were to be continued then the probability is that United States Pro-Consuls abroad and all their minions would incline to treat all foreigners who had not the power to resist their demands, as inferiors outside the law, as, shall we say, Aryan Negroes.[35]

After several years of mildly rancid pro and anti-American frothings, the *Leader* felt bound to print in 1949 'One American's Opinion.' L. G. Hart, apparently an Irish immigrant to the United States of long standing, wrote to say that for many years he had agreed with a general pro-American stance but had come to the conclusion that Americans were propagandised by newspapers owned by a small clique of rich conservatives. American foreign policy was a cleverly designed device to further the purposes and interests of a small and powerful group of people. Many Americans were indeed well-motivated people, but there was 'a lot of violence, inequality and racism in the United States—it's not heaven.' Furthermore, the Marshall Plan, whatever its apparent generosity to other countries, was fundamentally designed to further the interests of the United States.[36]

By 1951 Seán Ó Faoláin, exercised by this hostility to his beloved America, felt impelled to run a symposium in his own influential little magazine, the *Bell*, on the phenomenon of anti-Americanism. Ó Faoláin, son of an RIC policeman, was one of the best-known Irish literary figures of his time. He had served in the Old IRA and had had books banned under the ultra-severe censorship of the time. He had also published well-known books that rehabilitated such historical figures as Daniel O'Connell and Hugh O'Neill, and he had argued for a historical liberal tradition in Irish culture and politics that had been partially repressed by clericalism and insurrectionist republicanism.

He kicked off his symposium with a little ten-page polemic entitled, rather awkwardly, 'Autoantiamericanism.'[37] It was in part an irritated and amused rejoinder to a letter from a popular and respected trade union leader, Louie Bennett, founder of the Irish Women Workers' Union and sometime president of the Irish Trades Union Congress. She had protested against the newly founded Industrial Development Authority (IDA), in actuality a rather brilliantly thought-out arm of the inter-party Government, co-operating with Marshall Aid schemes to encourage American investment in Ireland and Irish exports to the western hemisphere in particular. (In the coming decades the IDA was to turn out to be one key to Ireland's belated but phenomenal economic development.) Bennett's main argument against Marshall Aid and American investment in Ireland was to the effect that any such project would ensure that Ireland became entangled in American foreign policy initiatives, seen by her as warlike and right-wing. She rounded off one of her letters to the editors with the Virgilian phrase *Timeo Danaos et dona ferentes* (I fear the Greeks, especially when they bring gifts), referring to Virgil's restatement in the *Aeneid* of the distrust of Cassandra, the Trojan priestess, for the wooden horse left, stuffed full of Greek infantry, in the city of Troy as a poisoned gift.[38]

Ó Faoláin's reaction to Bennett's letters was to rubbish them genially and to describe her position as merely emotionalism with no factual argument behind it. He was pro-American, saw the United States as a beacon of freedom and had done postgraduate work at Harvard University in the twenties. In the near future he was to write stories for *Playboy*. He proceeded to outline a complete theory of anti-Americanism in Ireland. He proposed four interacting sources of the ideology or prejudice: firstly, there was British cultural influence, driven by snobbery and resentment at the loss of empire; secondly, a general loss of philosophical or religious belief, due to the catastrophic recent past of Europe; thirdly, a simple and rather traditional Irish suspiciousness; and lastly, an honest patriotism which was, in his view, being misapplied. There was also a traditional distrust of all great powers, which was perfectly understandable, given the history of the island.

However, British cultural and intellectual influence in Ireland was inevitably immense, particularly in the form of the leftist periodical *New Statesman*, then under the charismatic and cantankerous editorship of Kingsley Martin. The British had lost their worldwide empire and had suddenly become a second-rank power, and they disliked their coming down in the world. Some of the Irish of 1951 simply aped, rather pathetically, a British tradition of sneering at America, he argued. Cuttingly, he remarked, 'Evelyn Waugh once called their [British] sourness "the snarl of the underdog at his benefactor".'[39] He continued, rather entertainingly, to note that he personally found the *New Statesman* a good read.

[The *New Statesman*] is the organ of genuine socialists. It contains good literary articles. It is also the British bible of every washed-up Liberal, soured Conservative, lapsed Catholic, half-baked Grammar School intellectual, the new technical school boys whose knowing twang you hear on every bus, every manic depressive Orwellite, fissurated Koestlerite, prehistoric Fabian, antique Keir Hardyite, flaming anti-Roman Catholic, like Mr. Trevor-Roper or the editor himself, Mr. Kingsley Martin, and every other unhappy misfit, pink and pacifist whose sole prophylactic against despair, if not suicide, is a weekly injection of Kingsley Martin's Bottled Bellyache.[40]

Other English papers shared this rather silly anti-American tone, Ó Faoláin observed. The second source of this hostility to the Americans and the Marshall Plan was simply *unbelief*. By 1951 all the isms were wasms. No-one in Europe really believed in either religion or socialism; cynicism was general, and the modern generation of intellectuals believed in nothing. The intellectual and spiritual exhaustion of Europe was complete. The third source, Ó Faoláin claimed, was simply *suspicion*. This mood was one of *cui bono*? (for whose benefit?). The Americans, some claimed, were simply supplying aid to shore up capitalism and feather their own nests. Ó Faoláin's answer to that was simply to say, So what? At least their self-interest seemed to be pretty enlightened, and he pointed to American generosity in pumping money into developmental schemes in deprived parts of Europe, particularly southern Italy and Sicily, parts of a country seen as particularly vulnerable to communist infiltration, subversion and takeover. A last, more traditional source of anti-Americanism, Ó Faoláin argued, was an old-fashioned and essentially honest, if naïve, *patriotism*. This involved a fear of cultural colonisation by American films, entertainment, comics and literature. In general, he accused his targets of mean-mindedness.[41]

Two months later, reactions to Ó Faoláin's polemic came in the form of four short essays. The first was from Louie Bennett, who argued that American methods of mechanised production were unsuited to Ireland, because they drove out labour by substituting capital for it. Furthermore, the confrontation between the United States and the Soviet Union that had set in almost as soon as the guns had gone silent in Europe and Asia in mid-1945 demanded a peace-loving European 'third force.' This was a local anticipation of the anti-American ideas of General de Gaulle a few years later. Hubert Butler, a much-admired liberal essayist of the time, argued for free speech, pointing out that all sensible Americans acknowledged that the United States, like all countries, pursued its own interests and argued that Ó Faoláin should not be complaining about Irish anti-militarism and pacifism. Brigid Lalor argued a straightforward traditional nationalist case, for nationalism, isolationism and social democracy. One D. Sevitt argued a straight Soviet Stalinist line: 'America wants to involve Ireland in her plans for conquering the world.' Fear of American economic might and of militarism were the main themes of these reactions.[42]

However, the Dublin dailies generally supported the idea of the United States being the leader of the western democracies and welcomed it as a fact of international relations.[43] Seán Murray, a veteran Irish communist from the Glens of Antrim, attacked Ó Faoláin's pro-America stance, pointing out quite accurately in the monthly *Irish Democrat* that there was no anti-American writing in the public 'bourgeois' press.[44] He had a point; but anti-Americanism was not particularly popular in Ireland; nor was any pro-Soviet stance particularly liked. On the death of Joseph Stalin in March 1953 the *Irish Democrat* published a piece by one R. W. Hardy that described the old monster as 'one of the greatest men of the twentieth century.' During the Second World War the old nation-killer allegedly 'wept at the frightful sacrifices the Soviet Union had to endure.'[45] This was very much a minority opinion. The mainstream papers were resolutely anti-communist and unpersuaded of Stalin's essential humaneness. In the memory of this writer he was certainly seen at that time as an evil man and as a mass murderer.[46] The perception was accurate and shrewd, if under-informed.

The Irish left remained small, divided and sectarian, in the sense of being doctrinaire and exclusive. What was evolving instead of a move to the left from the late forties onwards was a growing interest in Europe, a new reconstructed Europe that appealed to the intellectuals, annoyed the British and was approved of, and ratified by, the Americans, because of their concern about the Soviet Union. A prosperous Europe was also attractive for purposes of mutual trade between the United States and Europe and of American investment in a resurrected continent.

Seán Lemass had written about a future united Europe as a young man of thirty in 1929, inspired by the United Europe movement of the time and also by the example of the prosperity of the vast single-country market of the United States of his time, a country that he admired greatly.[47] He wrote this prophetic piece just before he became an architect of Irish economic autarky on the pragmatic grounds that everyone was doing it and therefore that no Irish Government had any other choice. Lemass was a philosophical free-trader who had to gainsay his own economic principles in the face of the protectionist world of the Great Depression. Europe in the fifties appealed to an old instinctive Irish 'Prester John' yearning for a Continental saviour, whether it be the Spaniards in the seventeenth century, the French in the eighteenth century or the Americans in the nineteenth century. In the twentieth century it was, for a while and for some, the Germans. Later it was a combination of the Americans and the 'Europeans', principally led by the international Christian Democrat tradition, a tradition to which the Irish subscribed almost without realising it.[48] Lemass was to preside over an Irish opening to a new Europe by dismantling in the years after 1957 the protectionist apparatus that he had built in the thirties. However, he had always been a free-trader; he simply did not live, and the Irish did not live, between 1929 and the fifties in a free-trade world but in a world of warfare, militarised economies, disrupted trade and tariff barriers.

THE CRISIS OF THE MID-FIFTIES

The inter-party Government staggered on after the Mother and Child disaster until June 1951, and it did surprisingly well in the general election of that month, newspapers actually predicting a new inter-party Government. Clann na Poblachta did badly, indicating that MacBride was being blamed for the betrayal of Browne more than was Fine Gael or the Labour Party. (Browne had excoriated him publicly in a well-known release of private letters to the public press, and Browne became a popularly acclaimed hero in working-class Dublin, as opposed to MacBride's demonised villain.) Furthermore, a cloud of independent deputies was elected, reflecting in part a probable dissatisfaction with all the big parties. Fianna Fáil managed to cobble together a Government with independent support, and it came back to power with an uneasy majority.

In February 1953 the *Economist* published an article that commented on the repetitiveness of Irish politics; 1953 was just like 1950, it opined, with parochial disputes over milk prices and health policy and rows over the management of rural post offices. This mixture of inconsequence and repetitiveness was symptomatic of an underlying ailment in Irish politics. It reflected a blocked polity, where decisions that should have been taken were essentially under silent veto. Although the paper did not say so specifically, small farmers, the Catholic Church, trade unions, professional associations or state-sponsored bodies that wished to prevent private enterprise competing against them wielded this joint veto. This syndrome of repetition, commented the paper, 'arises almost entirely because of decisions that must be taken in Irish politics; these have been avoided with great skill for years.'[49]

By this time de Valera, although still Taoiseach at seventy-one, was increasingly coming to be seen as a figurehead, while the dominant forces in the Government were MacEntee, seen as being on the right wing, and Lemass, seen as being left of centre. De Valera still felt entitled to take months off to have his nearly blind eyes treated by doctors in the Netherlands. Lemass had clearly emerged as a managerialist in the tradition of James Burnham.[50] MacEntee was seen as being on the conservative side of the party; however, as a Belfast engineer and a fearsome political infighter he shared, as another townie, Lemass's almost contemptuous disregard for farming as a potential industry. Left versus right, however, continued not to mean very much in Ireland, and agrarian versus off-farm employment became a far more salient division. In March 1954, having lost two by-elections, de Valera called a general election.

In May an inter-party Government was returned, de Valera commenting wryly, '*Beidh lá eile ag an bPaorach*' (There will be another day).[51] The new inter-party Government decided yet again to put scarce American money into agricultural science; the Fine Gael obsession with agriculture as the potential motor of economic development was again evident.[52] Many commentators reported a general atmosphere of popular unease in the mid-fifties. In July 1954 the new Taoiseach, John A. Costello, said that the main obstacle to economic recovery was the public's lack of confidence in the Government's ability to put its policies into operation. A student in University College, Cork, wrote at the same time about modern Irish youth: 'Modern mass democracy is something which the majority of young people despise.' They would have preferred, it seemed, a king or a dictator, according to this very young writer. The economy was a shambles that had better be fixed quickly to avert a general political collapse. The country would have to revive Irish and decentralise government. The editorial of the same day noted with some alarm that skilled workers and even middle-class people were leaving the country, essentially concluding that it was washed up. The absence of any real political thought was evident.[53]

In May 1954 the *Standard* weighed in in the person of its regular columnist Manus O'Neill, who ascribed much of the country's problems to the gerontocratic tendencies of its elites.

> In all my conscious life, which covers a few more years than the lifetime of the State, I never remember any period that was more subdued, grey, unexciting and empty of promise in political and social matters. One gets the feeling, almost from the air, that the state has grown old and weary before its time and is sinking comfortably into that somnolence in which some of the little principalities of the old Germanies used to wallow before they and their independence were engulfed . . . We have come to the end of an era of Irish life. The impetus of the revolution, which carried us through three decades, declines with the decline of the men who made that revolution.[54]

O'Neill was on to something, and subsequent academic research has confirmed that generational tensions, the growth of something that looked like gerontocracy and the exclusion from power of younger people, rather than any real ideological differences, conditioned much political passion in the fifties and were not resolved until the next decade.[55] The reluctance to cultivate a younger generation of political leaders, even though such a generational change was inevitable, seems to have been linked to a traditional Irish peasant farming resentment of the young and to a fear of being dispossessed by younger, stronger and more energetic people.

'Aknefton' of the *Irish Times* commented on the general atmosphere of insecurity and worry in July 1956.[56] Éamon de Valera, Erskine Childers and Seán Lemass all detected this mood while being in hopeful opposition but thought it exaggerated and easily dispelled once the country experienced a period of united, resolute and ambitious government—evidently a government run by themselves. From his own viewpoint Aknefton made a similar point in September when he or she described Irish politics despairingly as 'incoherent.' In the same issue the *Irish Times* referred to Ireland in almost defeatist tones as 'a nation marking time.'[57] Bad temper seemed occasionally to overcome an internally divided and somewhat besieged Government. Owen Sheehy Skeffington, an indefatigable opponent of corporal punishment in schools, where it sometimes achieved horrific levels, was shouted down in the Seanad by the Minister for Education, Richard Mulcahy, in mid-1955. Mulcahy accused him of pushing for a non-Irish, alien system of discipline and child-rearing.[58] Through the smoke of sham-battle the growing stature of Lemass was noted by Aknefton as early as October 1955.[59]

1956 was to be a year of economic crisis, and it was seen as such by the newspapers. Industrial leaders stressed publicly in February that home interests needed to be protected from the economic whirlwind. There was a real fear of cheap imports from the 'Far East', an Aesopian way of referring to Japan, at the time going through an extraordinary economic transformation.[60] The *Irish Times* screamed that Ireland was 'FALLING BEHIND' in the international economic 'race.'[61] Lemass announced almost apocalyptically in the *Press* that the issue now was one of national 'survival.'[62] In May the *Standard* announced: 'This country has fought long, and it has fought honourably, for political freedom. The time would now seem to be opportune to launch the battle for economic freedom.' This emphasis on economic well-being was combined with a fairly frank assessment of the plight of the poor a generation after independence.[63] This was itself a rare display of uneasy conscience.

Emigration was quite accurately seen as rocketing, and the *Irish Times* announced a 'national emergency' in June 1956.[64] Lemass asserted that tax incentives would have to be given to industry and that in future 'the country must rely on the development of industry in the main.'[65] Sweetman and Costello in Fine Gael had come to the same conclusion independently. The *Irish Times* implicitly accepted this view in an editorial in late February 1957, just before the general election of that year.[66] De Valera, apparently already scenting a fall of the Government and a consequent general election, announced at a Cork by-election campaign meeting in August 1956:

> All is set for a new national advance. The infancy and early adolescence of our state is over. We only need now the adult, manly determination to succeed—to advance together as a community in a steady, ordered, disciplined manner towards the ends we have in view. As a people we must be enterprising and bold, and gird ourselves for the efforts necessary to reach and maintain our proper place in a competitive world. Should this daunt us?[67]

'Operation Harvest,' the IRA campaign in Northern Ireland, was launched from the South by a resurgent IRA of young disillusioned men filled with the usual mixture of religious affect and irredentist nationalism. Although the campaign had been clamped down on by Dublin in late 1956, it was, according to Gerard Sweetman, Minister for Finance in the dying inter-party Government, distracting the authorities from thinking clearly about the economic crisis. The Government seems to have been actually frightened of a resurgence of popular nationalist anti-partitionism of a militarist character. The evidence actually suggests a fair amount of passive sympathy for the insurgents but a general indifference to the entire issue on the part of most of the population. Sweetman pronounced the IRA to be 'a group of men with no authority or representative capacity of any kind what-soever.' He was speaking in Tralee, Co. Kerry, in the heart of an area with a persistent, if naïve, IRA tradition—a tradition many years later characterised wonderfully and accurately by Prof. John Kelly of UCD as one carried forward by a bunch of 'demented hillbillies.'[68]

In Belmullet, Co. Mayo, on the hustings, de Valera announced: 'This election is particularly important because the country is in a serious economic condition, and if Fianna Fáil is returned to power we will not merely get it out of this condition but make it the start of a new era.'[69] In the ensuing general election Sinn Féin, the IRA front party, was to take four seats in western Ireland but threw away their opportunity of becoming a serious force in politics in their traditional fashion by refusing to take the seats. The election took place on 5 March, and Fianna Fáil was able to form a Government—not so much because its vote rose but because voters hostile to de Valera's party but despairing of Fine Gael and its allies stayed at home or cast protest votes for the tiny IRA-Sinn Féin bloc. Fianna Fáil lost votes to its illegitimate little half-brother Sinn Féin, or it would have been a landslide by Irish standards.[70]

SPRINGTIME FOR LEMASS

Lemass returned to his usual post at Industry and Commerce. A wide-ranging public debate on economic policy, involving economists, political leaders, industrialists, senior civil servants and even the occasional bishop and educationalist ensued over the following three years, coinciding with an unmistakable upturn in the economy, starting in 1957 and led yet again by industry and not by agriculture. Intelligence was suddenly in demand and was found not to be in short supply. In March,

Charles Carter, a well-known British economist of the time, gave his famous lecture, reprinted in *Studies* in 1957, on the essential irrationality of Irish governmental economic policies and on how easily the situation might be set to rights. He apparently found the Irish political situation idiotic and quite unnecessarily preventive of success. He didn't make the point, but interest-group politics, when permitted to run riot and even encouraged by authoritarian governmental fiat, do tend to produce irrationalities of a surreal kind, as later chapters argue. Partition was a red herring, he argued, and was used by politicians and commentators as an excuse for their own persistent underachievement. Reunification he adjudged to be a 'fantasy'. Old freedom-fighters, he suggested, did not necessarily make good administrators.[71] However, chance remarks he made also in 1958 in view of new Government initiatives indicate that he felt that if the Republic were ever to get its act together the poorer Southern tortoise might eventually get the better of the richer Northern hare.[72]

A start was made in the late fifties with dismantling Government controls on the economy and trade and lowering tariff walls, although the complete abolition of tariffs did not occur until the late seventies. Carter's comments broke a strange silence, and a torrent of complaint about Irish industrial backwardness hit the papers over the next few years. A typical example is a tirade by T. R. Ashley, a management consultant, in the *Irish Press* in January 1959:

> The fact that businessmen had managed for so long without rational policies of capital investment has been compared to the feat of crossing the Atlantic without a map, compass or sextant.[73]

The strange official silence about education, essentially generated by the Department of Education's historical terror of the Catholic bishops, was finally broken in the late fifties as well;

something would have to be done about the politics of Irish education, or rather about its non-politics.[74] How the journalists of the time dealt with these issues is outlined elsewhere in this book. Uneasiness and a lack of political self-assurance persisted and seem to have driven much of the debate on new departures in economic and social policy.

As late as November 1957, however, Alexis Fitzgerald felt able to write a mildly pessimistic article about the prospects for the survival of democracy in Ireland. Sinn Féin was a revolutionary menace, he felt.[75] This fear of revolutionary violence ignored the actual abject weakness of the Irish left and the political absentee-ism and primitive incoherence of the republican insurrectionists. It also ignored the fact that all Irish people had the option of Exit rather than rebellious Voice, thereby choking off Voice, to use the terms of Albert Hirschman: you could vote with your feet and leave the country.[76]

Prof. Myles Dillon, a well-known Celtic scholar, denounced the use of partition and of Irish as means of avoiding real issues and problems; these extraneous issues were simply 'bedevilling Irish politics.' The cowardly use of the Irish-language requirement to be permitted to pass one's Leaving Certificate examination or to qualify for a civil service job as a way of covertly discriminating against a person's religion or nationality was 'evil.'[77] Noel Browne, already evolving into a sort of martyr-hero figure, announced in November 1958 that 'our gunmen' turned politicians since the twenties had 'between them in over forty years . . . created this socially decadent, economically bankrupt and intellectually arid gombeens' paradise.'[78]

The country was a failure in the minds of many. The experi-ence of weak and unstable Governments in the 1950s seems to have had something to do with this demoralisation. This strengthened Fianna Fáil's determination to do away with proportional representation by means of the single transferable vote. The issue surfaced in the silly season of August 1958, possibly as a kite-flying exercise.[79] The Fianna Fáil line was that PR led to fragmented party systems and eventually to the collapse of democracy and the coming of dictatorship; the unspoken precedent was, of course, the utterly different case of Weimar Germany. No-one made the point either that PR with single transferable vote, although certainly very different from the Anglo-American 'first past the post' system, also differed wildly from the Continental list-PR systems so commonly blamed for party fragmentation, chiefly in that it was PR with a totally free choice given to the voter to vote for *candidates* rather than for a party ticket or 'list'. The Irish system permitted the voter to vote a ticket, vote for one individual, vote for a few candidates or vote for virtually everybody on the ballot in rank order while omitting the candidate least preferred, therefore throwing all the other candidates against the hated one. This crucial point was completely and bizarrely omitted from the public debate, perhaps because nobody knew anything about the Continental systems. The idea of voting merely for a label with a list of names provided by a party central office was alien to a culture that was heavily localist and personalist.[80]

The effect of this system was to encourage cross-class and cross-ideology parties and alliances of parties, uniting left and right. Fianna Fáil was a classic cross-class 'catch-all' party, and the Labour Party together with Fine Gael constituted a similar pan-ideology alliance—incongruous, perhaps, but obedient to the iron logic of the system. The standard text on Irish democratic representation, James Hogan's *Elections and Representation*, touted to the public in the Government bookshop, seems to have spread this particular piece of Irish convenient confusion.[81]

It was also never pointed out that, in practice, PR with single transferable vote had produced one big party and a few others, one of which was quite large, which ganged up on it—scarcely a total fragmentation or an invitation to chaos and dictatorship.[82] In small homogeneous countries one big centrist or centre-left party versus an alliance of the rest is a common pattern. Instead it was commonly suggested that Fianna Fáil wanted the 'first past the post' system so as to have a permanent majority in the Dáil. There was something in this; Neil Blaney, Minister for Local Government, blurted out the subtext of the proposed change in January 1959: 'If this referendum goes through, Fine Gael will have had it.'[83] The *Independent* suspected that the referendum was really designed to distract public attention from economic problems and unpopular economic remedies.[84]

More interestingly, Lemass appears to have favoured the abolition of PR because by making political competition so cut-throat it discouraged the potential involvement in political life of the kind of business leader and intellectual he valued for Ireland's economic development.[85] The reverse side of this seems to have been his low opinion of many of his own backbenchers. Unlike de Valera, Lemass was eager to attract to Fianna Fáil people of talent who were not of his own political tradition. As is well known, he tried at one time to attract the young Garret FitzGerald to the party. FitzGerald went on to become leader of Fine Gael, Minister for Foreign Affairs and eventually Taoiseach.

In June 1959 Lemass became leader of Fianna Fáil, and the PR referendum was held simultaneously with the presidential election. De Valera won the presidency fairly easily, but multi-seat PR survived the onslaught of Fianna Fáil, mainly thanks to a Dublin vote in favour of the status quo, expressing a city-dwellers' distrust of cute culchies, perhaps; rural constituencies favoured its abolition by narrow proportions.[86] It seems that the unpopularity of the campaign against PR denied Dev a last landslide; certainly the cunning old veteran tried to use his own famous coat-tails to get his pet amendment through the popular contest, and he nearly got away with it. However, not quite this time.

Lemass became Taoiseach immediately after, a tired work-aholic and aging man in a hurry, fighting the onset of ill health and a fading of energies. He was to succeed brilliantly, in a premiership of seven years still remembered as perhaps the most successful Irish premiership ever. He used to make characteristic black jokes about his own 'decrepitude'. An era had come to an end, and clearly something new and very different was about to happen.[87] (Later chapters deal with what had happened at work, in education and in economic policy in the fifties to make this new departure possible.) Old uneasiness and uncertainty persisted, however, to re-emerge during later times of tribulation.

As late as September 1960, when the boom was obviously in full swing and good times were coming, the *Times* commented that the Irish party system was ill-geared to dealing with the problems of economic development. 'It may even be unjust to ask political parties who were born out of the gravest political crisis in this country, now to turn to the more thought-provoking problems of building a new economy.'[88] The transition from arguing about the symbols of independence to debating the ways and means of building a modern economy had actually been made in the 1950s, perhaps the major political achievement of the decade. What had not happened was the emergence of any serious debate about education and about the kind of culture and citizenry the Republic needed.

Comhairle Cathrach & Contae Phort Láirge
Waterford City & County Council
Leabharlann Dún Garbhán
Dungarvan Library
Borrower Receipt

Customer name: Headd Elizabeth

Title: News from a new republic : Ireland in t
ID: 30004003854854
Due: 05-01-19

Total items: 1
05/12/2018 13:17
Checked out: 1
Overdue: 0
Hold requests: 0
Ready for pickup: 0

Thank you for using the self service system.
Visit us online at www.waterfordcouncil.ie
Tel 0761 10 2141

K1

Chapter 3

DUBLIN NEWSPAPERS AND THE CRISIS OF THE FIFTIES

DUBLIN NEWSPAPERS IN THE POST-WAR WORLD, 1948–62

Dublin daily journalism, in the virtual absence of radio and television, was well served by three national newspapers, the *Irish Press*, *Irish Times* and *Irish Independent*, during the era 1945–62. While the *Irish Press* was obviously and explicitly the mouthpiece of Fianna Fáil and echo of Seán Lemass, theoretically the *Irish Times* and *Irish Independent* were non-partisan. In reality the *Independent* was Fine Gael. As a middle-class newspaper that was more popular than its political ally, the *Indo* had to moderate its leanings and be respectful to Fianna Fáil opinion, a stance that the *Press* did not reciprocate in its attitudes to Fine Gael.

The *Irish Times* was the heir to the unionist tradition in the Republic. It was already in the process of transforming itself into a liberal nationalist paper, but it had not quite got there yet. Even in the fifties the *Times* had clearly developed a loyalty to the Dublin state and was beginning to develop cautiously a liberal line on partition and the Catholic Church.

The *Independent* had by far the largest circulation, followed by the *Press*, while that of the *Times* was tiny. The *Independent* was also by far the richest paper. The *Press* group was the youngest of the three, the *Irish Press* dating only from 1931. There was, and still is, a niche for a gadfly press in Dublin; chief among these at that time were the *Bell*, founded by Seán Ó Faoláin, the *Leader*, a survivor from the pre-revolutionary period, the impoverished communist monthly *Irish Democrat* published by the Connolly Association in London, and the weekly *Standard,* a paper that reflected most completely the confused and self-contradictory ideological currents of the Irish Catholicism of the time. *Hibernia* in this period evolved from an organ of the Knights of Columbanus to a relatively liberal intellectual fortnightly paper. *Dublin Opinion,* a monthly humorous journal, provided gentle commentary and caricature of political and social life.

FARMING AND THE ECONOMIC CRISIS

One immediate and evident contrast between the three Dublin dailies was their attitude to farming. Both the *Times* and the *Independent* assumed that the economic future of the Republic was agrarian. The idea that Ireland's future lay in off-farm employment was not exactly scouted but rather was not fully grasped by commentators. Articles on agriculture, the extreme reluctance of the young to go into farming and the need for agricultural education were commonplace. Both papers had a large-farm readership; the old thirties argument about the cow versus the plough had already been settled in the former's favour. In stark contrast, the *Press* was determinedly pro-industry while remaining equally determinedly nostalgic about the small-farm ancestry of its readers; generally it ignored farming in favour of industry and vocational training. It never discussed farming as a serious career choice. Behind the *Press* there lurked the strong views of Seán Lemass, who knew little about farming and cared less.

A Darwinian process of elimination of the less fit was going on in Irish farming, but it was inevitably going to operate slowly; it would take a long time for an efficient and modern agricultural 'industry' to emerge. In practice Lemass acted during his years as Minister for Industry and Commerce and later Taoiseach as though the long-term stagnating effects of the Land Acts meant that farming would have to be bypassed by industrial development. In January 1948 he remarked in the pages of the *Press* that Fianna Fáil was not a class party but 'a workers' party.'[1] By this he seems to have meant a pretty inclusive sense of the term 'worker', including members of the nascent national business class. He saw the *Press* as the voice of an emergent cross-class patriotic alliance that transcended sectional interests.

All three papers published articles on agriculture, but the *Independent* and the *Times* were far more likely to publish articles of interest to more commercial farmers who wished to use 'scientific methods'. This is not to say that the two papers neglected industry but rather to note that they did not share the *Press's* view that industrialisation was the only real way out of the trap of stagnation. Lemass wanted to bypass completely what he saw as the morass of Irish agriculture. So did others: in October 1948 *Dublin Opinion* published a cartoon portraying a farmer and his wife commenting on rural electrification: 'This improvin' of rural life is wonderful . . . Now the children will be able to study till all hours of the night for the Civil Service.'[2]

In March 1948 the *Independent* published an editorial commenting on an official report on the condition of the land. It had huge potential for pasture production, but much of it lay unused.[3] By way of illustration, in May 1949 the paper pointed out that the pig industry had fed the country in 1931 and had provided pig products and live pigs for export. According to the *Indo*, the Government had subsequently virtually regulated the industry to death.[4]

Rural life was commonly seen as superior to urban life, but the young disagreed and expressed that disagreement with their feet. Despite that verdict, agriculture was still seen as so central that nearly all Marshall Aid funds were sunk in it. In July 1951 the new Fianna Fáil Minister for Agriculture, Seán Moylan, commented on the low educational attainments of Irish farmers.

The farmers in the past paid very little attention to a boy who was going to occupy the farm. Immediately he was able to take a fork in his hand he was put out on the land. The money the farmer had saved was spent on the education of other members of the family and that was why they had not had the progress in agriculture that they should have had in this country—because the farmers were being denied the education to which they were entitled.[5]

In one of his rare references to farming Lemass suggested in January 1952 that Irish agriculture was old-fashioned. He thought that eventually a process of the elimination of the unfit would lead to a modern agriculture.[6] Later in the month the *Times* wailed, 'On almost every side of agricultural life there is the same melancholy story of decay; but there is no sign that the decline will be arrested.'[7]

In July 1953 the *Press* editorialised that all the efforts at industrialisation behind tariff and quota protection had just about managed to absorb the surplus population leaving the land. As agriculture mechanised, rural employment would shrink and rural productivity would grow.[8] A now vicariously frightening letter was published in the *Irish Times* in September 1952: 'During the last hundred years we have been living on our capital of phosphorus in the soil, which is now in a great many areas almost exhausted.' Other vital minerals were also disappearing. The cattle were starving amid apparent plenty.

In February 1953 the *Economist* of London, as reported in the *Irish Times*, commented on Irish political paralysis in the face of certain obviously necessary decisions that were being avoided. Irish agricultural production had been stagnant for a century, it claimed.[9] In February 1954 the Organisation for European Economic Co-operation (OEEC) observed that Ireland's agricultural output had not yet recovered to the level of 1929.[10] But Cardinal John D'Alton intoned in early 1953:

Those who laboured on the land were more closely in touch than others with nature in its various moods, and could be more in touch with God, Whose providence was clearly discernible in the yearly round of the seasons.[11]

A thoughtful editorial in the *Times* in July 1954 noted that skilled workers and professionals were emigrating and were not interested in leading the nation. The power of the Big House,

like its shattered stones passed into the hands of farmers and smallholders, who are only now, slowly and warily, beginning to come together out of the barren isolation which they enjoyed for so long. With a static agricultural production and a dwindling supply of labour, one wonders how unmixed a blessing the Land Acts really were.[12]

As early as May 1954 the *Independent* noted that industry was developing faster than agriculture.[13] In June it reported a big slump even in processed agricultural products.[14] The *Independent* also reported in the same month that agricultural scholarships were not being taken up, but the under-equipped vocational education system could not keep up with the demand from eager young people wishing to acquire skills that would enable them to earn their living outside agriculture. Despite all these obvious straws in the wind, the *Independent* announced in an extraordinarily defensive editorial a few days later that industrial development in Ireland had actually 'reached its limit,' and more money would have to be poured into agriculture.[15] In October, however, it announced 'Big Jump in Industry' and a 'Marked Industrial Expansion' of an almost incredible 8 per cent in 1953, compared with 1952.[16] The paper was suffering from a curious intellectual schizophrenia and was ignoring an obvious piece of data: nascent Irish industry was showing a dynamism that modern Irish agriculture had never experienced. Alternatively, it was echoing a national condition of indecision.

In March 1954 the *Press*, always more single-minded than the *Independent*, rebuked James Dillon, sometime Minister for Agriculture, for ridiculing the prospects for industrialisation.[17]

The *Press* suggested in 1954 that the Land Acts lay behind the pathologies of Irish agriculture. It concluded by arguing that agriculture would have to learn to compete.[18] Fianna Fáil's aggressive scepticism about agriculture was articulated yet again by Seán Moylan in May 1955 in his off-the-cuff remark that 'many people who praise the dual purpose cow did not realise that in many herds we had a no-purpose cow if the profits had to be fed back in concentrates.'[19] In August 1956 the *Standard* lamented:

Now the Irish, bitter and grumbling, leave Ireland to work in Britain because the farmyards are too muddy, the villages too depressing, local transport too bad, wages too low, food prices too high, houses too few, work too scarce—under the Government they themselves elected freely, unhampered by any man, uninfluenced except by the common techniques which are the stock in trade of politicians everywhere—the mixture of promises and prejudices which by nature seems to succeed the highest ideas on all sides in the rigid and paralysing framework of the party system.[20]

Hibernia, still the organ of the Knights of Columbanus but showing some tendencies toward liberalisation, published a revealing article a little later in the year by Father Michael O'Carroll, a well-known member of the Holy Ghost Fathers. The census had just indicated a new wave of emigration, and O'Carroll voiced an echo of an old fear of race death. Irish emigrants in England, he wrote, are well-paid, they enjoy amenities they cannot have at home, they have larger opportunities for self-improvement and self-advancement. They are not hopelessly held back by barriers thrown up around certain classes and groups.

Irish society was unattractive, careers were often blocked by vested interests and young people simply wanted to escape from it.[21]

In November 1956 Martin Smyth wrote in the *Times* that many farmers were lazy and did the minimum of work on the land. Anticipating Raymond Crotty by a generation, he proposed a land tax that would be inversely related to productivity.

As long as these men control a large proportion of Ireland's best land, and believe in this policy, they can effectively block the progress of the whole country, and this is exactly what they are doing at present.[22]

Cyril McShane responded a week later in a brilliantly argued and empirically informed article, arguing that farm output varied wildly, and that a land tax was not politically feasible. The dual-purpose cow existed because meat was only a secondary product. On small farms more cattle were reared than could ever be brought to maturity, so they had to be sold on to larger farms. These half-starved animals were the only ones the larger farmer could buy. Intensive feeding would be wasted on such animals, and they had to be got rid of at three or four years old. In such a market efficient modern farming was pointless, was the devastating conclusion.[23]

In March 1957 Smyth pointed out that half of Irish farmers had no title deeds to their land, and it was difficult to get bank credit against landholdings, partly because of this legal lacuna.[24] Jack Lynch, now Minister for Education, asserted that education had been seen for too long as irrelevant to farm life.

As late as 1959 the *Independent* stuck to its agrarian guns, editorialising that 'the land is, and must long remain, the chief source of livelihood for our people.'[25] Dillon defended the farmer valiantly in July 1959, claiming that farmers could double their output if incentives to do so existed. He also asserted that most of the exporting to Britain during the post-war years had come from agriculture. He also revived the old and increasingly irrelevant plough versus cow or farmer versus rancher division that had underlain the Fianna Fáil versus Fine Gael cleavage in the 1930s. The *Irish Times* finally changed sides in 1959, specifically rejecting the view that agriculture was the necessary basis for economic progress. On 9 May 1960 the *Independent* finally went to Canossa and accepted openly for the first time that Ireland's industrial development would have to be given priority over agriculture in Government policy and economic leadership.[26]

THE SLOW ACCEPTANCE OF INDUSTRIALISATION

Back in 1948 the idea that Ireland would have to become a successful exporting country, and that such success would mean far more than exporting cattle and food to Britain, was only beginning to dawn on policy-makers, journalists and the general public. In January 1949 Daniel Morrissey, in Lemass's traditional ministerial seat, declared the economy to be in good shape, with no external debt. 'Our greatest need in relation to industry was the shortage of skilled technicians and trained executives.'[27] The new industrialists seem to have occasionally felt themselves to be unpopular, envied and vilified. The communist *Irish Democrat* spotted this weakness in the new and superficially successful Ireland of 1951.[28] The new bourgeois and commercialised Ireland of Lemass was built on shaky psychological and material foundations.

In reality, farm productivity had scarcely changed, the gap between rich and poor was widening and 'the whole rickety structure of prices and luxury living for the middle class' was built on very shaky foundations, the paper claimed. *The Irish Press* argued generally over the years for a wager on the strong: big farming, industry, the new and growing skilled working class and the new capitalist entrepreneurs. However, Irish industry remained solidly protectionist in the early fifties, and the Government was vacillating.

In opposition in 1949, de Valera obediently expressed in public his private doubts about the entire system of controls, tariffs and quotas that his own party had built up. He put this in the context of the American drive towards freeing European trade and spoke not in Ireland but in Strasbourg.[29] However, a fear of damaging the protected industries often surfaced. William Norton and Frank Aiken, of the Labour Party and Fianna Fáil, respectively, voiced their unease in late 1949, opposing the idea of a European customs union.[30] Norton, a Post Office worker and trade union leader, was a convinced industrialiser and protectionist, whereas Aiken, an IRA veteran from South Armagh, was a team player who followed the industrialising line that was pushed by Lemass and blessed by de Valera.

Having shelved the transatlantic air service as a waste of money in 1949, the inter-party Government sold off the five Lockheed Constellations to a delighted British Overseas Airways Corporation. It then proceeded in 1950 to close down the CIE heavy engineering project, another brainchild of Lemass's. Lemass, a brilliant propagandist, or someone associated with him, reported anonymously some months later:

CIE fitters had tears in their eyes, at the sight of the finest machinery in the world going to loss. Must we always be satisfied with assembling here parts from Britain? Were we not going to get on to the manufacturing process some time?[31]

In March 1950 Morrissey announced in effect that the new Industrial Development Authority was to plan future industrialisation.[32] There was some vague sense in the papers of the potential of this new agency. However, Lemass took time to grasp its importance, because he distrusted its Fine Gael provenance. The man who seems to have really understood its significance was Morrissey: he pointed out that very little information about Irish industry was available even to industrialists themselves and that the first job of the IDA would be to collect such information and make it available.

Lemass changed his tune when he returned to Government in 1951.[33] Back in office for more than a year, in late 1952 he remarked that the country was indeed running down its external assets and that they would be all gone in a few years. Then there would be a crisis. However, the Fianna Fáil Government would be ready for it. It was increasing investment in cement, sugar, shipping and electrical plant. Half the capital was being provided from private sources.[34] In early 1952 the *Times* feared a reversion to protectionism and self-sufficiency, arguing that the country would have to brave the risks of modern international trade if it were ever to escape poverty.[35]

In June 1953 Lemass was positively gung-ho about developmental prospects. He spoke about investment in infrastructure, electricity, land improvement, housing, health, and education.[36] Repeatedly he gave the public ideological pep talks in an almost single-handed attempt to change the psychology of the people from one of passivity to one that encouraged energy and optimism.[37] More soberly, a *Press* editorial noted that industrial development since 1932 had just about absorbed the surplus labour leaving agriculture as agriculture mechanised and increased production while shrinking employment.[38]

Despite all the bad news, something was indeed changing in an almost underground way. As early as 1953 Aknefton of the *Times* wrote that the business pages of the newspapers reflect the state of growth of Irish industry and latterly have shown, beyond all doubt, a development which is new in so far as this country is concerned—the emergence into full prominence of a managerial class as the leaders of Irish trade, industry and commerce.

However, industry was still intellectually backward, and managers continued to be reluctant to discuss innovative changes with their workers.[39] The *Indo* relieved itself of the strange opinion in June 1954 that Irish industry had developed to its absolute limit and that future investment therefore should be in agriculture.[40]

The cacophony and disunity were extraordinary. In July 1954 Norton lamented the lack of technical skills necessary for the new industrial ventures.[41] Erskine Childers remarked that greater productivity required a change of attitude on the part of three-quarters of the population, changes in the educational system and a campaign of instilling confidence in the future.[42] The *Independent* in December 1954 reported that France had moved away from the 'strangle' of protective tariffs.[43] There was a general, if rather confused, sense of new possibilities, although not yet a consensus about what the general lines of policy should be; nor did the will quite yet exist for a genuine new departure. People were evidently hunting around for new ideas.

Morrissey of the second inter-party Government was attempting to tiptoe around the protectionist mentality of some senior civil servants, in particular the implacable and legendary opposition to free trade of J. C. B. McCarthy, Secretary of the Department of Industry and Commerce, and many, but not all, of the manufacturers. In this he had the sympathetic hearing of Gerard Sweetman, who had a background in economics and who listened also to Whitaker, Lynch and others.[44] Morrissey remarked, rather alarmingly, that Britain and Northern Ireland were attracting plenty of American investment, while the Republic was not. The fancy-free Americans merely took one look at the apparent hostility to capital in the Republic and went elsewhere. Government-imposed price controls, survivals of wartime, were another turn-off. There was a general air of entrepreneurial frustration in the country, despite Lemass's boosterism.

In the same month Joseph Griffin, a well-known Dublin businessman, published a well-publicised paper on the significance of the price structure in the economy. He had an early version of Cathal Guiomar's 'designer economy' in mind. He argued that Irish economic success, such as it was, occurred *despite* the economic and political framework in which it had to operate. The Irish had an 'underdeveloped country and the potential for an expanding economy and population . . . Only an ideal was lacking.'[45] The usual lamentation was recited. Agriculture was underdeveloped and achieved only 50 per cent of its potential. Manufacturing potential was unexplored and unexamined. Industry was sluggish, and in services, education and culture progress was slow and underdeveloped. 'Frustration and cynicism are apparent in all walks of life and at all levels of society.' Price controls depressed economic activity; in Britain and America the price structure was closer to the ideal.

In February 1956 Costello urged the encouragement of foreign investment, but only for export industries, a proposition that Lemass was to echo faithfully a year later.[46] The economic crash of 1956 was now on its way, and the population was shrinking as emigration reached record levels and even the middle class were leaving. The *Press* announced: 'Emigration of Professional Groups Deplored.'[47] It claimed that the real incomes of professional groups, people who had easily transferable skills and therefore itchier feet than some of the less privileged, had declined by 30 per cent since 1939, partly because of taxation.[48]

There was now a slowly growing consensus among all the political leaders that something would have to be done, involving foreign investment, serious cultural change and educational development. Education was not really emphasised. Hindsight wisdom tells us that this was part of a general pattern that was characteristic of the decade; education could expand only through private effort and by stealth.[49]

NEW DEPARTURES

Common Europe was coming, and the long Irish love affair with Europe was beginning. In February 1957 the manager of Gateaux Ltd, a successful food manufacturer with a clever line in cartoon advertising, expressed the view that Ireland could not afford to stay out of the coming Common Market. People who had been protected for generations in their industries and who had never exported anything were getting 'too loudmouthed' about this issue, he asserted. He hoped that when the decision was made their opinion would be assessed only in relation to their real and rather inconsiderable contribution to the Irish economy.[50] Fianna Fáil swept back into power in March 1957.

In April it was reported that Hungarian refugees, horrified by Irish poverty, were going back to communist tyranny in Hungary. As the black joke of the time had it, the wolf was at the door, howling to get out. Lemass growled again: 'Those who are still pulling long faces and making gloomy forecasts about the future, will look just as foolish, when the future arrives, as the Jeremiahs of the past.'[51] He then announced that the Control of Manufactures Acts were to be amended and, in a silent tribute to the power of vested interests in post-war Ireland, an incredible twelve years after the end of the Second World War, wartime price controls were to be abolished. James Ryan admitted that abolition had been opposed by many in Fianna Fáil; for electoral purposes controls could be represented as protecting the poor against the rich.[52] John Conroy of the Irish Transport and General Workers' Union, the largest union in the country, argued noisily that controls didn't work.[53] As usual, a step had been blocked for years by what amounted to a conspiracy between Fianna Fáil back-benchers, employers and unions against the public interest. In August, Lemass claimed that foreign firms were beginning to wake up to the productive potential of Ireland.[54] He began to emphasise a new theme in 1957, that of efficiency in production.[55]

A few weeks later, as if on cue (and possibly actually on cue), the OEEC recommended that Ireland should go in for more private and less public productive investment and that the Government should be more supportive of business. It should also afford the maximum scope to make profits and boost production. Secondly, public funds should be directed less at social investment and more to productive schemes. Dependence on the British market for sales of meat and dairy products should be lessened by an active search for other foreign markets.[56]

In February 1958 the *Press* observed that industrialists were reluctant to hire technicians. Jack Lynch commented that Irish people still saw no connection between education and the capacity to earn a living.[57] The president of the Federation of Irish Industry pointed out that the output of technically trained people per head of population was a quarter of Britain's, a tenth of America's and an eighteenth of that of the Soviet Union.[58]

In March 1958 Lemass said that whatever free-trade regime emerged from the negotiations going on in Europe, the Irish people would have to get used to the idea of working in an internationalised economy, where 'protection would no longer be the main instrument of industrial policy.'[59] After a generation of protectionism this was an almost revolutionary declaration. Whitaker's *Economic Development* was saying what a very large proportion of the population wanted to hear from the Government: that a new departure was overdue; in his case, the people were hearing it from a source they trusted. In effect, the politicians were forced to hide behind the civil servants.

The newspapers had gradually converged on a similar position, regardless of their traditional allegiances or, in the case of the *Times* and *Indo*, their deep-rooted commitment to agrarianism. There was a general sense of change occurring and being inevitable and of the overwhelming necessity of cultural change in particular to cope with the economic shifts that were about to happen. Joseph Griffin said with an air of new hope in November 1958, with reference to Whitaker's team and their White Paper outlining a four-year plan for economic expansion:

We in Ireland are beginning—only beginning—to throw off the pall of gloom that has been darkening our days, confusing our minds and our policies, and distracting our intelligence and our energies. I sense it in many walks of life . . . The doctrine of our poverty in material resources continues to plague and debilitate our people like a dark and brooding mediaeval superstition. Our educational system has not done enough to dispel it. It is not merely among workers or small farmers or the little people of the country that this doctrine survives, but among the educated in business and commerce in industry and agriculture, in public administration and, alas, in our educational institutions. This doctrine of poverty destroys hope and where there is no hope there is no courage. Instead there is a sort of counter superstition. This myth of our [inevitable] poverty must at all costs be destroyed.[60]

In July 1959 the Taoiseach, Seán Lemass, with exquisite timing, announced:

We have now the element of an accepted national economic policy. The fact that organisations representative of every economic interest accepted and supported the Government's economic programme is a splendid beginning.[61]

The economy began to grow in 1957, and by 1959 it was becoming obvious that a benign syndrome of economic improvement and growing public optimism was occurring. The *Times* editorialised in November that Irish industry's resistance to free trade was now finally fading. However, the paper also emphasised that such resistance would have been very determined in 1949, and it would very probably have been successful; protection would itself have been politically protected ten years earlier.[62] The third report of the Capital Advisory Committee, headed by John Leydon, Lemass's right-hand man since 1932, was published at the same time in what was presumably a co-ordinated move. It listed three serious weaknesses: poor education, a lack of enterprise and a tendency to substitute subsidies for effort, combined with a tendency for most capital investment to be redistributive rather than productive. The echoing of Whitaker is evident. 'Standards of consumption are pushed up toward the British level, but real income per head is little more than half that in Britain; private savings are low.'[63]

That old Irish sense of hopelessness was at long last being addressed, and it looked as though something might finally be done about it, under pressure of a sense of emergency or even calamity combined with a new and still rather frail sense of hope. In January 1960 Lemass declared it to be a critical year. Ireland would have to learn new markets and become internationally competitive.

In industry in particular, we have just about reached the limits of development based on present home market possibilities alone. The policy of high industrial protection on which we relied for industrial expansion heretofore has now nearly spent itself. It is no longer very effective as a stimulus to industrial growth. It may indeed become something of a handicap, to the extent that it may operate to preserve inefficient or obsolete production methods, or shelter restrictive labour practices, or other high-cost factors, which could not survive in more competitive conditions ... we cannot remain in business, much less expand, if our production costs remain out of line with the rest of the world.[64]

D. A. Hegarty of Dublin Port and Docks Board made a similar point at about the same time. Irish people were far too insular, inward-looking and inert. Irish management techniques were utterly obsolete and self-defeating. Employer-worker relations, the training of managers and work study were non-existent or extremely primitive. He pointed out what many already knew: Europe had developed a 'new industrial thinking' since the war, and this had resulted in an 'unparalleled prosperity' in an unprecedentedly small number of years.[65] There was a general sense that Ireland's problems were psychological and cultural rather than material or structural. An inherited sense of second-rate status, inherited from the days of empire, had reinforced a strong tendency to be content with mediocre performance. Things, however, were changing; by 1960 Ireland was waking up from what many *contemporary* commentators saw as a very long sleep.

| FROM FIELD TO FACTORY

FROM FIELD

In the early twenties the *Irish Independent* had absorbed the old Parnellite *Freeman's Journal,* which seems to have broadened its ideological scope somewhat. As late as the fifties Fianna Fáil and the *Irish Press* still were twitting it for its notorious urging on of the executions of the leaders of Easter Week 1916, its support for the Treaty of 1922 and its encouragement of the Provisional Government's prosecution of the war against the anti-Treatyites in 1922–3. The two 'party papers' had continual and entertaining slanging matches in the fifties about their respective political ideologies and political histories. The *Irish Times* was still the 'Protestant paper,' sympathetic to the Ulster Unionist case, unlike the other two papers, which still stuck to an anti-partitionist orthodoxy. It tended to attempt an Olympian aloofness from the squabbles of Fianna Fáil and Fine Gael.

In the sixties the *Times* experimented with a Sunday paper, the *Sunday Review,* which folded quickly. There was also an evening 'Protestant' paper, the *Evening Mail,* which sickened and died in the 1950s and early 60s, just as the *Press* group produced a set of Sunday and evening stable companions to the daily paper. However, even in the fifties the *Times* had clearly developed a loyalty to the democratic Dublin state and was beginning to develop cautiously a liberal and very mildly anti-clerical line with regard to the Catholic Church and to social issues, such as adoption, emigration and education. The *Independent* had by far the largest circulation, followed by the *Press,* while the circulation of the *Times* was tiny and mainly confined to middle-class Protestant Dublin; in parts of rural Ireland it had to be sold under plain wrapper, almost as though it were contraband. The *Press* was later to shrink, while the increasingly liberal *Times* was to grow considerably and to lose its perceived status as a sectarian and anti-national paper; but in 1948 these developments lay far in the future. The *Press* group was to be the only group to die (and the death, in the late twentieth century, was a very curious one). The other two groups had long pre-independence histories.

As observed in the previous chapter, one immediate and evident contrast, even touchstone, between the three main Dublin daily newspapers in the 1950s was their attitude to farmers and farming and their role in the perceived economic and social future of the country. Denmark, which had indeed modernised through agriculture, was the tacitly idealised model, following a tradition that dated back to Horace Plunkett and the late nineteenth century and perhaps even back to Gladstone, who famously took up the cause of home rule on seeing the successful Norwegian experience of self-government in the late nineteenth century. The *Irish Times* and the *Independent* regularly lamented the evident dislike of farming life shown by the young and the equally evident wish of the new generation to live in towns and cities and to get as far away from agriculture as they could. Both papers had large-farm readership. The *Irish Press,* on the other hand, was determinedly pro-industry. As Brian Farrell has pointed out in his biography of Lemass, as far back as 1931

there was . . . a definite indication of Lemass's own deepest sense of political identity in the deliberate way he challenged and linked the conservatism of agricultural Ireland against the claims of the urban poor. 'I am not, never have been, and probably never will be, a farmer', he told the Dáil, arguing that emigration represented 'the fruits of the policy of allowing the farmers to do what they liked with the land, regardless of its effects on the community'. Again, he placed it on the record: 'I represent Dublin, and I feel justified in speaking especially about the position in Dublin because of the fact that unemployment in Dublin is worse than in any other part of the state.'[1]

Lemass went on to observe that urban and rural interests were not opposed but complementary; but he argued that until the system of land use was changed so as to generate more employment, and industries started up to absorb the rural surplus population, depression in the economy was likely to be endemic.[2] He was occasionally notorious for actually forgetting about farming, omitting it from his somewhat visionary economic plans produced in opposition in the mid-fifties. I have suggested elsewhere that Lemass's Parnellite background seems to have had something to do with his disregard for agrarianism and farmers.[3]

Early in 1949 the *Irish Times* editorialised sadly that economic policy would continue to be driven by interest-group activity more than by a purposeful and steady pursuit of the national interest. 'Like it or not, we must face the fact that passion and prejudice, self-interest and sectional demands will continue, in large measure, to shape the course of events in economic and industrial development.'[4] Even the *Independent* noted as early as April 1949 that, even at that date, agriculture accounted for less than one-third of the country's gross national product.[5] In March the *Irish Times* commented in a rather Olympian fashion: 'Far too many farmers are content to let a percentage of their holdings go to waste, because they lack either the money or the energy to bring the derelict portions into use.' In April it complained about the ingrained traditionalism and low productivity of the farm community.[6] A few weeks later it returned to this theme at greater length in an editorial, suggesting that land in Ireland was not seen as a productive resource but as a source of social status and, most of all, a sort of insurance.

> The reason for this sad state of affairs is not difficult to find. In this country the land is not regarded primarily as a source of national wealth; we still tend to consider it with the hungry eye of a tenant, as a source of individual security. The size of farms is not regulated by the dictates of maximum output; it is dictated rather by considerations of minimum subsistence. The division of labour has made little progress up the farming ladder, and the small farm, with the farmer combining in his person a number of diverse and highly skilled occupations— grower, buyer, seller and accountant—is still the rule. This system, or lack of system, does not make for all-round efficiency. The diagnosis is simple, but it is considerably less easy to decide what can be done to bring output up to a civilised level. Fixity of tenure is a principle that has been so strenuously fought for that the farming community is not likely to relish its revocation, even in the case of farmers who are manifestly abusing their land.

It went on to quote Thomas Drummond, a Scottish engineer and Chief Secretary for Ireland in the 1830s and a great friend and ally of Daniel O'Connell, to the effect that property had its duties as well as its rights. The original remark had been levelled by a Scottish liberal at Ireland's much-hated pre-Famine landlords. The irony was not to be lost on Irish people in 1949, particularly farmers, many of whom had internalised many attitudes toward landholding that originally characterised the old landlords; anthropologically speaking, they were *tiarnaí beaga*, or 'little landlords.'[7] Although the editorial did not specifically make the point, because of attitudes essentially derived from nineteenth-century feudalism, a form of entail or inheritance by a son led to a situation where there was no real free market in land, thereby aggravating the pre-commercial character of much Irish farming; Irish land was literally priceless.

However, in January 1949 Erskine Childers of Fianna Fáil, son of the famous writer and martyr of the same name, half-English and a Protestant by religion, was given prominence in the *Press* for an optimistic, even hortative diagnosis on economic prospects. He apparently had no quarter-to-quarter quantitative estimates of the country's economic output, as a modern political leader certainly would.

> The years 1948 and 1949 should be boom years both in industry and in agriculture. For the first time in Irish history in one hundred years the following conditions were present, self-government, no national struggle, no civil war, no continuous decline in cattle prices, no world depression, no economic war, ample materials, machinery imports improving, guaranteed prices for farmers, help from the u.s.a., sound credit, fertilisers and Fianna Fáil reconstruction machinery.
>
> But there was hesitancy, there were so many outcries against the cost of living that businessmen feared taxation, workers wanted more and more wages. The Ministers for Finance and Social Welfare spoke in different languages. One moment there was to be high protection, the next moment the direst warnings were given.[8]

In January 1950 President Seán T. O'Kelly made ritual obeisance to anti-partitionism and linguistic revivalism; but his real, some-what paranoid ire was directed at British and American attitudes towards the economic role of Ireland. British economic policy 'of course falls in well with Britain's plans and with the plans of the [European] Recovery Programme experts, both of whom seem to regard Ireland solely as a supplier of food to British workers.'[9]

But rural life was commonly seen as superior to urban life, even by some in Fianna Fáil. In 1950 Phyllis O'Kelly, the President's wife, proclaimed: 'If we can make country people realise that their way of life is superior to all others, we will soon readjust this balance, and send the people back from the towns.'[10] The President was himself a Dubliner, but his wife came of a well-known Wexford farming family. As we have noted, agriculture was seen as so central that nearly all Marshall Aid funds were to be sunk in it. The Fine Gael Taoiseach, John A. Costello, announced in June 1950 that the land was the main source of national wealth.

They had in the land of Ireland a noble inheritance and it was their responsibility to ensure that not only was it cultivated and developed but that no effort was spared to improve its condition, increase its fertility and extend its limits. The land . . . was the main material source of their real wealth. They must direct unrelenting energy towards reclaiming of land neglected under alien rule.[11]

In the same month the *Irish Independent* editorialised happily that Marshall Aid to Ireland had 'given a decisive impulse to both agricultural and industrial production.' However, the paper's pro-agrarian focus was evident in the editorial.

Assistance under the Recovery Programme has taken the form of raw materials and machinery. The gratifying increase in the production of pigs and poultry, on which the small farmer so greatly depends, could not have been achieved without the provision, under Marshall Aid, of wheat and feeding stuffs. There has also been a considerable importation of machinery for purposes that should bear fruit in future, such as land reclamation. It is possible that the most valuable form of assistance is the opportunity provided to study technique, principally in agriculture, abroad. There are many forms of research that cannot, for one reason or another, be easily pursued in this country; and it is well that results obtained abroad should be available in this country.[12]

The Minister for Agriculture announced in July 1950 that an Agricultural College was to be set up. As a result of the usual infighting between vested interests, in this case the universities (particularly UCD and UCC) and Catholic clerical interests, it ended up being delayed, finally opening as the Agricultural Institute in 1957. It was to develop into a high-powered and very successful institution, but in the 1980s it was amalgamated with other para-statal bodies.[13] The *Times* commented in May that the inter-party Government had a strong agrarian bias, despite the fact that farmers used primitive methods and Irish food was very overpriced. Later in the year it noted yet again that much agricultural land was falling into waste.[14]

In October 1951 the *Independent* editorialised about the 'flight from the land' in view of the results of the 1946 census.

The number of farmers fell by 9,000; the number of assisting relatives, who are less closely attached to the land, fell by 41,000. It appears that the decline in numbers occurred almost exclusively on farms of under thirty acres. There was an increase on the numbers at work on farms of 100 acres and over in size. This carries its own comment on the process of [Land Commission] sub-division as it is at present carried out ... The basic cause, no doubt, is that a better living can be got more easily in industrial employment in Ireland or in the United Kingdom. Even granted, however, that some small farms are uneconomic, the question must be posed whether many more of them can be made to yield a living by more enlightened State assistance. Better technique rather than higher prices is surely the proper policy; and it is the duty of the Department of Agriculture, and often of the Land Commission, to show the way.[15]

Not many educational scholarships were offered young people, and those that were offered were skewed towards agriculture and farming, despite the fact that demand by students was very obviously biased towards off-farm skills and employments. The *Independent* commented in December 1951 that even the sons and daughters of farmers were not particularly interested in scholarships. 'It appears that young farmers will not apply for these scholarships unless they intend to become agricultural inspectors.'[16]

In February 1952 a returned emigrant opined that rural Ireland was far more sophisticated than it had been twenty-five years previously.[17] This urbanisation of the rural mind was viewed with great unease by the many powerful people who were still ideologically committed to the idea of a rural Irish civilisation. In March 1953 the *Press*, of all papers, published an admiring article on Danish industrialisation, noting that much of it was derived from agriculture, particularly food-processing and farm machinery.[18] In July it editorialised that all the efforts at industrialisation behind tariff and quota protection had just about managed to absorb the surplus population leaving the land for urban centres and non-agrarian work. As agriculture mechanised, rural employment would shrink and rural productivity would grow, it asserted.[19] This was to be an over-optimistic perception in view of the wave of emigration that overtook the country in the mid-1950s. An Old IRA veteran interviewed by the *Press* described his disappointment and disillusion.

I didn't fight for a divided Ireland, or an Ireland where one creed or particular interest would dominate. I fought for a united country where everybody would have a fair chance of education and jobs and a future where things would be decided not on your bank balance, but on merit. Now we are still partitioned and one of the most conservative countries in the world.[20]

As early as May 1954 the *Independent* noted that industry was developing faster than agriculture.[21] The *Press* gave what seems to be its measured diagnosis of the ills of Irish agriculture in November 1954, suggesting that the Land Acts lay behind the pathologies of Irish agriculture.

> Unlike our manufacturing industries, which made a fresh start in the nineteen-thirties, agriculture has been burdened with a bad inheritance.
>
> The land came into the ownership of the farmers within the lifetime of men now living. The incentives to improve and drain the land were few in the past. When other countries were bettering the soil and adopting scientific methods of culti-vation, the Irish farmers were fighting a land war. Until they had security of tenure it would have been foolish for our farmers to put their savings into farm improvements. Their reluctance to invest capital in the land has unfortunately persisted right down to the present. All this is not just a matter of past history. It is essential to an understanding of neglect of our land . . .

The *Press* concluded by arguing that Irish agriculture would have to learn to compete with its rivals, even though they were far more advanced.[22] At almost the same time Bishop Cornelius Lucey of Cork made his extraordinary remark that it would be a mistake to raise the school leaving age, as this would have the very undesirable effect of making young men not want to be farmers.[23] Evidently these envisaged farmers would be of a very traditionalist kind and would be easy to control culturally in the good old way. His argument was a variant on the old idea that people should not be educated beyond that station in life to which it had pleased fate or God to call them. Despite this kind of thinking in some high places, a slow earthquake was under way. The Organisation for European Economic Co-operation (OEEC), as outlined in the *Indo*, noted in a prominently publicised report in December 1954 that the country had experienced a 'striking increase' in industrial output.

> Ireland's longstanding urban unemployment, which was aggravated by the minor recession of 1952, has been reduced to more accustomed proportions by a striking increase of industrial production. But the unemployment figures do not measure the full extent to which the Irish economy is at present unable to absorb the natural increase of the population since one person out of three emigrates.
>
> Some countries, because of overpopulation, look upon emigration as being in itself beneficial, but in the case of Ireland where the density of population has the effect of removing people early in their working lives, [it] now constitutes a serious obstacle to the development of the economy.[24]

The report added that Ireland had much unrealised industrial potential, particularly in the making of specialised products using local material content. In 1955 the *Indo* thought things agricultural were looking up. In March it announced a huge increase in cattle exports.[25] However, in October it published six articles on rural life that drew a rather pessimistic picture. In the first it reported that there was no Irish tradition of peasant prosperity, that there was a great wish for security, and, it claimed in a fascinating aside, that there was a real fear of envy.[26] The

Spectator, a conservative London weekly, commented at some length in April of that terrible year of 1956 that the Irish were actually much more prosperous nowadays than they once had been, even though Irish agriculture remained 'prehistoric.' Irish industry had developed respectably, and the state-sponsored bodies were a particularly big success.[27]

The *Press* reported in November the opinion of a business-man—Joseph Griffin of the Irish Glass Bottle Company—to the effect that agricultural production was only 50 per cent of its potential. In July 1956 Seán MacEntee, a veteran Fianna Fáil leader, made doubtful allegations that of $128 million in Marshall Aid funds $77 million was spent on the importing of wheat, $35 million on tobacco, $4 million on cars and only $6 million on new plant and equipment.[28] A *Times* editorial in September stated that farmers needed scientific training, but the Agricultural Institute was delayed because of the operation of vested interests.[29] In September 1957 a TCD economist said that the chief weakness of Irish agriculture was its dominance by the store cattle trade to Britain. Bovine tuberculosis was also a menace even to that trade.[30]

Jack Lynch, now Minister for Education, asserted in May 1958 that education had been seen for too long as irrelevant to farm life.

> For too long we had been inclined to divorce education from the practical things of life. For too long we held that the farmer needed no more than the ability to read and write. The successful farmer must be reasonably well-educated with a knowledge of a number of the sciences which underlie modern farming.[31]

In May 1958 Bishop Cornelius Lucey announced that the disappearance of the small farmer would be tragic; as usual, the fear of losing social and political influence, as well as recruits to the clerical career, lurked behind this annunciation.[32] By way of contrast, the *Irish Press*, assessing the Spring Show exhibition put together by the Department of Agriculture, pronounced it ungrudgingly as 'simply terrific.'[33] In January 1959 E. R. Richards-Orpen pointed out that because of bovine TB large areas of Britain were closed to Irish cattle, and for other reasons Irish cattle were shut out of the European Continent.[34] In February the *Indo* noted that 70 per cent of Britain was closed to untested cattle and that shortly it would be 100 per cent.[35]

Even as late as 1959 the *Independent* stuck to its agrarian guns, despite all evidence, editorialising: 'the land is, and must long remain, the chief source of livelihood for our people.'[36] James Dillon of Fine Gael defended the farmer valiantly in July 1959, claiming that farmers could double their output if incentives to do so existed. Between 1947 and 1957 they had produced the lion's share of exports and also tripled the value of their exports.

The great reservoir of fertility that could have been in this country was destroyed by the Fianna Fáil propaganda that grass was a reproach to the farmer. That propaganda had deluded many farmers into withholding adequate fertilisation from the grassland of the country. It was 'cracked' to try to follow the example of Holland and Denmark in the growing of cereals when their countries had an average annual rainfall of twenty-one inches whereas the average annual rainfall here was forty-one or forty-two inches.[37]

As we have seen, the *Irish Times* finally changed sides, specifically rejecting in January 1950 the view that agriculture was the necessary basis for economic progress. There was a quiet acceptance of emigration and population decline in Ireland, the paper observed, the calculation being that if the population were smaller there would be more to go around: fewer mouths to feed. This was erroneous, it claimed. The paper displayed a kind of despairing patriotism at a time when things were actually taking a decisive turn for the better.

> Since agriculture, however our methods may be improved and modernised, can no longer be trusted to take up the slack, it is clear that those economists are right who contend that we must increase our industrial exports or consent to our doom as a dying nation.[38]

Eight months later the paper editorialised against all the evidence that trade trends were still discouraging but displayed slightly more gumption.

> If we as a nation are not, as one sometimes despairingly feels, obsessed with some kind of a death wish, we must no longer tolerate the fumbling attempts of ageing governments, feather-bedded industries and backward farmers to toy with our destiny.[39]

In September 1959 Bishop William Philbin pleaded for the rescue of the small family farm. Small farms should be made viable, he argued; too many smallholders were selling up and leaving the country. 'This development was the most alarming kind of emigration.'[40] The *Independent* reported in October under a characteristically schizoid headline, 'IN SEVEN YEARS 67,000 PEOPLE LEFT THE LAND. Industrial employment improves.' Between 1951 and 1958, the paper announced, agricultural employment decreased by 67,000 and construction declined by 15,000, while manufacturing rose by 7,000 between 1951 and 1955, declined by 5,000 during 1955–7 and made a partial recovery of 2,000 during 1957–8. A prominent civil servant, William A.

Honahan, one of the bureaucratic intelligentsia that had a huge if sometimes unadmitted intellectual and even political importance in that era, remarked in November 1959 on the demographic and cultural peculiarities of Ireland. Regarding the population,

> he traced the decline to the long-term effects of the Great Famine of the 1840's, which were not only material but created in the minds of the people a hard-headed and somewhat irrational scepticism about the prospects of material betterment in Ireland.[41]

In 1959 the *Standard* published a rather moving 'lonely hearts' column, inviting spouse-seekers who were devout Catholics to write to the paper so that they might be put in touch with possible partners. Hundreds of letters poured in. Typical letters described farmers in their forties looking for suitable wives in their thirties, and women in their thirties looking for men in their forties, not necessarily farmers. One angry and tragic letter came from a man of forty-four living on a farm where the parents, presumably in their late seventies, enjoyed the old-age pension and also handled all the cash in the family business.

> Why not take down the pensions of these people who hold on grimly to the farms until their sons and daughters are in their middle age, still mere servants to 'Daddy' and 'Mammy'? . . . A child of forty-four years old afraid to mention marriage to 'Daddy and Mammy,' though not marriage shy.[42]

On 9 May 1960 the *Independent* finally followed the *Times* in its acceptance that Ireland's industrial development would have to be given priority over agriculture in Government policy and economic leadership. This was in reaction to an OEEC report on the Irish economy and to the long self-evident, politically inconvenient but much-ignored fact that a stagnant Irish agriculture, stoutly defended by an agrarian electorate, was increasingly being outstripped by a newly dynamic industrial arm.[43] The chronic and obvious stagnation of agriculture had been met with a deafening silence by some journalists, politicians, civil servants and academics.

TO FACTORY

The new industrialists occasionally felt themselves to be unpopular and even under siege. Denis McCullough, old IRB veteran and now chairman of the New Ireland Assurance Company, complained about anti-capitalist attitudes being expressed openly.

> [Our assurance companies] are deeply interested in the development of Irish industry and they are gravely concerned at the propaganda that has been going on for the past few years and which has been intensified quite recently, pilloring [sic] Irish industries and Irish industrialists as a class which tended to batten on the community. That is very unjust and unnational propaganda which can lead only to one result—the beginning of class hatred. Those who invest money in Irish enterprises which stand an equal chance of success or failure deserve a good return for the chance they took. I hope that those at present in charge of Ireland's destiny will make it clear that they are prepared to accept private enterprise and the profit motive as the basis on which Irish industrial development will be built, and that the attacks on those who have invested in Irish industry will cease.[44]

The communist *Irish Democrat* spotted this weakness in the new and superficially successful Ireland of 1951 in an article by Flann Campbell.

To the superficial observer Eire today may seem more prosperous than at any time since the Treaty. Wealth in its nouveau riche form may be seen in many Irish towns; and Dublin particularly with its smart restaurants, chromium-plated pubs, shining American cars and well-filled luxury shops shows all the signs of solid bourgeois affluence (so long as you keep to the main streets and middle-class residential areas). To watch the smartly tweeded farmers' wives at Leopardstown Races or to observe a well-to-do Dublin businessman eating steaks in Jury's Hotel [in Dame Street] is to realise how triumphantly the Catholic middle class has arrived in Eire.

It has been a long and stony road from the few barren acres of bogland or the miserable huckster's shop which was usually all the native Irish could hope for in the eighteenth century down to the lush pastures of Meath or Guiney's emporiums in O'Connell Street [Clery's department store] which are so typical of the middle class today, but the Catholic bourgeoisie have completed the journey at last, and show every sign of complacency at their achievement.

At first sight there seems solid economic basis for this new-found prosperity. Irish farmers, by far the biggest group in the country, are making more money than ever before. For every £100 they got pre-war they now get between £250 and £300. Industrial production has risen about forty per cent since 1939, and more people are employed in manufacturing than at any other time in Irish history . . .[45]

But in reality, Campbell argued, farm productivity had scarcely changed, the gap between rich and poor was widening and 'the whole rickety structure of prices and luxury living for the middle class' was built on very shaky foundations. Food production had been static since 1900, and a few thousand people dominated agriculture, industry and commerce. They controlled both major parties, he claimed in good Soviet style, and the poor were getting poorer. A decent family wage would be £7 per week, but many tried to get by on half that, and the unemployed got 35 shillings (£1.75) per week, or little more than a quarter of £7.[46]

However, a veteran American investment banker turned ambassador, George Garrett, opined in March 1950 that the country had a very bright future. 'Ireland will get more and more financial investments from the United States. She is now getting her own people to realise the value of investing their capital at home.' Ireland had always suffered from underinvestment, but now its people were finally beginning to take their money out of London and were putting these funds to use in their own country. Thus they would get better returns, both tangible and intangible. Poverty would be significantly lessened, if not eliminated. He predicted:

> In the next ten to fifteen years Ireland will surprise everyone by her progress. The tremendous building programme will pro-vide jobs for the next five to ten years for the skilled craftsmen who are coming back to Ireland from England with the realisation that they can get jobs there now, and certainly they can get more food than in England. Emigration is thus not the same problem that it was . . .[47]

The *Irish Press* echoed obediently the Lemass line on development. Without quite saying so, the country should bypass small-farm agriculture and wager on the strong: big farming to some extent and, in particular, industry, the new and growing skilled working class and the new capitalist entrepreneurs and managerial elites.

In March 1948 the deeply conservative new inter-party Minister for Finance, Patrick McGilligan, announced that there would be no transatlantic air service, as planned by Fianna Fáil at the instigation of Lemass. The five Lockheed Constellations, the most up-to-date airliners of the time, bought with scarce American dollars, were to be sold off to British Overseas Airways Corporation and used to revive British transatlantic aviation.[48] BOAC could not believe its luck, as hard-earned or borrowed Irish dollars had enabled it to mount a serious post-war challenge to the American airlines on the Atlantic. Lockheed had set up its European servicing at Shannon, and there were already Dutch customers, the *Irish Press* wailed in April. There was plenty of work for young Irish technicians, the American manager announced, and he claimed that the vocational schools were well capable of training them.[49] On 19 April the service was officially cancelled.[50] William McMullan, general president of the ITGWU, bluntly accused the new Government of being hostile to industrialisation.[51]

Lemass, when asked about the abolition of the transatlantic air service, said to a student audience in UCD that

he thought that the service had considerable possibilities. Part of the capital invested in the giving of skill to our own people had been lost. The government decision was deplorable, because the one thing needed here was to increase occupations which involved a high degree of technical knowledge and training.[52]

Lemass, in opposition, called for a general 'bold industrial drive' in January 1949.

He said that his experience as Minister for Industry and Commerce had convinced him that industrial progress was largely a matter of morale, which was the product of confidence. If the whole spirit of the nation was vigorous and enterprising, we would make progress against any difficulties.

In relation to industry, confidence could be created by the clear enunciation of a practical policy—a policy which public opinion accepted as practical and desirable—carried out vigorously and decisively. Those who undertook industrial development must have confidence that the Government was on their side. That did not mean merely assurance of support against external attack, or against difficulties inherent in our economic position. It meant also support against ill-informed or malicious hostility at home.[53]

He also commented that the general lack of any real experience was a central problem and that industrial leaders and workers should organise themselves more or less like an army. The trade unions must also be brought into the national campaign to industrialise, much as in Labour Britain at the time.

In January 1949 the trade union movement demanded the nationalisation of the transport system, which had already come about, producing that fairest flower of Irish bureaucratic corporatism, Córas Iompair Éireann.[54] In January also Daniel Morrissey, inter-party Minister for Industry and Commerce, promised 'never' to abolish tariffs as long as Ireland's infant industries needed them, to retain state control of any new industries and to build up technical knowledge in the country. There was, he lamented, far too little of it. American capital was to be welcomed, but only on a minority basis; there were too many examples of foreign capital's lack of concern for Irish national interest in the behaviour of its Irish branches.[55] His rather cautiously worded developmentalism does not seem to have been shared by his Fine Gael colleagues. In February the road grant was cut, and road improvement schemes were curtailed, partly at the instance of the railway interest. The reaction of the *Irish Press* was swift and brilliantly opportunistic, while incidentally letting the railway people off the hook.

So roads are a luxury? At any rate, Mr. Morrissey thinks so . . .
The cut in the road grants has, naturally, led to protests from
almost every County Council in the country. The Councils
have to strike a rate for the roads and, once the cut begins to
operate, there will—if road improvement is to continue—have
to be a heavy increase in the rate.[56]

Otherwise, the paper said a few days later, there would be serious
drops in county council outdoor employment.[57] The *Irish Times*
editorialised in January 1949 that it was the Marshall Plan that
had accelerated the Government's change in policy from all-
round protectionism to a greater emphasis on export-led
growth.[58] However, Irish industry remained solidly protectionist,
and the Government was vacillating.

In February the Old Lady of Westmoreland Street returned to
the fray, asking:

How can the desire of this country's industrial organisers to
free themselves from official controls be reconciled with their
all but unanimous claims to protective tariffs or other state-
sponsored privileges? How can recurrent demands for higher
wages and shorter hours of work be made consistent with the
need to bring down the market prices of life's necessities and
the production costs of goods for export?[59]

In May 1949 William H. Taft of the European Cooperation
Administration (the US agency administering the Marshall Plan)
told the Irish people that the development of a healthy export
trade was a priority for their country.[60] In opposition, de Valera
obediently expressed in public his private doubts about the entire
system of controls, tariffs and quotas that his own party had built
up over the previous two decades. He put this in the context of the
American drive towards freeing European trade, and his remarks

were made not in Ireland but at the European Consultative
Assembly in Strasbourg. He urged it to open discussions with the
Americans

> with a view to finding an agreement on the most practical
> means of putting an end to the compulsion exerted on nations
> to protect their monetary reserves by high tariffs, low quotas,
> oppressive exchange restrictions, competitive currency
> depreciation or any of the modern trade war devices for price
> cutting and subsidisation.[61]

However, an understandable fear of damaging protected
industries and of a possible deindustrialisation surfaced occasionally. In December 1949 the *Times* argued that Marshall aid would
dry up by 1952 and that the vital supply of dollars would vanish.
Emigrants' remittances, American tourists and exports to the
western hemisphere would be the only sources of the precious
currency, so important for the nascent recovery of the still ruined
European continent.[62]

Having shelved the transatlantic route as a waste of money in
1949, the inter-party Government proceeded in 1950 to close
down the CIE heavy engineering project that the Fianna Fáil
Government had instigated—another brainchild of Lemass. The
Press headlined the decision in its inimitable half-Americanised
English: BASIS OF GREAT PRIMARY INDUSTRY LOST.

> Inside a CIE building at Jamestown Road, Inchicore, Dublin,
> there is silence. At CIE works at Broadstone station there are
> huge crates of machinery and under heavy tarpaulins there are
> other machine parts. Those machines and heavy industrial
> equipment were to set the silent building at Inchicore
> throbbing with a new Irish industry—a CIE chassis-
> manufacturing shop, in which work for more than 500 skilled
> and unskilled men was planned.

Concept of the industry was the necessity to build up, in the national interest, a heavy engineering industry that would serve not alone CIE, but the country's entire industrial economy. Beginning with one chassis component, production was to be advanced, component by component, until the Inchicore factory was manufacturing an entire chassis from completely raw materials. Chassis building includes engine manufacture, and this aspect of production was regarded as of outstanding importance. There is no other industry in the country capable of producing oil and petrol combustion engines. The planners of the factory envisaged the Inchicore works as an engineering centre around which the industrial, especially the heavy industrial, arm of the country would pivot. Its initiation would have been the beginning of a new era here—the opening up of new possibilities for every Irish schoolboy and for the country itself in the future.

On the Government's instructions this project—estimated to cost £590,000—has been shelved. First of the heavy machine parts, that were to turn out Irish-produced buses and lorries, arrived in Dublin towards the end of 1946. Others followed until there was assembled machines of various types, at a cost of about £200,000. Suddenly orders from Cabinet level stopped assembly. Into a corner of Broadstone's broad spaces the crates of machinery that had been destined for the only factory in this country capable of making precision engineering components and of undertaking turning, milling, grinding, gear-cutting and heat treatment. A few of the machines have been distributed to other CIE repair and construction shops. Most of them may go back to Britain, their wooden casings unbroken and rope knots untied . . .

Irish industry would have a tool-making industry to speed progress in the industrial field. Special stress was laid on the ability of the factory to manufacture spare parts, a heavy recurring item in running costs. The agreement with Leyland Motors would have slashed large overhead expenditure on design, research, development and technical assistance . . .[63]

As we have seen, Lemass's *Irish Press* made propaganda out of both closures; they demonstrated the inter-party Government's hostility to industrialisation. However, in March 1950 Morrissey commented that in 1926 there were 102,000 workers in industry and services, and by 1949 there were 200,000 in industry alone. The real increase was probably 2½ times, he said, but it was still too small as a proportion of the total work force; Ireland was probably the least industrialised country in western Europe. The IDA was to plan future industrialisation.[64] John Leydon, a senior civil servant of the time, was also originally somewhat uneasy about the idea, and he influenced Lemass in his initial hostility. Lemass changed his tune when he returned to Government in 1951.[65] In April the *Irish Times* political correspondent, 'Aknefton', remarked of the Federation of Irish Industry:

> While condemning 'bureaucracy' and controls, the members of the Federation, nevertheless, welcome the Industrial Development Authority and ask for Government help with the export trade, for Government licensing of industry, for a Government ban on foreign trade mark transference and for a continuation of Government financing for expansion of industry. All these demands, of course, can only serve to strengthen that same 'bureaucracy' which the Federation condemns when it is a matter of inspection of production costs or social security.[66]

Aknefton later commented on the extreme wariness of Irish workers and on their conservatism, instancing the refusal of workers in a factory to co-operate with work study, despite being recommended to do so by their own union.[67] The bill setting up the IDA was actually denounced by some representatives of business interests, meeting under the auspices of the Federation of Irish Industry in, of all ironic places, the Shelbourne Hotel in Dublin, where the Constitution of the Irish Free State had been drafted under the aegis of Michael Collins in early 1922. They objected in particular to the power that it was proposed to give the new body to examine witnesses in a quasi-judicial manner, enforceable by fines of up to £50 (in an era when £7 was seen even by communists as a decent weekly wage).

Rightly, the industrial leaders claimed that the powers of semi-judicial compulsory inquiry that the Government proposed to give to the IDA were probably unconstitutional. Later it turned out that these powers were unnecessary, as the benefits of co-operating with the IDA became obvious and as industry queued up voluntarily to co-operate with it and get advice, information and grants. Workers were wary of employers, and both sets were wary of government. The *Irish Times* was quite sympathetic to the workers' traditional distrust of the establishment, whether it was the state, the bosses or even the union leaders. The following year the paper remarked:

> No objective-minded person can deny that the Irish working-class suspicion is well-founded. Every attempt that is made to improve their living standards is met with hostility. One has merely to think of such socially beneficial legislation as the Social Security Bill or the Mother and Child scheme to realise this.

True to form, the Federation of Irish Manufacturers was now opposing workers' involvement in the management of industry.[68]

In October 1950 the *Press* complained that the Department of Industry and Commerce's bureaucratic permit system for imports was slowing down and interrupting industrial production. It instanced a Co. Wicklow textile factory that was allegedly in danger of being closed down by such governmental interference.[69] In February 1951 the Federation of Irish Industry complained that industrialists were 'surrounded by an artificially created hostility provoked mainly by utterances mainly made by public men who ought to know better.' Lightning strikes, he added, were used to intimidate employers and workers.[70]

Also in October the *Times* painted a dark picture of the country's future and commented that Ireland was running down its sterling assets and that this artificially raised the standard of living temporarily; eventually there would be a reckoning. The truth was, the paper observed quite accurately, that the Republic was a poor country and that, compared with Britain or even Northern Ireland, its industrial resources were quite negligible.

The *Irish Independent* editorialised in February 1951 about the modest industrial expansion that was occurring. Its main concern was with the growth of Dublin and the heavy bias toward Dublin and Leinster evident in this expansion. Its underlying concern was the wish to use limited industrial development to underpin a mainly rural and agrarian society.

It is unnecessary to stress the importance of producing at home as much as possible of the manufactures that the country requires. But there is more in this matter than merely supplying our own needs to the greatest possible extent. There is the necessity to curb emigration, to stop the ruinous export of the strongest and healthiest elements in our population. It has been the dream of every thoughtful Irishman for generations to see provided in Ireland remunerative work for the large numbers of young men and women who, if they cannot find jobs in their own land, must seek livelihoods abroad to the great loss of the nation. Our best hope of meeting this long-standing problem lies in the growth of native industry.

In one respect, however, recent developments have not been entirely satisfactory. Dublin and its immediate neighbour-hood, already top-heavy in relation to the rest of the State remain a powerful magnet for industrial promoters. As Mr. Morrissey pointed out, they still show, in spite of inducement and persuasion to the contrary, an unmistakable bias in favour of the capital. The result is that, of the whole number employed [in industry], no fewer than 42 per cent are engaged in concerns in Dublin and Dun Laoghaire.

Leinster as a whole has 62 per cent of the State's industrial workers, whereas the whole province of Connacht has but 7 per cent and the three Ulster counties of Cavan, Donegal and Monaghan only five per cent. It is not in the national interest that there should be so excessive a concentration of factories and workshops in one comparatively small area. If industrialists were to go thoroughly into the whole question, they would find that in most cases their operations could be conducted at least as economically and profitably in the South, West or North-West as in the overcrowded metropolitan region, with its exceptionally high rates, rents, labour costs and other expenses.[71]

By way of counterpoint, back in office for more than a year in late 1952, Lemass admitted openly that he foresaw agriculture eventually being rationalised through the weaker farmers being squeezed out of the work force in favour of the stronger, more efficient ones.[72] In early 1952 the *Times* feared a reversion to protectionism and self-sufficiency, arguing that the country would have to brave the risks of modern international trade if it were ever to escape poverty.[73] A few weeks later a prominent unionist politician, J. E. Warnock, argued that the South was a hopeless case, for no better reason than a perverse politics.[74] In an uncharacteristic piece of support for industry, the *Indo* editorialised in praise of Irish industry in March 1952:

In the far-off years the institution of Irish Week was a brave gesture of defiance rather than of hope. The native manufacturing industries were then few and weak; the regime of the period offered them little encouragement and less practical help. With the coming of political independence all that was changed almost overnight. Successive Governments set out to give direct help and protection to infant industries; capital was encouraged to seek new and wider fields in the home market; industries once thought to be far beyond the capacity of this country took root and flourished. Were it not for the native industries which had been established before the outbreak of war in 1939 the community would have fared badly indeed during the years of isolation which followed.

For that alone the Irish industries would deserve well of the Irish people. But their claims rest on surer ground than mere gratitude. They are able to base their claims to support on quality, on price and the employment they give to Irish hands and brains.

Unfortunately there is no denying the fact that some people—a dwindling section, no doubt—still have the mentality which permits them to think that Irish goods are in some way inferior to the imported commodities. It will take time yet before that residue of foreign rule is eradicated.

Meanwhile two major factors have emerged which make it more imperative than ever to give first preference to Irish products. The first is the menacing state of unbalance in our external trade. The second is the growing menace to the race caused by emigration.[75]

Shortly afterwards the *Irish Times* published an interesting little survey of informed opinion about the country's economic problems, quizzing a leader of the Irish Housewives' Association, a farmer, a senior ESB official, a businessman, a drapers' representative, a well-known trade unionist and a representative of the service and professional associations. The usual suspects were cited: economic sluggishness was due to many factors, in particular to retail price maintenance, too much protection, too many middlemen parasitic on the economy, poor marketing of agricultural produce, high taxes, restrictive practices, unfair apprenticeship systems, too much Government interference, price controls, international tensions, external circumstances beyond the country's control, unions forcing up costs, a small tax base, and industrialists influencing politics in their own interest.[76]

In April 1952 the *Irish Times* proclaimed 'HARSHEST BUDGET WE EVER FACED.' The editorial, headed *'Dies Irae'* ('Day of Wrath'), pointed out that Marshall Aid was gone and that only one in sixteen workers paid income tax.[77] The Stacy May Report on the economy, written by American experts, observed an anti-materialist ideology and an authoritarian and heavy-handed governmental style, according to a quite accurate *Irish Times* story in November 1952. The report commented that Ireland's potential productive capability was enormous and almost completely untapped.[78]

In early 1953 the *Press* was boasting of the impressive expansion of the vocational education sector that was finally occurring under Seán Moylan.[79] In June, Lemass announced that the country was going to get state-aided infrastructure in the form of new electricity generating plants, land improvement, housing, health and education, all of which were needed to produce higher levels of economic activity.

This country has not got vast natural resources—hardly any at all except the land and the capacity of its people to work. It has no prospect of getting foreign aid. We have to pull ourselves up by our own strength, and we can do it. Since 1932 an economic and social revolution has been accomplished here under

Fianna Fáil leadership, although its extraordinary character is often forgotten.[80]

In August 1953 Lemass predicted a 'great period of national development and economic expansion.'[81] In July 1954 William Norton, changing his rhetorical tack, expressed a willingness to look at the tariff regime again with a view to lowering or abolishing some tariffs in exchange for concessions by other countries on free trade. He asked for an industrial consensus on the issue.[82]

Daniel Morrissey (Fine Gael and ex-Labour) and William Norton (Labour Party) had in many ways more in common with each other than they had with the majorities in their parties, and they had much in common with Lemass. All three were philosophical industrialists and pragmatists, although they differed about their proposed means. Their differences seem to have been more of emphasis, style and political tradition than of real ideological conflict. Norton lamented in July 1954 the absence of technical skills necessary for the new industrial ventures.[83] Erskine Childers, often an acute observer despite a covert in-house dismissive attitude in his party towards the son of Dev's martyred friend, remarked in September that greater productivity required a change of attitude on the part of three-quarters of the population, changes in the educational system and a campaign of instilling confidence in the future. The pervasive sense of hopelessness had to be dispelled.

The changeover from production with minimum capital risk and maximum war scarcity plus protection, to intense production was the only way of increasing the income of the whole people. We are all agreed on that. The present system, Mr. Childers said, was more proof against the effects of world depression, but brought progress to a standstill.[84]

People were evidently hunting around for new ideas, occasionally to surreal effect. In January 1955 Norton asked Irish Shipping to investigate the possibilities of the transatlantic passenger trade, or of an Irish transatlantic liner service. This was just at the point when transatlantic airliners were outstripping the classic ocean liners in passenger numbers, and it was coincident with the introduction of the Comet, Caravelle and Boeing 707 'jetliners', which were to revolutionise air travel and make the ocean liner obsolete for other than luxury travel. Lemass hit the roof when he heard of this silly proposal.

> The idea is fantastic, coming from a Government which wrecked the project for an Irish air service to America. It would be better ... for Irish Shipping to consider establishing a tanker fleet than waste their time on a project which would have no chance of success.[85]

Interestingly enough, Irish Shipping decided to acquire a modest amount of tanker tonnage shortly after this exchange—just in time to run into the Suez crisis of 1956 and the closing, in what were essentially wartime conditions, of the canal.[86]

In July 1955 John O'Donovan, a UCD economist and Fine Gael Government minister, claimed quite accurately that Ireland was on the threshold of a breakthrough on the agricultural and industrial export fronts. An adventurous minority of industrial concerns was already moving cautiously but bravely into the export markets.[87]

Lemass, in opposition in 1955, outlined his own thinking. The *Press* gave prominence to his speech and reported that his plan was to create 100,000 jobs in five years by means of state-led private enterprise.

> In other words our view is that the Government must carry the main burden in the first instance, but must so arrange its

programme that it can gradually fade out of the picture leaving private economic activity the main basis of national prosperity. It is clear that the scale of the public expenditure which will be required to bring national outlay to full employment within five years will be very considerable. Fianna Fáil reject the view, which is sometimes propagated in the press and elsewhere, that the sole object of Government policy should be to keep public expenditure at the lowest possible level.[88]

The inter-party Government, under its equivalent of Seán Lemass, Daniel Morrissey, defended its tentative attempts to attract foreign investment and get around the Control of Manufactures Acts (1933–4). In November 1955, in the Dáil, Morrissey defended this rather timid, but creative, new departure.

There was apprehension among urban people at the recent statements the Minister had made with a view to attracting outside firms to produce here. Home industry should not merely get preference but should get whatever measure of protection that it required. While giving the fullest protection, they might, however, be sure that merely because a firm was Irish it did not mean that it could become a monopoly sheltered completely from competition. There were some firms in this country who protested vehemently, not only against competition from foreign firms, but from Irish firms as well.[89]

Although the Control of Manufactures Acts could be evaded in various ways, the fact that they were on the statute book meant bad publicity for the Republic. Most stingingly, the American entrepreneurs went next door to Northern Ireland. Government-imposed price controls were another turn-off. There was a general air of entrepreneurial frustration, if not despair, in the country.

Possibly it was a symptom of this sense of frustration that impelled Lemass to have an aggressive go at the bankers in January 1956. They seemed, he said, to be indifferent to the widespread consequences of new surcharges.

> I have expressed the view that the inadequate part which the Irish banks have played in national economic development in the past was due to the character of those who control them rather than to weakness of the system itself . . . they give an impression of contemptuous indifference to the effects of their actions.[90]

In January, William Norton, a putatively leftist workers' leader, was in the United States voluntarily wooing American investors. He expressed a willingness to offer tax concessions to foreign investors; and the old protectionist psychology, together with the classic republican distrust of foreign capital and 'big business,' was slowly but quite visibly fading away.[91] In October 1956 the *Times* editorialised to the effect that a national economic development plan should have been put together 'thirty years ago.' However, there was no mention of education in an otherwise progressive article; hindsight wisdom tells us that this was part of a general pattern that was characteristic of the decade. The traditional farmer's view that education was not particularly relevant to economic progress prevailed. The old idea that education should be denied to the poor lest they should develop views beyond their station in life persisted in many minds.[92] Furthermore, there was very probably a nervousness about any aggressive approach to educational expansion and reform because of fear of clerical backlash.

In December the *Times* announced that 1956 had been 'one of the worst years which this State has experienced.'

The great inertia that oppresses this country is not the result of two or three years of inaction, but of thirty years during which it has been economically rudderless—or, perhaps, steered in the wrong direction.[93]

Lemass then suddenly announced that the once-sacred Control of Manufactures Acts were to be amended. He also made his abrupt announcement that wartime price controls were to be finally abolished, on the grounds that they were obsolete and were a major deterrent to outside investment.[94] He explained:

> The system of official price control which now operated derived largely from regulations brought in during the war. The survival of these war-time price controls long after all scarcity had ended operated as a major deterrent to Irish industrial possibilities. They had been interpreted by people outside Ireland interested in the promotion of new under-takings here as implying a hostile attitude to industrial profits. It was proposed now to dismantle that war-time price control structure.[95]

James Ryan, a senior Fianna Fáil figure, admitted that the abolition of price control had been opposed by many elements in the party, presumably for electoral purposes; they could be represented quite easily as protecting the poor against the depredations of the rich.[96] John Conroy, president of the ITGWU, ratified this action rhetorically in what seems to have been a co-ordinated move, arguing repeatedly that controls and restrictive practices just didn't work.[97] In August, Lemass claimed that foreign firms were beginning to wake up to the productive potential of Ireland.[98] Lemass began to emphasise a new theme in 1957, that of efficiency in production and an end to traditional make-do and half-trained sloppiness. Productivity, he announced in September, was the key to the solution of most of the country's economic and social problems. A little later he insisted that productivity was too low, and protection would have to be phased out.

Increasing emphasis on efficiency was now essential, and those industries which were not getting themselves out of the condition of having to rely on high protection would have to be looked at again. Obsolete production techniques, restrictive practices, and other factors making for high costs would have to be eliminated from them. A high protective tariff can be exploited, to the public detriment, not only by the owners in any industry, but also by the workers in it. Where improper exploitation of a tariff is developing from any cause, it is better to appear to be cruel now in order to be kinder later. If high costs are eliminated now, these industries may have a chance of surviving when their tariff protection has to be reduced or withdrawn. If they are allowed to go on relying on high tariffs to support unjustifiable costs, then there can be no other prospect than complete collapse in the new free trade era. So urgent and important is that matter deemed to be that the Government is prepared to pay up to half the cost of the services of expert consultants employed by any industrial firm which wished to overhaul its organisation and methods.

Restrictive practices resulting in inefficiency may, in my experience, just as likely be found affecting the policies of managements as of workers. There are too many Irish business leaders who pay tributes to the virtues of private enterprise in public and then meet in private to enter into agreements and covenants to eliminate competition between themselves and in that way to deprive the public of the major benefit which free enterprise can confer, which is the continuing compulsion to seek the greater efficiency and the lower prices which competition enforces.[99]

On 14 November 1957 Seán MacEntee warned industrialists that they should prepare for free trade and that all tariffs against foreign produce would be abolished within fifteen years.[100] The *Times* editorialised that the people had had a fright in 1956 that briefly woke them up, but now they were showing distinct signs of going asleep again.[101]

In January 1958 the Federation of Irish Manufacturers announced that it would appoint a committee to examine the position of Irish industry under a free-trade regime.[102] In February an expert commented in the *Press* that industrialists were very reluctant to hire technicians and scientists. It was actually difficult also to find qualified people of that kind, as the demand 'elsewhere' was so great. Eventually, when industrialists decided to get into laboratory work, they would have to recruit from the newly expanded vocational schools. Jack Lynch, the new Minister for Education, commented that Irish people were far too prone to see no connection between education and the capacity to work and earn a living. Farmers, he observed, were particularly likely to have a disregard for education and training.[103]

The economy began to grow in 1957–8, and there was growing public optimism. In late 1959 the *Press* trumpeted 'NEW PHASE FOR INDUSTRY. Well into Era of Bigger Projects.'[104] On 30 October the paper boasted in a front-page headline, 'ECONOMY IS EXPANDING.' In November it expanded on this by heading its report of the the Lemass speech at the Fianna Fáil ard-fheis 'PATRIOTISM THE MOTIVE POWER.'[105] The *Times* editorialised in November that resistance among industrialists to free trade was now finally fading; ten years earlier it would have been far stronger.

It has been adhered to far too long and over too comprehensive a field in this country and indeed has, as an increasingly un-popular policy tended to overshadow the real achievements of

Irish enterprise and skill in the industrial sphere . . . Ireland, like Portugal, is financially rich but economically poor, and her needs lie more in intangibles like enterprise, ideas and ambition, than in any shortage of physical capacity for progress.[106]

In other words, capital was not a problem; land, skilled labour and enterprise were the problem. Political leadership was badly needed and was not being supplied. Simultaneously, J. I. Fitzpatrick, president of the Federation of Irish Industry, rather revealingly announced, in an almost confessional way, that the era of protection was over and that it should have been brought to a close years earlier. This was in November 1959. It had also overshadowed the very real achievements of modern Irish industry. Government and industry were, hand in hand, finding new markets for Irish products, he announced.[107]

In August 1960 D. A. Hegarty of Dublin Port and Docks Board expanded on his general theme of Ireland's relative backwardness being due in large part to cultural and psychological factors, combined lethally with intellectual incuriosity.

Many of our problems during the past forty years . . . stem from immaturity and the failure to realise that democracy is not just the right of the ordinary citizen to vote to elect a government. It is created only by the existence of a very strong and positive sense of partnership on the part of all citizens and by each possessing a well-developed and indeed compelling sense of public duty.[108]

Chapter 5 ∿

WHAT WE HAVE WE HOLD: THE WORLD OF WORK

CAPTAIN LUDD: PROTECT OUR JOBS

Post-war Ireland was still possessed of a traditional psychology, one that looked upon the world at large, and in particular the world of work, as a zero-sum game: anything you gained I lost. Reciprocally, if I were to gain you would have to suffer. The economy was static, and therefore the population would have to be static, or even be expected to shrink so as to let the remaining people have more. After the Great Famine of the 1840s an attitude gained currency that Ireland was overpopulated and that emigration was therefore in the interests of those who stayed at home, and that it was simply fate that drove thousands from Erin's shores into exile. Exile, seen traditionally as a sad condition, where one mourned the bright hills of Mother Ireland, was declared to be all for the best in this best of all possible worlds. The *Irish Times* commented on this psychology as late as 1959, editorialising that there was a 'quiet belief' that emigration was a good thing: it meant that there was more of a fixed supply of work to go around in a depleted population.[1]

Certainly Gustave de Beaumont was struck by this zero-sum mentality, and was apparently rather shocked by the collective psychological and spiritual collapse that he felt it reflected, as early as 1863.[2] The result of this way of thinking was a weakening of collective patriotism and the justifying of selfish, anti-civic and 'familial' styles of material and cultural defence; charity began at home and often failed to go much further. In the phrase of Robert Banfield, something of the moral basis of a backward society persisted in much of post-war Ireland, much as it did in Banfield's southern Italy in the fifties.[3] Banfield himself referred to the syndrome as one of 'amoral familism.'

This habit of mind and behaviour extended far beyond the family. The churches defended their kingdoms in education, the professions and the hospitals; some bishops tried to discourage the education of farmers' sons on the perfectly rational grounds that education would make them wish not to be farmers and therefore less likely to be producers of young priests and nuns; skilled workers defended familial preference and tried to shut out competitive recruitment; farmers resisted being taxed and avoided what was sometimes seen as unnecessary and state-imposed schooling for their children—schooling that might permit the freeing of their labour for non-farm purposes; farmers quite literally defended their territories, regardless of the productivity of their land.

In the late forties there was a growing general awareness among the political class that economic progress was being hamstrung by archaic work-restriction practices, much of it having been exacerbated by protectionism and the emergency controls on trade, including the rationing of essential products, that characterised the war and post-war years. Unions, employers and Government all tended to engage in practices that could be legitimately described as being in restraint of trade, sometimes very seriously so.

One commentator, Brian Inglis, wrote in 1951 that many Irish common practices in restriction of trade would be illegal in the United States.

For many years . . . unwritten agreements have existed between firms, that they will not trespass on one another's territory. In Ireland, particularly, the tacit *concordia* with a rival not to cut his throat if he will refrain from cutting yours has long been common. The present fuss is not over something new, but over the sudden transformation of these gentlemen's agreements into organised large-scale 'rings'—trade associations— designed to do much more than merely to eliminate cut-throat competition. Some of them have attained considerable power: and it is the growth of these states-within-the-state that is frightening the Government, and the public.

Before we take a look at some of these 'rings' in order to see how they work, and what effect they have on our lives, it is important to realise that trade associations are not illegal. They are, to a considerable extent, outlawed in America. If Ireland were tomorrow incorporated as the 49th State in the Union, quite a number of our most respected business figures would find themselves facing a sojourn behind bars. But in the Republic these men are perfectly within their rights. We may decide that 'rings' are anti-social: we may come to the con- clusion that legislation was evolved to put an end to them: but we cannot fairly condemn businessmen for trying out this method if they think it will benefit them. As the law stands at present, they are perfectly entitled to make the experiment.[4]

Rules and practices in restraint of trade, to use the American phrase, were generally legal, if not precisely legitimate, in the emergent industrial and trading Ireland of the early 1950s.

Any sense of urgency about the issue was weakened by the general orthodoxy or underlying instinctive sense, shared by many in all three major parties, that agriculture was and would remain Ireland's major source of work and wealth and was the key to the country's economic development; or, alternatively, that it was the prison-house in which its poverty presided. The idea that non- farm work was the future was held by a few but was not yet the consensus opinion. The principal division was still between two sets of agrarians: between those who looked to an Ireland of small to medium-sized farms engaging in a mixed agriculture combining arable, dairy and export cattle, on the one hand, and those who looked to ranching and the bulk export of cattle, on the other: farmers versus ranchers, or the plough versus the cow.

Back in the late forties the idea that a future Ireland might be industrialised, with agriculture relegated to a subordinate and even minor role in the economy, was unimaginable to very nearly everyone, with only a rather isolated minority seriously thinking about a post-agrarian, industrialised Ireland. Even fewer imagined that services, based on highly trained and educated workers, rather than light and heavy industrial manufacturing, might be the dominant part of a future Irish economy. The further, more general proposition—more immediate and urgent at the time— that non-agrarian work and production was the true future of the country, and that this vital activity was being stymied by existing circumstances and practices, was dimly grasped by some, but not by enough to trigger an immediate political reaction. With some exceptions, the disease of restrictive practices was allowed to continue to run through Irish society.

In February 1949 the *Irish Independent* editorialised in its usual anti-statist and anti-socialist vein that one of the greatest sources of monopolistic and restrictive economic behaviour was the state-sponsored sector, or the dozens of state-spawned institutions that ran an airline, generated electricity, supplied public transport, owned tramp steamers, harvested bogs, ran the post offices and ran licensing systems for private industry. The paper claimed that the 'semi-states' performed no better than private industry, were sources of political patronage, and actually had the effect of crowding out private enterprise and capital.[5] Much of this crowding out of private economic activity was quite deliberate and calculated, the paper claimed. The *Indo* returned to this theme in March the same year.

There is something slightly amusing about a Government which, while itself setting up monopolies on a grand scale, at the same time initiates an enquiry into other alleged monopolies. From the point of view of the public, there is little to choose between a combination created by means of nationalisation and one brought into being by arrangements between commercial enterprises. Both, as a rule, take little heed of the interests of the consumer, who undoubtedly would be better served by the operation of healthy competition.[6]

In November 1949, in a typical comment of the time, the president of Cork Chamber of Commerce remarked that not only did high taxes inhibit economic recovery but many walks of life were closed to youth, as a result of what amounted to possibly illegal conspiracies between tradesmen, unions and public-sector employees.

Ministers had deplored the lack of skilled tradesmen in the building industry, but it should be realised that most of these trades were closed and the ministers were making no effort to remedy that state of affairs. No boy who was not an immediate relative of a tradesman would be accepted as an apprentice in most trades and this was seriously affecting the general position. This situation was repugnant to the Constitution.[7]

At about the same time the Minister for Industry and Commerce, Daniel Morrissey, alluded to

unscrupulous attempts to exploit the consumer, purely arbitrary advances in prices without any justification, creation of artificial scarcities, price manipulation to the disadvantage of the consumer, and activities of organisations whose avowed aims are to frustrate deliberately any movement to restore normal competitive trading.[8]

"We've got to admit that the evidence given last evening was pretty convincing."

THE PAYBOY OF THE WESTERN WORLD

September 1948

"*This improvin' of rural life is wonderful. . . . Now, the children 'll be able to study till all hours of the night for the Civil Service.*"

"*Why did my mother ever put me into the Civil Service?*"

October 1949

STALIN WAITING UP ALL NIGHT FOR THE RUSSIAN ELECTION RESULTS

"*Try this for size.*"

December 1951

" *I was thinkin', father . . . that is . . . if you'd consider it . . . how about me thinkin' about gettin' married and settlin' down?* "

September 1952

DUBLIN

July, 1956
Price Sixpence

OPINION

The National
Humorous
Journal of
Ireland

OUT OF OUR CENSUS

July 1956

"Get to work! They're saying I've no future."

September 1957

However, the most insidious and nasty restrictive practice was the various forms of closed shop, enforced by employers and by organised employees, which permeated the Irish employment system. Between October 1949 and March 1950 the *Irish Press* published a fascinating series entitled 'Any Jobs Going?', which gave job-seekers in post-war Ireland a run-down on 117 different careers in the labour market of that time. The series attracted widespread interest and was later reprinted in pamphlet form at public request; historians and sociologists of modern Irish labour should (but don't) treat this series as an intellectual first stop. The articles typically outlined in a clinical, helpful and non-emotional way the general standard of education and training expected of applicants, the amount of fees charged for apprenticeship, if any, and the presence or absence of restrictive practices limiting employment typically to the sons of those already in the trade. The restriction of employment to trade union members was sometimes hinted at rather cautiously, the *Press* being the Fianna Fáil paper and Fianna Fáil being a party that was very dependent on a big labour vote.

On 8 February 1950, however, the paper published a rather affecting story about a young man who had been committed to a borstal school for a series of petty larcenies. He had learnt a trade as a carpenter while incarcerated but could not get a job afterwards, because he was not a member of a trade union. Apparently he would not be permitted to join a union, though there was plenty of work available. This, commented a sympathetic district justice, was quite a common way for unions to treat veterans of borstals and industrial schools.[9]

The paper reported the many alleged merits of Artane Industrial School in May 1950—'THEY MAKE NEARLY EVERYTHING AT ARTANE'—noting again that the unions unofficially barred ex-borstal labour, operating a closed-shop system against the graduates of such schools, thereby closing off a source of skilled labour and, presumably, encouraging young offenders to return to a life of crime, there being little alternative other than immediate emigration to a country that was willing to use their energy and skills.[10]

The 'Any Jobs Going?' series was well researched and quite comprehensive. If very substantial expenditure on third-level training or education was necessary to qualify for employment in a skilled profession or other career, the articles spelt out quite bluntly the often considerable amounts needed. The type of income one might expect to earn after qualification was also usually specified. The range of employments was impressively wide and comprehensive, the only major omission being the traditional post-Parnell yeoman owner-occupier farmer of the kind that dominated the work force of the time—the underlying and unspoken assumption being that such farming was something to be escaped from, particularly by the readership of Fianna Fáil's *Irish Press*.

Significantly, 'scientific farmer', veterinary surgeon, poultry instructress and, perhaps, blacksmith were the only professions with some farm connection to be included in the series. Blacksmiths at that time spent much of their time shoeing horses and repairing agricultural equipment. Presumably this extra-ordinary range of skills, ranging from army private, carpenter, waitress and welder to actuary, architect, barrister and vet, reflected the 'new class', or perhaps more accurately new classes, that read the paper. It also reflected the ambitious and upwardly mobile character of the paper's mainly Fianna Fáil readership, nostalgically post-rural but rather determinedly urban, ambitious and modernist in self-image and purpose.

The *Irish Press* was the most wholeheartedly modernist newspaper of the three Dublin dailies in its general outlook and view of the world. It was also probably the paper that was most thoroughly aware of the importance of the United States to

Europe and Ireland in the new post-war world; the paper and its parent political party had an American feel to them, echoing in part the Irish-American dollars that had originally financed the founding of the paper in the early thirties.

The list of careers open to young readers offered by the *Press* series of 1949–50 follows below. The standard title of each article was 'How to Become an X?' Restrictions to recruitment are marked here if enforced by traditional familial considerations (*), by union restrictions (†) or by both together (‡).

Carpenter,‡ dentist, hairdresser, waitress, radio officer, army officer, nurse, confectioner,* architect, electrician,‡ Guinness's, military pilot, gardener, chemist, air hostess, chiropodist, motor mechanic, dressmaker, barrister, national teacher, civil air pilot, optician, cabinetmaker, milliner, physiotherapist, photographer, telephonist, air mechanic, Fire Service man, Garda Síochána, barman, industrial chemist, draper's assistant, marine engineer,‡ librarian, veterinary surgeon, scientific farmer, [cinema] usher or usherette, salesman, civil engineer, chartered accountant, plumber,* bus driver or conductor, quantity surveyor, dress designer, hotel manageress, doctor, printer,‡ prison officer, almoner, incorporated accountant, ship's master, poultry instructress, engine driver, men's hairdresser,† law clerk, auctioneer,† tailor,* forestry officer, postman, grocer's assistant, bricklayer,* solicitor, welder, chef, linesman, mechanical draftsman, creamery manager, stockbroker, projectionist, bookbinder, dietician, decorator,* (ship) stewardess, silversmith,* welfare officer, post office clerk, locksmith, watchmaker,* upholsterer,‡ bank clerk, coach builder, vocational teacher, certified accountant, baker,* boot-repairer, advertiser, blacksmith,* (lighthouse) lightkeeper,* commercial artist, fitter and turner, plasterer, cost accountant, radiographer, mechanical engineer, customs officer, tiler,* valuation surveyor, jockey, radio engineer, secondary teacher, butcher,* army private, dental mechanic, brass finisher, railway clerk,* instrument-maker,* clerk of works, glass worker, insurance official, laundress, railway clerk (female), boilermaker,* actuary, ESB clerk, meteorologist.

The newspapers of the period tended to be silent about other restrictions that were well known at the time but that were sensitive and not talked about loudly in polite society. Guinness's brewery, a major employer in the small and rather poor city of Dublin, restricted employment at the white-collar level to Protestants. A general pattern of routine and unquestioned religious preferment characterised many walks of life, including nursing, teaching, and many businesses and professions. Many professions also restricted the numbers of cadet posts, thereby depriving young people of employment while driving up wages and restricting competition. The old skills of printing, bookbinding and silversmithing were notoriously restricted.

Schools and universities were commonly and routinely sectarian in their hiring practices. Catholic schools hired only practising Catholics. Jobs tended to be confined to one or other sex, males being generally preferred to females, in obedience to the assumption that the ideal situation was one job per household, that job being normally held by the male head of household. Some jobs, however, such as midwifery and nursing, could be done only by women, for reasons of modesty or tradition. Also, and very obviously, many of the jobs listed in the *Irish Press* cost a lot of money to qualify for, particularly those involving expensive and very hard-to-get third-level training, as in the case of architecture, engineering, medicine and teaching. This restricted such employment automatically to the small and privileged middle and upper classes.

It should also be reiterated that up to 80 per cent of young people left school at the ages of twelve to fourteen with very primitive levels of education and unfitted for any work beyond low-level manual labour. Even those with the educational level of the Leaving Certificate (taken at the age of seventeen or eighteen) were rather thin on the ground. Many of the half-educated young people turned out by the Irish system ended up in England working on the roads or as maidservants, earning relatively low wages and often in very poor circumstances.

A rather defensive editorial in the *Press* noted that restrictive practices of various kinds were common internationally, and it argued that the Irish situation was scarcely out of the ordinary; even the much-admired Americans indulged in this kind of thing. Captain Ludd was a much-vilified chap who had a very understandable grievance.

> In reality these practices are common in every country in the world where free trade unions exist. The United States is no exception. Indeed, in some respects the Americans have carried the technique of restriction furthest. The fact is that restriction of output is as old as the trade union movement itself. In the early years of the nineteenth century, the Luddites, who were the forerunners of the modern trade unions, threatened by breaking up machines and destroying factories to call a halt to the industrial revolution while it was still in its infancy. By their own lights they were possibly justified.[11]

Restrictions on trade, pricing, employment and even long-distance selling were regarded as understandable and perhaps legitimate, if only to underpin a traditional way of life; even a relatively forward-looking and developmentally minded paper like the *Irish Press* evidently felt it had to take into account the short-term disruptive and often oppressive effects of a free market in labour, work practices and technological innovation. It is also evident that the writers of the *Press* editorials were looking over their shoulders at a powerful and popular trade union movement with a vested interest in defending existing employment practices and patterns and a strong ideological bias, reinforced by a Catholic traditionalism, towards male labour. It is also probable that more Irish workers at that time voted for Fianna Fáil than voted for the two Labour Parties combined.

The *Press* felt forced to throw a sop to the unions, although, like the *Irish Times* and the *Irish Independent,* it probably quietly disliked restrictive practices and realised the importance of eliminating 'stickiness' in the labour market as in economic activity generally. However, in October 1949 the paper did report the opinion of Seán Ó hUadhaigh, chairman of the committees set up to oversee the Apprenticeship Act (1931), to the effect that many apprentices were being exploited as cheap labour; some were not learning anything at all, and this was the case even in some of what he termed the 'properly organised trades.' There were many places in the country where nobody was looking after these young men and women in any fair or competent way; they were being underpaid and neglected, he claimed. The provisions in the act guaranteeing suitable conditions and instruction to apprentices had been formally accepted by only four trades: furniture, painting and decorating, 'brush and broom' and hairdressing.

The Department of Industry and Commerce felt that many trades were unaware of the provisions of the act and that if it were better known there would be agitation to get other trades to adopt its provisions. The act was framed as a voluntary one, based on agreement between employers and workers.[12] Ó hUadhaigh added:

The larger concerns . . . were usually reasonably good employers, but exploitation of apprentices largely arose in the case of small employers, with whom the problem of inspection was usually difficult.

Monopoly enforcement or rent-seeking was common in the Republic in the 1950s and was even regarded by many as the norm. The authorities seemed to be either tolerant of the tendency or actually complicit with it, in what amounted to a tacit understanding between labour and management or even a conspiracy against the public. Although known and understood, the idea of a completely open and free market appeared slightly alien and even threatening; protection had reinforced traditional and essentially peasant subsistence attitudes that reinforced caution and a what-we-have-we-hold mentality in economic and political life. Such attitudes were in fact quite popular and received considerable public support. Rural shopkeepers felt threatened by travelling shops and traders who could undercut them and damage their little local monopolies; city grocers were worried about competition from what were termed the 'payantakes' or 'cash-and-carry' shops, which, by not offering delivery by van or cyclist messenger boy, could sell food and other household goods at cut rates. These shops were the ancestors of the supermarkets, sometimes almost literally, their owners begetting sons who became the first supermarket magnates, sometimes enjoying the ancient Irish surname of Quinn.

There was a tendency in the fifties, in effect, for the traditional shops to conspire to keep prices at a level suited to the seller rather than to the buyer. The Retail, Grocery, Dairy and Allied Trades Association (RGDATA) was at the centre of much of this activity. Government licensing systems, for mechanical organisational reasons, aggravated local shopkeepers' irritation with irregular travelling traders, the latter being able to evade Government regulation by their almost black-market status. They were among the guerrillas of the Irish economy, notorious as it was and is for 'nixers', or work done off the books by all kinds of workers, from politicians down to landless labourers, so as to avoid tax, regulation and 'restrictive practices', or, for that matter, price-fixing by bigger concerns.

For example, among other things the travelling traders could buy eggs casually from farmers while settled shopkeepers had to have a licence and a fixed address to do so. It is strange to think that a lot of innocent and casual local trading was technically illegal.[13] It is impossible to estimate it half a century later, but, given the inadequacy of Irish economic statistics, anecdotal evidence strongly suggests that the informal economy must have been quite large in the aggregate, even though it consisted of very small traders and worker concerns. There were very many small traders.

> It has long been recognised that persons engaged in the professions or in commerce are within their rights in forming associations for the promotion and protection of their legitimate interests, just as salary-earners and wage-earners may combine for the same object. Complaints, however, have arisen from time to time that in the matter of admission of apprentices and in other ways some trades unions have introduced restrictive practices injurious to the national welfare. Recently, also, there has been an outcry against the activities of certain associations of traders which have been accused of seeking, under one pretext or another, to make it difficult or impossible for anybody else to enter their line of trade.

The *Irish Independent*, in an editorial on 20 April 1950, came out against 'restrictive practices', emphasising the bad habits of some of the trade unions in particular, as was the Fine Gael paper's wont; but it did advert to the analogous practices of employers. Some of the unions had restricted the number of apprenticeships to their trades, the paper observed. Traders had sometimes attempted to make it difficult for new entrants to trade in competition with established and well-organised traders. Rings and monopolies had the effect of fixing prices at higher than the true market level and, of course, 'enriched their originators at the expense of the community.' Much of this the paper saw as originating in the time of wartime controls, such controls being extended into peacetime at the behest of vested interests. It called on the Minister for Industry and Commerce to look into the matter.

Nobody can have any doubt that the creation of rings or monopolies is inimical to the public interest. Invariably such devices aim at keeping prices at an unjustly high level, for no other purpose than to enrich their originators at the expense of the community. Any attempt to withhold, or to force manu-facturers or wholesalers to withhold, supplies from parties who either will not or cannot conform to the selfish demands of a particular association must be viewed as a grave injustice. Interference with the individual's right to earn a livelihood in an occupation for which he is qualified and suitable, or in which a beginner is entitled to seek training and experience, can only earn condemnation.

It is to be feared that the conditions of wartime, with its shortage of essential goods and the consequent application of quotas and unavoidable refusal of supplies to newly-opened establishments, have encouraged some traders in the belief that a similar system can be successfully imposed in times of com-parative peace and plenty. If such a belief does exist, and if there are good grounds for the allegations that efforts are being made to exclude or to cripple new entrants, then obviously the law will have to be applied to remove the mischievous notion, and to ensure to all merchants and dealers free access on equal terms to whatever merchandise may be available. The public will welcome the assurance given by the Minister for Industry and Commerce in reply to a question in the Dáil that the matter is being considered, and they will expect that whatever action may be necessary will be taken.[14]

The *Irish Times* took a similar if more muted line. On 9 June 1950 it editorialised that tariffs and quotas since 1932 had encouraged restrictive practices.

> Associations of manufacturers, importers, wholesalers and retailers are rapidly becoming a feature of the community's life. An association need not, of course, be a 'Ring' in the strict sense . . . Most of these associations, however, do establish a degree of commercial restraint over their members, either by restricting entry into the trade or by enforcing rules against price-cutting. To that extent 'Rings' exist, quite openly, in this country. They are not formed with sinister intent; rather they are the natural and inevitable consequence of our economic development over the past twenty years. Protection gave them their first opportunity when it reduced outside competition, and the war enabled them to consolidate their position.[15]

The tariff and quota regime set up under Fianna Fáil governments since 1932 had aggravated an older tendency towards restriction of employment in order to keep up wages and prices. The regime also had the convenient political effect in many cases of handing over control of employment to politicians and officials. 'Combinations' (primitive, usually illegal, trade unions) had existed in Dublin in the eighteenth and early nineteenth centuries, aiming at restricting employment to local workers and keeping out incomers from the countryside or Britain; and something of their tradition seems to have survived into the middle of the twentieth century.

The tendency to restrict became positively extrovert and self-righteous in the post-war years. In November 1950 the president of RGDATA proposed openly that only 'properly qualified people' should be permitted to set up as grocers. The *Irish Independent* commented that, although the august president had specifically denied that he wished to establish a closed shop in the retail food trade, it was to be feared 'that his speech will be looked upon as yet another manifestation of a recent tendency to try to exclude, except on terms that were dictated by these organisations, all new entrants to the particular businesses concerned.'[16] The editorial continued:

> In this matter there is another and a higher consideration to be taken into account—the public interest. While it is that those engaged in commerce should take all legitimate measures for the protection of their rights, care must be exercised to see that the community as a whole is not thereby injuriously affected. Already there has been an outcry against the introduction by other associations of restrictive practices which tend to sacrifice the public good for the benefit of sections who take it upon themselves to decide the conditions on which customers shall be served or not served. Indeed, the Government, as a result of many strong protests, already has this question under consideration with a view to the correction of certain abuses which are alleged to exist.

RGDATA also seemed to want the Government to provide a system of grants to enable grocers to make various structural alterations made necessary by new hygiene regulations.[17]

In December the *Irish Times* pointed to the self-evident proposition that state-imposed quotas on imported goods automatically handed a 'closed shop' to the wholesalers and retailers, who were then free to raise the price to the legal limit or even beyond, and it remarked that Government policy was effectually allowing free competition 'to be eliminated by restrictive trade practices and we are doing little to ensure that the monopolies are conducted in the public interest.'[18]

The extraordinary dominance of interest-group politics, particularly in all three major parties, was seen by some observers as strangling the nation and its economy. Unions, professional associations, cartels, religious organisations and trades tried to stake out territory and control entry and even exit; 'what we have we hold' seemed to be a national motto of sorts. The *Independent* returned to this theme repeatedly during the next twelve months, finally thundering to the attack in early 1951 in an editorial headed 'LOOKING FOR MONOPOLIES.'

A proposal has lately been made to the [inter-party] Government that the number of taxicars permitted on the roads should be limited. The underlying idea, no doubt, is that if too many are permitted they cannot all make ends meet. Of course, the same arguments could be used in favour of permitting only a limited number of plumbers or drapers or doctors or grocers to engage in business. It is the argument of those who want to restrict competition and thus to create a monopoly for their own advantage.

The Government should not listen to such proposals. What the taxicar owners ask to-day every other section of the community will ask tomorrow on the same specious argument. Restrictions of this kind have never proved to be to the public benefit. A British statute of half a century ago has resulted in the creation of fantastic monopoly values for publichouses. The late Government in this country placed restrictions, based on a similar principle, on the road transport business with disastrous consequences to the public. We are even now facing the probability that betting shops will be given a monopoly value because 'the existing facilities' are taken into account when a new licence is sought.

There is far too much of this tendency to demand monopolies and to eliminate competition. Many trade unions, approaching the problem from an equally selfish angle, have been endeavouring with much success to debar the youth of the country from occupations which they wish to adopt. The principle is all wrong. It is an unjust interference with the citizens' rights; it creates monopolies, whether of trade, labour or capital; it eliminates competition and benefits the few at the expense of the many. Instead of adding to the list, the policy should be to eliminate many of the monopolies already existing.[19]

A few days later, on 15 February, the *Independent* editorialised on the sometimes surreal irrationalities, price-fixings and cross-subsidisations involved in transport policy. These had intensified since the creation, in 1944, of a state monopoly of public transport.

It has been announced that passenger and freight rates are to be increased by Coras Iompair Éireann. However regrettable may be the necessity for the contemplated increases we are of opinion that it is better to raise the charges rather than to attempt to pass a deficit on to the taxpayer. The policy of CIE should be to make the services pay their way—to require those who use them to pay for them.

The practice of subsidies and grants has already been carried much too far and in too many directions in this country. It would be quite indefensible to compel those who make little or no use of the railways or omnibuses to pay, by way of state subsidies, for those who use them extensively. The businessman who travels by car and never takes a bus should not be forced to contribute, in the form of taxation, a subsidy to his next-door neighbour who always travels by bus. The bed-ridden old age pensioner should not pay, in the shape of taxes on his tea or tobacco, part of the train-fares of the young men who go by train to a race-meeting. Nor should anyone defend an arrangement under which a trader with his own lorries should be compelled to pay in taxes for the subsidising of a competitor who preferred to have CIE do his transport work.

As between the different sections of the community, so it should be as between the different localities. The people of one area should not be asked to subsidise the people of another area. Everyone knows that in Dublin the bus services not only pay their way but make a substantial profit. In these circumstances it would be quite unfair to raise the bus fares in Dublin in order to make up for a loss elsewhere. On the contrary, the question of reducing fares in Dublin should be seriously considered. The cost of living is oppressive enough in Dublin without making it still more oppressive merely to come to the relief of those districts in which the bus services are run at a loss. The users of the trains and buses should pay the economic price, wherever they may be.[20]

The *Indo* was a popular paper, but it is to be wondered how many different categories of voters would be antagonised in the Ireland of 1951 had any Government actually set out to obey these injunctions to follow a classical economic orthodoxy. Its favoured Fine Gael party paid electorally for believing in such maxims and for admitting to such a belief in public; Fianna Fáil, with its characteristic political *savoir faire*, tended to keep such beliefs to itself until they became slightly less unpopular. Many people actually believed in a popular version of the redistributivist ideology so much favoured by many of the revolutionaries of the 1900–23 period and much touted also by Catholic thinkers of a certain type. Understandably, the trade unions thought more of defending existing jobs than of letting new technology create new, more skilled jobs; as we have seen, leaders like the much-respected and liked Louie Bennett felt that mechanisation drove out labour.[21]

Later in the year the *Irish Times* pointed to the imposition by the Government of price controls as one of the original stimulants of rent-seeking in Irish trade. 'The reason is that the imposition of price controls brings retailers together in the face of the common enemy,' and they pushed prices up to the maximum permitted price, price restrictions being typically banded, maximum and minimum prices being set by statutory instrument.[22] The Catholic Church weighed in as well, in the person of Prof. Féilim Ó Briain of Maynooth, a well-known ecclesiastic and social philosopher of the period. Vocationalism was the answer to the problems of vested interests, he wrote.

At present unorganised groups of underpaid workers in town and country are the victims of well-organised professional, industrial, financial and trade-union bodies. The state depends on these strong bodies and must bow to them, legislate in their interests or accede to their demands, while the lower unorganised strata of the people must live just above the starvation level or emigrate. Social realities are disregarded; social and political forces are not coordinated for the common welfare, but are allowed to develop incoherently and in an unbalanced fashion highly dangerous to social and political welfare.[23]

Even the Irish Association of Civil Liberties got in on the act. In late 1951 one of its investigators, the writer Brian Inglis, wrote a report, alluded to earlier, on his findings. As we have seen, he painted a mildly alarming picture of a movement that went beyond normal price-fixing and that wanted to set up a state-within-a-state system to an extent that was actually 'frightening' the Government and the public. In the United States these practices of price-fixing and boycotting price-cutters would be illegal, but in Ireland they were apparently perfectly legal. He went on to look at price-fixing among radio dealers, car salesmen and RGDATA.

The 'ring' whose operations affect the public most directly is undoubtedly the Retail Grocers', Dairies' and Allied Trades' Association. And in their case, the emphasis shifts away from regulations about minimum facilities, to the maintenance of minimum prices.

As RGDATA have grown in strength and influence, they have gradually been increasing the range of goods that may be sold by grocers at, or above, an agreed minimum price. The object is quite frankly to eliminate competition, and thereby to ensure a 'fair' profit to the retailer.

What is a fair profit? The answer quite simply is that there is no such thing. Of two grocers in a village, one may make £1,000 a year by charging high prices, but attracting customers by giving good value in service, deliveries, credit facilities, etc.; while the other, operating on a cash and carry basis, may undersell his rival by a considerable margin, attracting in the process a much quicker turnover and also making £1,000 a year. Both methods are legitimate. What RGDATA is trying to do is drive the second class of grocer out of business, in the interest of the first. Its aim is to eliminate price-cutting, and with that end in view it orders manufacturers and wholesalers not to supply any shop which disobeys its minimum price rules. If a wholesaler disobeys, RGDATA instructs its members to boycott him. The wholesalers not unnaturally dislike both the threat and the practice, and not so long ago one of them effectually evaded the edict by delivering goods to a grocer's back door at night, in a plain van. The deed could not be done in daytime because the premises were discreetly picketed.[24]

The spirit of Captain Moonlight and the Whiteboys evidently lived on in an urbanising Ireland. In a slightly more murderous way, similar stories could be told about improving landlords in nineteenth-century Ireland or innovative inventors of agricultural machinery in early nineteenth-century England.

Things reached a head of sorts in 1952 when Thomas Connolly, a grocer in Dún Laoghaire, took an action against RGDATA, seeking an injunction against the association's officials to prevent them inducing or even forcing wholesalers to cease supplying him with goods at the usual prices. Connolly was trading on a cash-and-carry basis, using family labour and providing no delivery service. His prices were apparently lower than those of other local grocers, and he ran an efficient business, by all accounts. The wholesalers had boycotted him under aggressive pressure from RGDATA, including what one wholesaler witness termed 'threats from the organisation.'[25]

Patrick Lynch, formerly a well-known civil servant at the Department of Finance and latterly an economist and professor at UCD, argued as an expert witness that price maintenance as enforced by RGDATA on retailers and wholesalers was 'injurious to the public interest in the sense that it maintained at a level higher than they would under competition, the prices of certain commodities in the grocery trade.' The grocer who ran an efficient shop, was a good manager and perhaps used family as distinct from union labour and did not provide any delivery service was a low-cost trader able to undercut a high-cost trader, he argued. To Lynch's mind he had a perfect right to do so, and by so doing, far from doing something underhand or unfair, he was actually serving the greater public interest. The inescapable, if unspoken, implication was that the 'payantakes' were actually helping the poor by providing goods to the consumer at a lower price.

Lynch argued that the association's favoured term 'fair average price' was meaningless, as under free competition each trader had his own price, and high-cost traders would be forced to come down in price or be forced out of the business. A truly fair price, he implied if not quite said, would be the lowest one the grocer could charge and still stay in business; here Lynch was merely relaying standard economic doctrine. Ireland had too many shops, he said, each with a small turnover, and they were generally poor and inefficient.

The defence argued rather unconvincingly that travelling shops and price-cutters tended to give short weight and to supply inferior goods.[26] The RGDATA witness argued, for example, that 'in a half-pound of back rashers, for instance, the rashers in the middle would not be up to the standard of those on the outside. There had been cases which he could quote of short weight and the pawning off of inferior articles.'[27] The answer to that, presumably, would have been that such traders would have been out of business rather quickly under frictionless free-trade conditions. Lynch's opinions seem to have fallen on deaf bewigged ears, perhaps because Irish lawyers were, as usual, not very well up in basic economic theory. Connolly lost his case, and was held liable for costs.[28]

Interestingly, RGDATA's real target was almost certainly the cost-cutting effect of using family labour, a traditional complaint of trade unions also. The kind of trading Connolly exemplified was, of course, to win out eventually with the coming of the supermarket and the private car in the 1960s. It must be remembered that one reason for the little retail monopolies of the fifties was the simple fact that most people did not own a car and that the vast majority of the population did not know how to drive and were therefore automatically restricted to a small range of suppliers, typically within walking distance or bicycle ride in their own neighbourhood or 'in town' by bus journey.

Shortly after the Connolly case made headlines, in June 1952, Lemass, back in office as Minister for Industry and Commerce, raised the issue of the practice of limiting the number of apprenticeships to certain trades, with enforcement supplied by unions, by writing a public letter to the Irish Trades Union Congress. He threatened legislation to make such restrictions illegal. The *Irish Independent* editorialised:

As Mr. Lemass has emphasised in his recent letter, if the present state of affairs is allowed to continue the level of industrial output will decline. Indeed, he might have added that already in some branches of industry output has been retarded. It is common knowledge that in some crafts there is a marked shortage of skilled men because of unreasonable limitations placed on the recruiting of apprentices. Moreover, while a young citizen is free to enter any profession or any branch of the Civil Service or of commerce to which his ability can aspire, there is no such freedom in some crafts. This is indeed a strange perversion of democracy by those who should be its champions.[29]

The flaw in that argument was that it ignored the glaringly obvious fact that gaining entry to a profession was commonly subject to the ultimate restrictions imposed by class and status in a very class-polarised society: class, cash, culture and an expensive education. However, the editorial was making an important point: restrictive practices, whether enforced by unions, by professional associations or simply by custom and tradition, were also preventing large numbers of young people from earning their living in their own country; they were unable to 'break in' or to get a start in the trade because of artificial and anti-economic barriers.

Some months later Lemass warned organised labour against the policy of concentrating too much on protecting the interests of existing workers while ignoring the possibilities of actually increasing employment and encouraging the work force to expand. He was trying to face a classic problem of developing economies: the fact that the potential workers of the future had no political clout in competition with existing, employed and organised workers.[30] As a joke of the period put it, echoing the eighteenth-century parliamentarian Boyle Roche but showing a cynical understanding of fifties Ireland, 'Posterity be damned! What has posterity ever done for me?' Actually, posterity is commonly what gives the present some meaning.

Some days later Lemass expanded on this theme. Ireland had gone a long way but from a very bad beginning, and it had to do much more before progress would be ensured.

> All the economic progress of the last twenty years has not solved our national problems; at best we have done little more than stop the rot which a century of neglect has caused . . . What they need most is to get ideas moving in industrial and labour circles in that direction, to take the emphasis off the home market, and off security of profits and jobs behind protective tariffs and quotas, and on to the improvement of equipment, working methods and individual output, which might make exports to competitive markets practicable.[31]

Ireland's basic problem, he seemed to be hinting, was that the British government before independence was not concerned with Irish economic development but rather with pacifying the Irish people with hand-outs. The paradigmatic example was provided by the Land Acts of 1882–1904, which handed most of the land over to the sitting tenants at bargain prices without any regard for the tenants' capacity to develop their farms, productive ability or educational level. This formed a contrast with the successful and much-envied large farmers, most of them Catholics, many of whom bought their land from the British state in the post-Famine 1850s as serious agrarian business ventures under the Encumbered Estates Acts.[32] If Ireland were to develop economically, Lemass said a few days later, far-reaching changes in industrial and labour organisation would have to happen.[33] Efficiency was badly needed, but this would inevitably damage existing interests. He intended to introduce a bill designed to tackle the entire problem of restrictive practices.

> What was needed was a complete change of outlook . . . an 'across the board' re-examination of all existing procedures and policies, their deliberate adjustment so as to meet the requirements of economic progress and not because any law compelled that adjustment but because they recognised [that] national progress required it.

The *Irish Times*, quoting the Chamber of Commerce journal on 3 July 1952, commented on an open letter Lemass had circulated to the employers and the unions and described it as a blanket condemnation of restriction of entry to trades and a kind of declaration of war, as restrictive practices had by now reached an extreme stage of actually shrinking vital sections of the national work force.

> In effect the letter is an ultimatum to the unions that, unless the closed shop rule is abandoned and the unions concerned cooperate with employers in drafting a more liberal policy towards apprenticeship, the Minister will bring in legislation to deal with the matter. The fact is that restrictive rules have so limited entry to some trades that there are not enough men to do the work even with many hours of overtime, with additional expense to the employers and unnecessarily high costs to the consumers. In consequence, the national interest is

harmed, for a national policy of increasing output is nonsense if trades can counter it with their own policy of restricting output.[34]

In October the *Times* returned to the fray in a wide-ranging editorial essay, attacking not only trade unions but Government agencies, private employers and professional associations. The headline, quoting Lemass, was RESTRICTIVE PRACTICES ARE HAMPERING EXPANSION.'[35]

According to Mr. Lemass, the outside experts who have been called in recently to advise on the expansion of production in Ireland have shown on this issue [restrictive practices] a remarkable unanimity. If there is to be economic expansion, they agree, there first must be a reexamination of the policies and practices not only of Government authorities, but also of business organisations, agricultural associations, financial institutions and trade unions. All the experts have commented on the prevalence of restrictive practices in these organisations which, they have said, are hampering the expansion of economic activity. All of them have pointed out the folly of prating about expansion while practising restriction. They have found, and condemned, a disposition toward restrictive practices in every section of our national life. Too high a proportion of the time and effort of every section is devoted to consolidation of existing positions, and the protection of existing advantages and privileges. Too little of the time and effort is devoted to facing the hazards inherent in changing the practices upon which expansion of production, particularly production for export, depends. As Mr. Lemass said, the unanimity of these criticisms should be sufficient to jolt us out of any complacency about the country's position. Can any businessman, or any member of a trade union, who examines his conscience, aver that at no time has he ever been a party to any agreement that may limit production in his own interest? Such men must be rare indeed.[36]

The paper concluded, somewhat unconvincingly, that these practices were often well intentioned or at least well rationalised but admitted freely that they led to partitioned markets, commercial oligarchies, laziness, underemployment and stagnation. A traditional tendency to partition the market, much of it possibly rooted in a sectarian tendency originating in the eighteenth century to trade only 'with our own,' had become nationalised, reinforced and legitimised by the tariff regime introduced after 1932. The studies of Stacy May and other expert studies were politely and implicitly telling the Government and establishment that their approach to economic life reflected a subconsciously static view of economic development and that it threatened to strangle the economy completely if action was not taken by the Government.

According to Lemass, himself the architect of the protectionist system, protection had reached its limits or had even gone well beyond them by 1952. He admitted that most of the factors that were holding back progress were of 'our own invention and were certainly capable of being remedied by our own efforts.'[37] A bill aimed at 'smashing trade rings' was introduced in the Oireachtas a few days later, towards the end of October 1952. It was claimed that many items were overpriced by at least 20 per cent because of restrictive practices.[38] In the Dáil, Lemass announced a Government-led war against 'trade rings.'[39] There had been many complaints about such practices, he said, and many trade associations were in denial about it. He continued rather dramatically:

I want to smash trade rings, and use that term in the sense that the average man understands it . . . practices designed to

eliminate or restrict competition in the supply and distribution of any class of goods, or operated to deprive the
individual citizen of the right to engage in legitimate trade in
any class of business . . . The practice which had produced the
largest volume of complaints was that of refusing supplies of
goods on trade terms to persons who were not members of the
association, who were denied membership of the association,
or who could not get the approval of the association to engage
in the distribution of these goods.[40]

Here he was referring in particular to building materials, cars,
bicycles, newspapers and periodicals, paper bags and wrapping,
electrical goods and other products. The second-largest category
of complaint involved 'exclusive dealing arrangements.' 'Goods
were supplied to a trader on condition that he did not stock
similar goods supplied by a competitor.' Guinness was an obvious
culprit, with its system of tied houses—pubs that could serve only
the company's products if there were competing lines—but it also
involved producers and suppliers of petrol and cutlery.
Monopolies existed also, he said, in hides, rubber footwear, sheet
glass, screws, nails, and tacks. Wholesalers were forced to boycott
cost-cutting retailers; he mentioned in particular sales of petrol,
batteries, radios, pottery, cutlery, groceries, drapery, agricultural
machinery, veterinary medicines, paints, cigarettes and tobacco.
Lemass wished to outlaw the practice of excluding new entrants
to a trade whether it was by refusing supplies or by insisting on
unnecessarily elaborate working premises and conditions, the
expense of which would naturally have to be passed on to the
customer. He wished to stop people

imposing onerous conditions either as to the dimensions of the
trader's premises, the technical equipment he should employ,
or simply by the imposition of unreasonable conditions or
qualifications for trade discounts.[41]

Lemass received considerable cross-party sympathy for his general anti-monopolistic stance. The like-minded developmentalist in Fine Gael, Daniel Morrissey, of Industrial Development Authority fame, twitted him humorously with the example of the *Irish Press*, which commonly printed only the Fianna Fáil side of political controversies. William Norton of the Labour Party, a similarly like-minded figure, tacitly underwrote the Lemass line in an interjection some days later.[42] He remarked in the Dáil:

> Referring to manufacturers' agents, Mr. Lemass said he had had to make representations about a small clothing factory whose quota allowed it to operate only three days a month. He was told he would get enough [material] to work a full month if they paid fifteen per cent commission to an agent who never even saw the cloth. The individual had not even an office, and all he appeared to have was an attaché case and an order book. These agents were merely parasites, not merely on the backs of the manufacturers but ultimately on the backs of the consumers as well.

Lemass was not particularly impressed by either Morrissey or Norton. He saw Morrissey as inexperienced and conservative, while he felt that Norton tended to have silly and impractical ideas. Morrissey disliked Lemass ('I won't say I liked Lemass'), and rivalry for leadership in similar, although scarcely identical, ideological projects seems to have been part of the dynamic between the two men.[43]

One of the basic structural problems was that Ireland had a very large number of shops, as Patrick Lynch had quietly pointed out earlier, and many of them were small hucksters' concerns, poor and struggling to survive. The country had several times the number of shops as the Netherlands, proportionate to population, as Lynch had also pointed out. This was partly a result of the geographical concentration of population in the Netherlands and the sparseness and scattered nature of the population of the Republic; by comparison with the tiny, crowded Netherlands, Ireland was half-empty, although the paper did not make this fairly obvious point. The *Times* commented rather patronisingly in August 1953: 'There is something pathetic about the optimism that induces a citizen to invest most of his savings in a small shop in an area already oversupplied, as most areas are.'[44]

James Dillon made the often-repeated argument that it was the protectionist and statist system of Lemass that had produced these people.[45] Costello pointed to the restrictive practices of trade unions.[46] Almost parenthetically it must be emphasised repeatedly that restrictive practices were not confined to the private sector. In the form of job protection in economic activity that had little market demand it proliferated also in the public sector, particularly in what was effectually the state-controlled transport network. Branch railway lines in the west, which had long outlived their usefulness and carried virtually no passengers or freight, stayed open to protect the jobs of heavily unionised and politicised local officials and railway workers. They also stayed open because of the politicians' fear of the marginal voter. Under the Irish PR electoral system small groups of marginal voters had—and have—immense power to 'turn' an election result; even a few hundred well-organised voters in a marginal constituency could determine the destination of the last Dáil seat. Empty trains puffed up and down all over the west, effectually at the behest of small groups of voters, many of whom never or rarely took a train themselves. In 1949 radical proposals to prune the system were rejected by the inter-party Government, terrified of public reaction at the local level. Road-making grants were to be cut to pay, in effect, for the maintenance of these unused lines, and no cuts were to be administered to the moribund rail system.[47] Perfectly sane people were creating a perfectly insane transport system, and doing so with open eyes. The *Irish Times* commented:

> The only apparent reason for this policy is that the branch lines furnish employment for a limited number of officials, and that the Labour Ministers in Mr. Costello's Government are more keenly conscious of their Trade Union principles than the country's advantage. The effect, of course, must be that the public transport system will continue to drag a lengthening chain of debt, and that the benefits of a modern and efficient service will be denied to a large number of districts in the twenty-six counties.[48]

The much-hobbled and obstructed Merchant Lorry Owners' Association attacked CIE for having an obsolescent rail system. In August 1956 the lorry-owners called for the abolition of a series of bizarre Government-created legal limitations on private road haulage and demanded a pruning of the railway system. The limitations imposed on private lorry-owners were designed not to enhance the health and safety of the haulage service but to protect the public transport system against the threat of private enterprise. Hauliers could haul their goods only within their own county, for example. The private hauliers pointed out, in some heat and even desperation, that the Republic had only 2,200 miles of railway but 50,000 miles of roads.

It was only at the end of the 1950s that the redoubtable Todd Andrews was finally to take an axe to Ireland's Victorian railway network. The proposed remodelled Bray road was stopped by pressure from village shops along the way, and the *Irish Times* commented in 1954 that the road was stymied because all the 'noise' was from those who opposed the project, while those who were for it were unorganised and therefore unheard.[49]

Throughout the 1950s, however, a series of assaults on the extra-ordinary tangle of restrictive practices that festooned the Irish economy occurred. In January 1954 the new Fair Trade Commission, set up by Lemass to police such practices, investigated the radio trade. Its evidence included the following:

> Mr. C. P. O'Loughlin, electrical contractor Limerick, in evidence, said that he had been refused membership of the association although he had been selling sets for a number of years, and got the sets from a dealer who was on the association's lists. He had applied to the association to be put on the approved list in February, 1952. The association replied regretting that the control committee could not consider this application as it was not satisfied that he kept on his premises, whole time, a person capable of doing repairs. The witness said that in his application he had stated that he did not himself maintain repairmen, but he had the repairs done by a qualified man. No person ever came to his premises, he submitted, to investigate whether or not it was a suitable premises or whether or not he had suitable equipment.[50]

He actually employed three perfectly good electricians, apparently part-time, who were well able to fix radios, and he was refused sets by the wholesalers because he was not 'qualified' to be a member of the association, apparently because his electricians were not in permanent full-time employment in his firm. Other traders told similar horror stories in the early fifties.[51] A common, and unconvincing, defence was that price-fixing merely reflected the traders' practice of maintaining the manufacturer's recommended price.[52]

Publicity was, however, working, and in February 1954 a Controller of Prices was appointed. It was also announced that the Industrial Development Authority was to investigate restrictive practices and local monopolies in restriction of trade.[53] On 12 February 1954 the *Irish Times* wrote affectingly of the 'lost years' since 1945 in the tourist industry. The idea that Ireland had been marking time since 1945 gained strength in the Dublin media.[54]

The preferred mechanism of the Government in dealing with problems like restrictive practices was authoritarian: the imposition of price controls rather than the prohibition of monopolies, whether imposed by the state or by trade associations such as RGDATA. The promotion of free trade was mooted, but somewhat unenthusiastically. The *Press* published a comment by John O'Leary TD (National Labour Party), who

> referred to the closed shops in the bricklayers' and plasterers' unions, and said where there is a boom in building, Englishmen had to come to Ireland to supply the scarcity of tradesmen. There should be no such thing as a bar on any man's son to enter any trade.[55]

In October 1954 the *Times* commented darkly that free competition scarcely existed in Ireland and that the situation could scarcely be cured by the usual fiat, which tended to create as many irrationalities as it removed. In a slightly frightening article it announced roundly that a free market scarcely existed in the Republic.

> The question needs to be asked, however, whether free competition exists. In almost every branch of Irish commerce there are restrictive practices by which competition is reduced, or in some cases removed altogether. If it is desired to abolish these restrictive practices, the way to set about it is not to create price controls. On the contrary, the whole emphasis should be on eliminating controls—on freeing the market and allowing producers, the distributors and consumers to conduct their

bargaining without interference, either from the State or from self-constituted 'rings.'[56]

RINGS, CASH AND CARRY

In October 1954 it was reported that the prices of cars were effectually fixed collectively by assemblers and distributors. It was reported that most dealers apparently would be quite happy to sell at lower prices but would then have their supplies stopped. In early 1955 Fry-Cadbury's cocoa supplies were cut off from one trader because of pressure from RGDATA, together with the fear that other grocers would be compelled by RGDATA to boycott their goods.[57] The general policy of RGDATA, according to a spokesman for Bachelor's (Ireland) Ltd, was to impose one uniform price, and 'where one trader cut the price as against his neighbour, friction and irritation was created.'[58] Interestingly, some firms ignored RGDATA, including Bovril and Famor Foods. These seem to have been mainly firms that were big enough to control their wholesalers and to protect them from RGDATA pressure.

There was also a genuine problem with loss leaders, which could be used by large firms to crowd smaller firms out of the business by underselling, followed by subsequent raising of prices in a newly established monopoly situation. This loss-leader tactic, it was claimed, also prevented new firms entering the market with new lines and low prices.[59] There was a recent and increasing tendency for manufacturers to go directly to the retailer and to skip the Irish wholesaler. The depression of the mid-fifties reduced tolerance for price-fixing, and the Free Trade Commission was having some impact: restrictive practices and retail price maintenance were perceived to be on the retreat.

However, late in the year, in October 1955, Lemass unveiled an ambitious scheme to create 100,000 jobs, but he felt that restrictive practices might easily compromise these very ambitious job targets.[60]

Another significant development was the rise of consumer associations, often led by prominent and articulate women of the new middle class. The Consumer Association rebuked RGDATA for its campaign against cash-and-carry shops in February 1954.[61] Apprenticeship periods were far longer than in other countries, it was reported in March 1955; the international norm was three or four years for most trades, but Irish apprenticeship periods amounted to six or seven years of essentially underpaid labour.[62] It seems that the long Irish period dated from a time when young men were illiterate and had to be taught to read and write; parenthetically, it is not clear that literacy levels were all that wonderful in the fifties. However, in January 1956 it turned out that RGDATA had had the audacity to ask the Government in 1954 to limit hours of trading for non-union shops to ensure that they conformed to unionised shop hours.[63]

Back in 1949 a small businessman who owned two lorries reported that he was only permitted to haul turf in them and that he had been assessed for £1,400 back tax on profits assumed to have come from haulage. CIE had a monopoly of haulage outside big towns, but any firm was permitted to haul its own goods—but only its own goods—anywhere, which had the lunatic consequence of encouraging each larger firm to have its own fleet of lorries (rather like the great and irrational state trusts of the Soviet Union, ships going up the Volga empty passing similar ships going down the river equally empty, the two sets of ships belonging to different mega-trusts). Furthermore, the Supreme Court had, in its wisdom, decided that the owner of a lorry had the constitutional right to rent it out to anyone else he chose. CIE wished to close this loophole.[64] As late as August 1956 the railway unions were trying to get the Government to tax lorries even more heavily so as to protect and subsidise rail freight on a railway system much smaller and far more inflexible than the road transport system.

In March 1956 the Restrictive Trade Practices Bill went through all its Dáil stages, nearly ten years after its predecessor had reportedly been snuffed out by powerful interests in 1947.[65] However, RGDATA marched on and was reported in May 1956, while an economic crisis raged around the country, to be attempting to set up a Merchants' National Co-operative, which would be, the journalists claimed, 'a ring within a ring.' The general idea was to whip into line small 'individualistic' traders who sought small profits and quick returns. The *Irish Times* commented sagely that a true co-operative was run by consumers rather than by sellers.[66]

In September the railway unions called for the Road Fund to contribute to transport by rail and canal while denouncing the apparently widespread practice of illegal long-distance haulage by lorry owners.[67]

A general sense of there being something wrong with the political culture was touched on by many commentators, perhaps best summarised by Father Patrick Corcoran, who, late in the terrible year of 1956, opined that the Republic had wasted ten years and that Irish people had an immaturity of political outlook. There was a poor spirit in public life, there were financial frauds, 'sterile criticism of authority and a self-centred defence of privileges in contempt of the general interest.'[68]

Signs of a shift in thinking were evident. M. P. Linehan of the Irish Conference of Professional and Service Associations remarked in October that the basic problem was that public investment favoured social and redistributive objectives rather than being aimed at encouraging productivity and exports, a proposition later to characterise Whitaker's Grey Book. In October the Government began *allowing* (the verb speaks volumes) private companies to install modern tipping gear on their lorries, but strange weight restrictions on private hauliers remained so as to protect CIE haulage.[69]

In February 1957 the *Times* gave the inter-party Government the doubtful compliment of remarking that it had at least made the public aware of the seriousness of the economic situation.[70] However, a majority of industrialists still apparently favoured protective tariffs and quotas. But there were definite signs of a sea change in public opinion.[71] 1957 brought a widening of horizons, as the prospect of free trade being almost forced on a reluctant little country emerged. In June, D. A. Hegarty, chairman of Dublin Port and Docks Board, pleaded for more 'patriotism' in the school system while attacking the trade unions for their restrictive practices. The country was caught in a vicious circle.

> We have restrictive practices because of fear of unemployment. We have unemployment because of lack of purchasing power and of national income and this in turn is due partly to restrictive practices and so on around the vicious circle. We must find some way of breaking out of this vicious circle. I believe the trade union leaders would be prepared to do this if they could carry their men with them.[72]

A commonly expressed opinion was that sectional interests tended to be more selfish than the individuals who composed them; in modern parlance it could be said that the entire economy was suffering from a general systems failure. In October 1957 the *Times* editorialised a national wake-up call of a suitably military character.

> REVEILLE!
> Mr. Lemass has made it clear to our Irish manufacturers that they must get on or get out. Too many of them, he indicates, are comfortably situated behind a curtain of protective tariffs, and see no reason why they should bother about such national necessities as production for export . . . Our great weakness is the persistent tendency to eliminate competition.[73]

The paper apparently had the occasional attack of nerves. In November it editorialised that Sweetman's desperate remedy for the balance of payments crisis of 1956 had woken the people up briefly but that they now looked like falling asleep again.[74] In January 1958 it editorialised that 1957 had been one of the dullest and least progressive years in Irish history, but it at least had the merit of marking the time in which there occurred

the emergence of the Twenty-Six Counties from an insular seclusion which, if protracted, might have done us great and growing harm . . . We have lagged rather badly—especially in the sphere of agriculture—for too many years, and we can afford to be laggard no longer.[75]

In May 1958 the Government finally revoked the ban on married women working as teachers, a ban that had commonly been denounced as irrational for at least ten years before this revocation. The *Times* editorialised that the general standard of popular education was actually lower than it had been a generation previously.[76] In July, Prof. Desmond Williams, a UCD historian, felt able to comment that the traditional cant about the national language, partition and foreign policy was essentially 'paying lip service to dead or dying ideas.'[77]

Donal Barrington, of Tuairim fame, felt that the central question of Irish politics in 1958 was the 'transfer of political power from the old to the young.'[78] However, older habits died hard. In October 1958 a hairdresser named James Morton was prosecuted for working after hours, at half-past eleven on a Sunday morning, thereby offending most grievously against the strictures of church, state and union. T. K. Whitaker's Grey Book was published, curiously enough on a Saturday, 22 November 1958, thereby formalising the new departure that had been adumbrated in public discourse for many years, to relatively little effect. In December 1958 the Minister for Finance, James Ryan, was able to announce that manufacturing industry had expanded that year by a very respectable 5½ per cent.[79] Lemass was to refer to 1958 as an 'encouraging year' a month later.[80]

The construction of an 'East Link' bridge east of the loop line in Dublin, first mooted in 1929 and blocked by the shipping company Palgrave Murphy Ltd because it would have cut off anchorages that were rarely used, was mooted again in early 1959.[81] Parenthetically, this wonderful and paradigmatic example of Irish political paralysis was finally removed in the 1980s with the construction of the East Link Bridge by private enterprise in the shape of Tom Roche of Cement-Roadstone Holdings Ltd. In March 1959 the Government turned down an American offer of 50 per cent financing for a nuclear research reactor for Irish universities; the *Times* felt this was regrettable.[82]

However, in April the *Press* was able to announce proudly that national income had increased by an entire 3 per cent in 1958.[83] In October, Erskine Childers, Minister for Transport and Power, suggested indirectly that the defence of vested interests had cost the country dearly. 'Cynical indifference to Irish transport costs is not justified.' CIE had lost £21 million since 1949, or £27 million if one included the Great Northern Railway's operations within the Republic. He felt personally that if this money had been spent by the taxpayer on Irish-made goods, or if the money had been put into scientific education and fertilisers, more people would have been employed.[84] Jack Lynch stated at about the same time that restrictive practices would have to be abolished.[85] The *Indo* denounced such practices also.[86]

On 29 December 1959 the *Times* felt able to announce that, for the first time, industrial exports exceeded in value the cattle export trade.[87] There was a genuine sense in 1959 that a historic-ally significant point had been reached and passed and that the future would have possibilities unimagined by previous generations. That sense was accurate. The 1960s boom actually began in the late fifties as the country finally began to shake off a series of ideas, work practices and attitudes, some of them of truly archaic provenance and resonant more of the eighteenth century than of the world of post-war Europe.

The traditional search for monopoly gains did not end with Lemass, however, although it was much weakened by his efforts and by the efforts of many others.[88] Ironically, his earlier work had intensified that tradition. However, restrictive practices still exist. It took half a century to privatise Aer Lingus and abolish the Shannon stopover. It hasn't gone away completely, even in the Ireland of the twenty-first century.

Chapter 6 ∿

LEARNING AND TRAINING: THE EDUCATION WARS

EDUCATE THAT YOU MAY ESCAPE

As early as 1942 a senior officer in the Department of Education, Joseph O'Neill, wrote to Archbishop John Charles McQuaid in connection with the difficulties involved in running a dual system of education controlled by both church and state. This system had been devised by the British government in the middle of the nineteenth century and inherited by the Irish state on independence. Most Irish separatists had accepted the system as normal and desirable, inheriting in this a tradition of lack of real interest in education that dates back to the Fenian movement of the 1850s. O'Neill wrote:

Unfortunately, as Your Grace is aware conditions are changing in many ways not least in the attitude of various bodies towards the control of education. Sometimes, as in yesterday's article in the Sunday Independent this attitude expresses itself as a demand that the State should supply all the funds for building and repair of national schools, although the bishops have stated categorically that they consider this undesirable. At other times it takes the form of a demand that these expenditures and other things such as heating and cleaning should be put on the rates. It is quite probable that most of the advocates of this lessening of managerial responsibility and control do not realise it is the thin end of the wedge which another type of 'reformer' wishes to use in order to get our schools completely under public control.[1]

In the late 1940s education was the victim of a very Irish political stalemate. The country was rural, almost pastoral, but teetering on the edge of a plunge into the uncharted waters of full-scale developmentalism, partly at the urgings of the Marshall Plan officials and the government of the United States. It was sensed that great changes were coming. Some wished passionately for such a new departure, but a strange and inchoate alliance feared it and tended, out of structural circumstance, instinct or ideological conviction, to resist it. Farmers, secular clergy (as distinct from religious orders), the older, more craft-oriented unions, family farms and businesses were distrustful of the changes mooted by those who favoured mass education and training, the possibility of higher taxes and Government regulation, large cities and general modernisation.

It should be recalled that in the late forties only 10 per cent of the entire population paid income tax. In the early sixties pay-as-you-earn (PAYE) income tax was finally to be introduced, partly because of trade union pressure, with the ironic result that eventually most members of trade unions found themselves paying income tax. The intention had been to make the rich pay, but it meant that those of middling or even more modest means paid the lion's share of the tax bill, thanks to the trade union leadership of the time; the rich had their own ways of avoiding taxes. Those who feared change sometimes had a point.

Although the national newspapers in the forties generally favoured an expansion of the educational system and in particular the extension of the compulsory school leaving age from fourteen to fifteen, or even sixteen, deeply ensconced and shadowy political and social forces resisted any change, even though the leaving age had already gone up to fifteen in Britain and was shortly to be extended to sixteen, a fact that was widely known and publicised in the Republic. Inevitably the developmental role-models for the Republic were going to be the United States, Britain and, less immediately, the recovering countries of western Europe. The country had, and knew that it had, what was possibly the most underdeveloped vocational education system in western Europe, despite there being a strong and increasing demand for technical training and even though there was a dedicated and able cadre of teachers and technical instructors.

I have offered in an earlier work, *Preventing the Future*, some explanations for this strange and traditional hostility to the idea of mass education, among them ordinary people's disregard for humanist education, combined with the Catholic Church's insistence on humanist education almost to the exclusion of other types of education, farmers wishing to use their sons for physical labour on the farm, and the underdevelopment of vocational education partly because of episcopal obstruction back in the twenties. Some of these explanations were, oddly, dismissed by an occasional ill-informed critic as hindsight wisdom or, more simply, as imagination and illusion. Here the less easily contradicted diagnoses of contemporary observers will be examined.[2]

This archaic and primitivist contempt for humanist education has persisted into the twenty-first century, and Irish universities' humanities departments are still under assault by managerialist presidents and administrators, many of whom have had no humanist education themselves and therefore despise and resent it. Myles na gCopaleen caricatured the mentality brilliantly in the early 1940s.

The Plain People of Ireland: Dear knows some people are very smart, these County Council scholarships to the universities above in Dublin do more harm than good, young gossoons walking around with their Sunday suits on them on week-days when they're home at Easter, ashamed to be seen out with their fathers and O no thanks, I'm not going to give any hand with the sowing, I have to attend to my studies, I've an exam in two months. And that reminds me, I want five pounds for books. Sure it's all madness. You say you'd like a joke or two for a bit of crack and the finger of scorn is pointed at you. It's madness, the country's in a right state. Madness. There's no other word for it. Madness . . .[3]

In October 1947 William Norton, veteran trade unionist and now leader of the Labour Party, appealed to the Government in the Dáil to go for a policy of producing highly trained manpower, as had advanced European countries, such as Switzerland. He was speaking implicitly against a very entrenched mentality that regarded all training beyond a certain age as being a ticket to emigrate and, in the minds of some, a process of spiritual impoverishment.

In many respects we could usefully find examples in Europe of small countries which are well worth our emulation . . . Switzerland is a country which should provide us with an incentive to emulate her high standards of production and efficiency . . . I do not think she would have a chance of doing that [marvellous economic export performance] except for a systematic policy of insisting on efficiency and a scheme of technical education which gives them skill, technical knowledge and adaptability, unlike our people who are hewers of wood and drawers of water in countries where people are too wise to be hewers of wood and drawers of water.

I think if we are going to build up here an industrial position capable of producing good quality products and which will give the people decent rates of wages, it can only be done by the same methods which have given other countries a high standard of efficiency in the control and direction of undertakings, and the avoidance, by legislation if necessary, of inefficient methods of production and the recognition that our aim must be the production of goods for our own people and the provision of much-needed employment for our people at home . . .

It seems to me to be vain to cry out for more production while every boat leaving this country is packed with emigrants who cannot get work here producing the goods we need. Until we get down to the problem of harnessing the energy, ability, brawns and enthusiasm of all those who are now leaving the country, because they cannot get a livelihood in producing goods here, we shall have failed to tackle the problem of increasing production. No country in the world has been able to increase its production at the same time as it exported the cream of its manhood and womanhood. We cannot do it. Least of all can we do it with our slender and relatively under-developed industrial organisation. Therefore I want to see established a development commission for the purpose of surveying our natural resources, for the purpose of planning to utilise those resources in the manner envisaged by the present Government when it favoured the establishment of an economic council, in the days when it was in opposition.[4]

In February 1948 the president of the Association of Secondary Teachers, Ireland (ASTI), noted that the secondary-school system had not changed since 1922, but it had been reported to him that the school leaving age was soon to be raised from fourteen to fifteen and later to sixteen. Pigs were to have wings. As early as January 1949 Daniel Morrissey, echoing William Norton, remarked that the country's greatest lack, as far as industrial-isation was concerned, was the shortage of skilled technicians and trained executives.[5] The Intermediate and Leaving Certificates were accepted in England, with the intriguing exception of the

English course, which was seen there as being hopelessly old-fashioned.

The *Irish Times* described the educational system as 'lopsided' in August 1949; it was very humanist and classical, but it didn't teach children how to earn their living.[6] It was claimed by the *Independent* that the standard of spoken and written English in Ireland in 1949 was far worse than it had been around the time of independence a generation previously.[7] In September the paper called for a raising of the school leaving age to fifteen, a call to be repeated many times and not responded to by the Government for more than another decade.[8]

Rural interests commonly blamed education for prompting emigration because it imparted skills that were easy to sell in Dublin, England or America; it was seen also as having the undesirable effect of 'citifying' the children, thereby making them restless in their native acres.[9] This view was shared by many in power, in particular the Minister for Education in the Fianna Fáil Government of 1932–48, Thomas Derrig. It was shared also by some of the secular clergy.

The fear of the attractions of cities was populist, nationalist and very much a small farmer's and rural employer's view of things. Vocational education was commonly seen as, or was intended to be, a means of building up rural society rather than as a general agent of economic development. The trouble was that young people simply did not want to go into agricultural work, and some saw farming as an inherited prison from which they wished to escape.[10] Many of their elders feared vocational education as a means by which skills were imparted that made emigration easier and more attractive. Religious and patriotic instruction would have to accompany technical instruction, or laicisation of the culture would accelerate, the bishops insisted, as they had done since the twenties. If such instruction were not to be included then vocational education might not be provided with any support from the religious authorities, and that might be the kiss of death to the whole enterprise of technical training.

That education was by itself, and if uncontrolled by religious authority, a force for the secularisation and demoralisation of a simple but brave people seems to have been the underlying and often unspoken thesis. In June 1949 a Father Greany informed the annual congress of the Vocational Education Association:

> It was a matter for regret that the 1930 Vocational Act did not refer to religion as a formal element in instruction in our vocational schools. Memorandum V.40, published in 1942, supplied admirably for that defect, but the civil authorities had not yet sought the Church's formal approval for the regulations governing vocational education . . . . It is virtuous and makes for complete living to love this land of our birth, to learn its history, to honour our national heroes who have moulded our Irish way of life, to cherish our national language, so long a medium of thought for our people and a medium of prayer for 1,400 years. But we must be careful lest the utilitarian aspect of education and of life should prevail and weigh on the fiery spirit of the Gael. We must be careful lest preparation for life should be narrowed down to preparation for a livelihood. Mere efficient preparation for a livelihood would not have given us in our generation the men of 1916 or the missionaries of China and Africa.
>
> Educators must have a clear vision of the spirit that quickeneth in Irish education lest the heart of our young people grow gross. They must be preserved from the worldly outlook that would make them wiser in their generation than the children of light. The worldly wise prefer the odour of smoke from their factories to the odour of incense from their altars.[11]

He also urged that co-education in school, college or university should be reduced to a minimum.

In September 1949 Desmond Clarke, librarian of the Royal Dublin Society, agreed with the traditional opinion and thought that further education beyond a minimum level merely encouraged the flight from the land by encouraging an urban mentality.[12] This very widespread attitude seems to have been a major factor in inhibiting further education generally—something alleged to make one into a rootless cosmopolitan and more ready to seek out fresh fields and pastures new, in Dublin or outside Ireland. However, early in 1950 Seán MacBride, going against this traditionalist grain, announced that secondary and university education was no longer a luxury but absolute necessities for young Irish people in the new world that was unfolding around them. The *Irish Times* responded to this outburst in traditional fatalistic fashion, to the effect that an expansion of higher education would be a waste of taxpayers' money, as it would simply fuel emigration.[13]

An interesting article by Shane Leslie in the *Irish Independent* supplied a general assessment of the educational system in August 1950.[14] In accordance with other observers of that time, his central observation was that education tended to point children away from farming and towards city life. Farming came to be regarded as backward and impoverishing. If one were to ask national school children what their ambitions were, the answers would be pretty unequivocal, he wrote. He gave a telling little sketch of children's opinions:

The majority of girls would like to be teachers or nurses. Sometimes they will say nuns. Two professions are never mentioned, the domestic service or the housewife, but to be the latter the most are fated if they stay at home. The boys will readily propose being bus-drivers, teachers, engineers, lorry-drivers. Two professions are barely mentioned: those of the soldier or the farmer. When farming is chosen, there is a titter as though the boy were good for no other. There can be no doubt that the hallmark of success in the parents' minds is the ability to get into a town and the bigger the town the better. There can be no doubt that the schools and colleges are giving the education that the parents demand. It is an education which fits those who receive it admirably for taking up positions in England—with the exception of what they learn of Irish.[15]

Young people were not being educated as agriculturalists, foresters, market gardeners or carpenters, 'because such professions do not appeal to their parents or to the educational authorities.' They preferred to aim at white-collar employment and looked down on manual work; status seems to have been as important in many people's minds as monetary reward. In effect, education was in fact geared towards emigration from rural to urban places because of the conscious or subconscious wishes of the parents; young people were being prepared tacitly for life in Dublin, Britain or America. Despite sentimental yearnings towards a rural or even Gaelic life, Irish people wanted to live in cities, thereby echoing a general trend of humanity in the twentieth century. Agrarian civilisation was gradually dying everywhere, albeit at different rates. Cities were housing a steadily increasing proportion of the rapidly growing human race. This accounted in part for the widely perceived pointlessness of teaching the children Irish, which would be of little use to them even in Dublin or Cork and certainly of no use outside Ireland. The girls in particular found in England the well-paid, secular and free life denied to them at home, and commonly the Irish emigrants forgot their ancestral Catholicism unless they ghettoised themselves in the big cities—a common first-generation solution.

In 1950 the *Press* observed that the country was becoming richer and that the numbers of university students had grown from 3,000 in 1925 to 7,500 in 1949, medicine, architecture, engineering and economics being the dominant subjects sought out by, and monopolised by, the new middle class.[16]

The students of UCD were pretty patriotic, even chauvinistic, in 1950. When asked 'If we went to war on the Partition issue, would you fight?' 98 per cent of women students said they would, as against a mere 70 per cent of the men. However, they were all against the GAA's ban on 'foreign games', such as soccer and rugby.[17] A practical question got a negative answer, an impractical question an overwhelmingly positive one, reflecting the unreality not of Irish thinking but of Irish rhetoric. The *Independent* editorialised in April 1950:

> That the vast majority of Irish children leave school for good and all at the age of 14 years is a feature of our social order greatly to be deplored. The Very Reverend Canon Fitzpatrick, Vice-Chairman of the Dublin Vocational Education Committee, has suggested one way of lessening the ill effects of this state of things. He has urged employers to afford facilities to young persons in their service to attend the day classes in the Vocational schools. It is an excellent suggestion and we trust that it will meet with an immediate response.
>
> It would of course be far more desirable that the occasion for such a request should not arise. In our view the real remedy is not to get those who have left school at fourteen years of age to go back to school, but to ensure that they do not leave school at so early an age. In other words, we want the school-leaving age to be raised to fifteen, as has been done in other countries. A strong case could be made for raising the age to sixteen; but that no doubt must wait. It is unnecessary to repeat the arguments in favour of raising the school-leaving

age; they are many, forceful and unanswerable.

As far as we are aware not only are teachers and trade unions and employers strongly favourable to the proposal, but no political party, no social organisation and no body of citizens opposes it. We have pressed for the change again and again. The late [Fianna Fáil] Government rejected it on a most un-convincing and indeed most unhappy report presented by some un-named officials. The present Government should approach the question more courageously. And it should be one of the first cares of the Council of Education.[18]

In May 1950 the *Independent* reported that there was an increasing shortage of secondary schools, particularly in Dublin city and county.

Within the past twenty years the total number of pupils, both boys and girls, in the secondary schools has risen from 26,000 to 44,000. There has at the same time been an increase in the number of recognised secondary schools from 287 to 404. In Dublin city and county, where there were only 63 secondary schools twenty years ago, there are now 82.

Having regard to the growth in the population of Dublin and still more to the increasing anxiety of parents to give their children a higher education it cannot be said that an average of one new secondary school per year is at all gratifying. It is well known that many of the leading schools and colleges are reluctantly compelled to turn away large numbers of boys who seek to be enrolled.[19]

In October 1950 Basil Peterson pointed to the dearth of edu-cation and training for farmers, which seems partly to have been generated by a lack of demand for such a service by the majority of the young farmers of the time. However, the Economic

Cooperation Administration, a US government agency, pronounced itself very impressed by the young farmers its officers
encountered in the Co. Cork vocational education scheme.[20] Cork
educational services, partly because of the creative efforts of the
educationalists of UCC, led by Alfred O'Rahilly, were unusually
well developed by the standards of the time and place. Irish
distance education had its origins in this local initiative.

There was no consensus on the matter of extending education
to the poorer and more remote sections of the population. Many
called for a raising of the school leaving age from fourteen, but
still it didn't happen. In March 1951 the president of the Irish
National Teachers' Organisation called yet again, and in vain, for
the raising of the age by two years, from fourteen to sixteen.

By denying equality of educational opportunity to her children, Ireland is more than half a century behind the modern
nations of the world. Reorganisation of our educational system
is essential if the talented child of the poorer parent is not to be
debarred for ever from higher education and the full
employment of his God-given powers . . . Reform must begin
by scrapping the superstructure of the present education of
our democracy, and the training of our teachers which is based
on the philosophy of the National Board of 1831, a philosophy
that was anti-national, anti-social and anti-democratic.[21]

The *Times* took a cautious and somewhat contradictory line on
this kind of argument. It editorialised, quite rightly but essentially
kicking to touch, that the existing primary system had some real
strengths and that raising the school leaving age to sixteen would
probably provoke some short-sighted parents to resent it. Boys of
fourteen were well able to do errand-boy or farm work. To be in
favour of further education was a notion to be entertained, but
apparently it was not to be articulated in the presence of the

servants. But the paper did admit, rather reluctantly, that there was far more illiteracy in the country than was officially acknowledged.[22]

In July 1951 the Minister for Agriculture made a blunt and quietly devastating observation about the education of farmers, who, with their dependants and economic partners in transport, trade and food production, made up still the majority of the elec-torate. Farmers were very poorly educated.[23]

The clergy were very divided as well, and there was certainly no united clerical reactionary front against educational reform. In late 1951 the professor of classics at Maynooth, Father Denis Meehan, spoke eloquently and sadly of the sheer intellectual mediocrity of Irish education.

> We are a community ridden by mediocrity at every intellectual level and we shall always fall short of Grade A achievement unless as a community and through our authorities we succeed in making drastic readjustments ... There is a degree of cultural immaturity in all our young people, the dull ones and the clever ones, which militated against efficiency and achievement. Generally speaking students, even after they had graduated from the university, remained without a right attitude toward civilised things, without civilised interests, and consequently without education in the historic sense of the term.

He believed there had been a noticeable decline in general educational standards over the previous ten years.[24] At about the same time the *Indo* made its depressing observation that the sons and daughters of farmers were not interested in agricultural college scholarships aimed at improving farmers' knowledge of scientific methods, unless they wished to become agricultural inspectors—a white-collar job.[25]

In October the *Press* published an article about a commission reporting on unemployment among young people. Lemass had set the commission up in 1943, and it reported finally a very leisurely eight years later. It recommended that the school leaving age should be sixteen, that bars enforced by unions or by custom to apprenticeship should be removed immediately, and that there should be a vocational guidance service, a central council of education, grants for recreational and educational clubs, courses in manual instruction and domestic science and an agency to supervise the working conditions of messenger boys. Also, alternatives to industrial schools for juvenile delinquents and disturbed adolescents should be sought, and the setting up of a fostering system was suggested.[26]

Messenger boys, presumably mainly working for the RGDATA shops, were typically teenagers who left school at thirteen or so and were commonly exploited labour in what was unmistakably a dead-end and short-term job; generally they were fired when they became relatively expensive adult employees. By way of contrast to the weakness of demand for mainstream post-primary education, Dublin vocational or technical schools could not cope physically with the increasing voluntary demand for full-time continuing education and training by many young people.[27] In Dublin 'the need to round off the education received in primary school, regarded as imperative in 1926, was much more imperative today.'[28] Seán Moylan, a very activist Fianna Fáil Minister for Education during the period 1952–4, evidently agreed with this, going against the conventional wisdom that seemed to recommend passivity by saying in January 1951, while in opposition:

I am hopeful that the creation of extensive facilities for vocational training will create a capacity for, and a spirit of, industrial enterprise, long discouraged, and a lack of which has been a grave contributory cause of our emigration losses.[29]

In early 1952 the *Independent* documented the extraordinary under-financing of secondary schools by the Government, apparently with the connivance of the ecclesiastical authorities, anxious not to permit Government interference with their control and administration of the secondary education system. Capitation grants for secondary schools were at the same level they had been at in 1924/5; they had suffered a 10 per cent cut in 1931/2; a partial restoration of the cut occurred in 1938/9; and a full restoration of the cut occurred in 1946/7. Admittedly there had been significant deflation in the thirties as the value of money grew greater year by year, instead of declining, as is the modern experience; cuts commonly meant little change in the actual value of the grants and loans. There was also a heavy subsidy for teaching through Irish.[30]

In January 1953 the *Independent* editorialised about the apparently characteristic Irish disregard for education. Parents saw no relationship between educational achievement and financial reward, often quite rightly. 'Not so many years ago a member of the Irish legislature stated publicly that there was too much education in Ireland.'[31] In June 1953 the paper returned to the neglect of secondary education. It editorialised yet again:

Apart from very small items, the State contributes nothing to the cost of secondary education. For all practical purposes the burden for paying for such education falls on the Religious Orders and the parents. Both are far more heavily penalised now than they were in 1929. If we are ever to make of our country something approaching our hopes for it, we must provide the best possible education that promising intellect demands. It is no credit to us that money can so easily be found for purposes that cannot bring in a return while we neglect the hopes of the young.[32]

Shortly afterwards the *Indo* noted that only 5 per cent of Irish students received scholarships, whereas three-quarters of British students did so. Even at that time the contrast was shocking. 'It would be strange indeed if this country afforded the last remaining example of a university system to which entry depended on money and not on talent.'[33] In April Mairéad de Barra argued that BA graduates shunned teaching because there were few prospects of lay people being promoted in clerically controlled schools; senior managers were usually priests or nuns.[34]

In September the INTO pointed out that the chronic shortage of teachers could be ended immediately by removing the prohibition of the 1930s on married women teaching and on permitting graduates to teach in primary schools.[35] The ban on married women was finally removed in 1958. In early 1953 the *Press* boasted of a real drive in the expansion of technical education under Fianna Fáil.[36] Seán Moylan, now Minister for Education and still a strong advocate of vocational education in a rather hostile or at best indifferent political environment, asked in September 1953:

Are we satisfied that eighty per cent of our children leave the primary school at the age of fourteen and that we should not provide a further opportunity for them for the development of their characters and the training of their aptitudes?

Most of these children remained effectually illiterate, he remarked.[37] In November he mourned the lack of modern Irish writers, something that sounds rather strange coming from a member of a Government that presided over a set of formal and informal censorship systems that methodically denied to the public the works of many modern Irish and foreign writers of distinction. In July the *Times* noted that capitation grants to secondary schools were still unchanged since 1929. In September

1953 the training of doctors in some universities was declared to be inadequate by American medical authorities.[38]

The *Independent* continued to complain about the under-financing of secondary schools, the 'backwardness' of the school system and the impoverishment of the Institute for Industrial Research and Standards.[39] In 1954 it noted the growing popularity of the technical schools and the continuing apparent decline in standards of command of the English language.[40]

Michael Joseph Costello, something of a charismatic hero to developmentalists, commented on the fifty years that had been wasted since Horace Plunkett's time in bringing scientific knowledge to farmers.[41] In July, William Norton of the Labour Party pointed to a problem with the new industries that the tri-party triumvirate of himself, Lemass and Morrissey was counting on: the work force was not up to the standards demanded by the new, relatively high-technology industries. 'Many of them required a standard of technical competence which our people have not got.'[42]

In August the Council of Education's long-awaited first report appeared, displaying a fantastically complacent satisfaction with the existing system. In October the *Indo* reported that third-level education was expanding but was doing so very slowly.

> It will be a false economy to spend millions on capital development if we stint on the education of the technical services that such development will make necessary. Again, it is still a reproach that, apart from the comparatively few scholarships offered by local authorities, there is an almost complete lack of assistance for poor but talented students.

University attendance, the paper announced, had increased threefold in forty-three years, from 2,250 in 1909 to 7,600 in 1952, but this was mainly an echo of the growth of a new middle class that valued career-oriented professional education.[43]

In February 1954 Moylan seems to have experienced some fairly serious resistance from the craft unions to his efforts to expand trade skills. He felt eventually that he had to say: 'The suggestion that vocational training is an intrusion on the work of craftsmen is unwarranted.'[44] In June J. Edgar Simmons asserted that censorship was intended to keep the country adolescent in its mentality.[45]

In November the *Independent* looked at the explosion of higher education in the United States and, instead of admiring the American achievement, rather self-revealingly speculated on the dangers of the future growth of an academic proletariat in that country.[46] The idea that there might be a connection between general educational levels and economic performance had been entertained by the media but was not fully absorbed as a practical proposition; the older idea that mass education meant the creation of a large, discontented and therefore troublesome class of over-educated poor still lingered on. However, in December the *Irish Independent* editorialised:

The British people have been taught by the lessons of the war and post-war years that there is a close connection between higher education and both security and prosperity. Warfare has been deeply affected by scientific advances; in trade and production the need of the applied sciences has grown progressively greater. It is an old complaint in Britain that there is much research that is at a very high level but that there is insufficient provision for the practical application of its results.

In Ireland, the paper observed, graduate careers had been built by state-sponsored bodies, such as the ESB and Bord na Móna.[47] In early 1955 the paper returned to grinding its educational axe; it commented angrily that the persistent and evidently deliberate under-financing of poor but able students was 'scandalous.'[48]

At about the same time Éamon de Valera, once again out of power, complained defensively that the teaching of Irish in schools was being made to take the blame for everything that might be wrong with the system.[49] In April 1955 it was announced that Northern Ireland was to raise the school leaving age to fifteen. The *Indo* noted that officials in Dublin had recommended the same change years previously (in 1936) and that the proposal had been rejected 'for spurious reasons.' The early school leaving age automatically handicapped the poor, the paper claimed.[50] These were the people most likely to have to go to England in search of work, and their lack of education and training necessarily condemned them to low-paid and menial work. The paper returned to the question of the dearth of university scholarships in April, and this time it generated a certain amount of sympathetic public reaction.[51] Also in April 1955 the *Press* announced proudly:

Our vocational schools have done a great deal in the short time in which the value of vocational training has been really understood here, but the old idea that practical experience was one thing and college education another dies very hard. It has affected even our progress in agriculture, the industry on which all others depend. A speaker at Warrenstown College on Sunday commented on the lack of skill in their profession that hindered so many farmers.

However, progress on the vocational education front was now being made finally under the Fianna Fáil Government, the paper claimed.[52] Senator Liam Ó Buachalla described the vocational teachers admiringly as 'a body of nation-builders' in July 1955.[53]

In June it was reported that a well-known delegate to the Vocational Education Congress had observed that Irish apprenticeship periods were far too long; it was ridiculous that a young fellow had to put in seven low-paid years to become a journeyman bricklayer or plasterer, six years to become a plumber or carpenter, and scandalous that no apprenticeship was shorter than four years. In Germany, Sweden and the United States apprenticeships lasted only three or four years. The long apprenticeship terms discouraged applicants, encouraged drop-outs and were clearly restrictive in their effects; they operated to keep the numbers of workers down, the skills scarce and therefore more highly paid. This suited the unions and their membership.[54]

In September the well-known and much-loved writer Francis MacManus sensed a huge, if shapeless, cultural shift in Ireland in the mid-fifties:

> It's in the people themselves, in us, that deep and rapid change is taking place, and it's taking place because the whole complex of traditions, customs and ways of living that give us our character, is vanishing.[55]

Things were certainly getting a lot livelier on the education issue in the middle of the decade. The *Times* editorialised in September 1955 about the opposition of various Catholic and clerical worthies, particularly Alfred O'Rahilly and Bishop Michael Browne of Galway, to the projected Agricultural Institute, for which the Marshall Plan had put up generous funding. The institute had been held up for years by interest-group haggling and clerical intrigue. Concerning O'Rahilly and Browne, the paper commented acidulously:

> Both of these worthies take the line that agricultural education cannot properly be divorced from higher education in general—and from the teaching of religion, ethics and socio-logy in particular. A 'glorified technical institute'—the phrase is O'Rahilly's—which confines itself to the production of agri-cultural experts pure and simple is an abomination to them.[56]

Parenthetically, it should be noted by younger readers that 'sociology' in Catholic Ireland meant Catholic social ethics rather than study of the writings of Marx, Weber, Durkheim, Michael Young and C. Wright Mills.

In an apparent and rather clever riposte Canon C. M. Grey-Stack of the Church of Ireland asked a few days later whether O'Rahilly's insistence on links between religious training and agricultural education necessitated limiting agricultural education to Catholics.[57] In October 1955 the provost of Trinity College, A. J. McConnell, pointed out publicly that the few available county council scholarships usually specifically excluded Trinity from the list of acceptable colleges; quite reasonably and accurately, he suggested that this amounted to religious discrimination.[58] In the same month Archbishop John Charles McQuaid congratulated the Department of Education and the City of Dublin Vocational Education Committee:

I am grateful for the increase of time given to religious instruction and formation. Thanks to your willing cooperation, to the goodwill of the Department of Education and the Vocational committee, it has been possible, within the framework of the defective Vocational Education Act [1930], to achieve much for the supernatural welfare of our students.[59]

Also in October 1955 the Bishop of Kildare and Leighlin commented that Irish parents took little interest in their children's education.[60] At about the same time Erskine Childers claimed that other European countries offered ten times the variety and quantity of technical education to their young people.[61] The *Times* claimed in November 1955 that there was little interest in science in schools and that 85 per cent of Irish dentists emigrated. There was 'appalling overcrowding' in the national schools. Classes with more than fifty or sixty children were commonplace, but sometimes there were classes of seventy, eighty and even ninety pupils.[62] On the other hand, there was an unexpected but spectacular boom going on in western Europe, and even Irish exports were increasing mightily. Signals in the mid-fifties were very mixed.[63]

Irish change was finally occurring, almost independently of political or philosophical change in the leadership of the political system.

EDUCATE THAT YOU MAY BE RICH

In January 1956 the *Independent* complained again about the number and size of the county council scholarships, but it omitted to complain about the obvious sectarianism of the local authorities' ban on scholarships for Trinity, evidently echoing McQuaid's notorious ban on Catholics studying at that university.[64] In May the paper announced that the Minister for Education had reported four years previously that 10 per cent of all primary schools were 'virtually derelict.'[65] In July the paper editorialised that Norton had 'mentioned agriculture and industry as two subjects that should be taken out of party politics. We would ourselves unhesitatingly add education as a third subject.'[66]

Norton himself was pushing for a new liberalised apprenticeship system and was trying to get it past the entrenched and fantastically archaic trade unions of the time. He proposed to the unions, rather bravely, 'a relaxation of the present rigid rules for the admission of apprentices.'[67] Monsignor Pádraig de Brún, president of University College, Galway, and a well-known public intellectual, commented on the extraordinarily intense anti-intellectualism of popular attitudes to universities.[68]

The number of pupils in the vocational schools was growing quite quickly; Moylan's efforts were finally beginning to get results.[69] Furthermore, without any visible state encouragement, secondary school enrolments were creeping up, from 40,000 pupils in 1944 to 54,000 in 1953.[70] Nevertheless, in the mid-1950s there were 476,000 pupils in the national school system but a mere 83,000 in the *combined* secondary and vocational systems. This represented what would be by modern standards an appalling drop-out rate at the age of thirteen of more than 80 per cent. Even at the time this was considered disgraceful by many observers. Furthermore, what education the majority got in primary school was not always the best. The president of the INTO explained the built-in unfairness of the system in 1955. The national teacher, by tradition, educated 'the poor man's child,' he observed, but the education he gave was considered 'less important and of less value than that given to the children of the favoured minority.'[71]

In July 1956 the *Times* complained that the Government contributed nothing to the building or maintenance of secondary schools, unlike Britain, but that the state did finance primary schools, vocational schools and third-level colleges. This con-tinuing refusal to finance secondary education was, the paper said carefully, 'apparently with the approval of some of the strong religious orders.' The implication was that the orders valued their control over the nature of education given to the children far more than any financial contribution the state could give them in addition to the price they would have to pay in the form of state control over the curriculum. Since the Treaty of 1922 attendance at the secondary schools had trebled, but this improvement was dwarfed by British figures. The contrast between the two countries was becoming really shocking. 'There the aim is seemingly to provide a secondary education for as many as can benefit from it; here secondary education is designed for such as can afford it, and want it.'[72]

In early 1957 Jack Lynch, the new Minister for Education, suggested that there was a connection between what he termed the evident 'spiritual malaise' in Ireland and attitudes towards education.[73] However, this did not prevent him cutting capitation grants to secondary schools (already quite small and, incredibly, still the same as they had been in 1929) by 10 per cent shortly afterwards; education was still low man on the totem pole in the hierarchy of Irish Government departments.[74] In March the dissident Federation of Catholic Lay Secondary Schools urged an extension of secondary education. The proportion of young people in secondary education was the lowest in western Europe; all children should be kept at school to the age of eighteen, it felt. This was a really radical departure from the status quo and was even more advanced than most reformist positions of the time.

The Department of Education's lack of interest in modern educational aids, such as films, tapes and libraries, was deplored.[75] In early 1956 Seán Brosnahan, ex-president of the INTO, launched a violent and devastating attack on the entire school system. There was no integration between the primary, secondary, vocational and third-level branches of the system. There was a 'callous disregard' for 'subnormal' and 'backward' children. Classes were too large; there was no educational research; too many teachers were untrained; the buildings were unsanitary, overcrowded and badly lit; the programmes were overloaded, and the Primary Certificate examination was worthless. He denounced the fact that the majority of pupils left school at fourteen. 'Many of those who left were mentally immature and quite unprepared for the battle of life.'[76]

In April the president of the ASTI prophesied rather dramatically that 'the day may not be too far distant when our educational system will have to be scrapped in its entirety.' Everyone should be taught agricultural science, he argued somewhat pathetically.[77] In July 1956 Michael Tierney, president of UCD, had already announced that something like a knowledge revolution was necessary in the Republic.

University education, instead of being a luxury for a small group, has become a stringent necessity . . . It seems to be excessively difficult to persuade the Irish people and their political leaders that the same effort for higher education as is made in other countries is a first need of public policy here.

He went on to point out that third-level funding per head in Ireland was a mere one-third that of other western countries.[78] Pádraig de Brún pointed out rather frighteningly that Queen's University, Belfast, then the only university in Northern Ireland, got a greater government allocation than that given to all four universities in the Republic put together.[79] Thomas Nevin, a well-known UCD scientist, said in December that not enough science was being taught and that this absence in the schools was producing intellectually untrained and under-equipped students—a circumstance that was in turn crippling vocational education.[80] Martin Gleeson, chief executive officer of the City of Dublin Vocational Education Committee, in the course of a revealing interview in September 1956 described with some passion how his efforts were being obstructed by 'the white collar,' or the obsession with status; technical education was being squeezed out by humanist and literary educational styles equipping the middle-class young for white-collar positions in the professions, the clergy, the civil service and business management.

> He feels strongly that our economy is being strangled by the white collar, and that we must now get down in earnest to education for the practical needs of the country. If Ireland succeeds in advancing to greater prosperity in the atomic age, no small part of the credit will be due to the vocational school system and its devoted teachers and administrators.[81]

Soon afterwards Erskine Childers denounced the coalition Government's repeated cuts of 6 per cent in the vocational education budget, and he quite bluntly described the Irish educational system as the worst in western Europe.[82] Government economic plans made no mention of education, an extraordinary and irrational omission.[83] In December the president of the INTO, commenting on the shortage of teachers, equally bluntly described the ban on married women in teaching as 'stupid.' The new Minister for Education, Jack Lynch, eventually announced the abolition of the ban in February 1958.[84]

In January 1957 the president of the Federation of Catholic Lay Secondary Schools warned grimly that there was little room in the modern world for the uneducated but pointed out that until very recently a frightening 80 per cent of Irish young people had left school by the age of fourteen.[85] Lynch was evidently concerned about the general demoralisation of the country and had a persistent sense that it had something to do with the condition of the educational system and with people's cynical, utilitarian and passive attitudes towards it, or even disregard for it. This in turn fed into the minds of the teachers, gave them a sense of the pointlessness of their efforts and made them dispirited.

> I cannot help feeling that if we were to take a greater interest in our system of education the teachers would feel less isolated in their battle for the minds of the country's youth, and would feel more at one with the country generally and that far-reaching effects might be achieved which are not being achieved at present.[86]

The chairman of the Dublin City Branch of the Vocational Teachers' Association claimed that the 6 per cent cut in vocational education threatened the future of any economic revival. Prophetically, he warned that any future boom might be stifled by the absence of trained manpower. He was to be proved right in the boom years of the sixties, when trained workers had to be imported from England and elsewhere.

A comprehensive report drawn up by representatives of industry, commerce and the professions shows that there must be a considerable expansion in the technological courses, if an attempt is to be made to train the people necessary for the industrial development of the country. Time lost within the next few years, with such rapid expansion taking place else-where, may condemn the country for many years to the backwater of underdevelopment.[87]

The cuts in the vocational budget were raised in the Seanad in February 1957.[88] Prof. P. M. Quinlan of UCC remarked in March: 'We are criminally negligent in developing the scientific potential of our young people . . . If we are going to have emigrants I would much prefer to see them going as engineers rather than as dock workers.'[89] In April the president of the Vocational Teachers' Association, Thomas Carney, stated:

It appears that a proper appreciation of the place of technical education is as far from us as ever. While other countries are expanding their schemes, the Government here, at the beginning of the school year, announced reductions in the grants to Vocational Education Committees.

Technical skills were vital to the cause of national economic development, he said.[90] In the same month the *Times* called for more investment in education, commenting that Northern Ireland outperformed the Republic in the sector by far.[91] In August 1957 Labhrás Ó Nualláin, lecturing at a social science conference, spoke of the 'need for training facilities for managerial personnel and skilled operatives.' He also urged the expansion of industrial research and in particular called for the investigation of potential new markets and products.

All our Governments since 1922 had underestimated the task of developing the industrial arm of the economy ... the policy of protection had had some success, but industry had not expanded fast enough to absorb surplus labour from the land or our natural increase in population.[92]

Seán Moylan, shortly before his death, observed that the common and traditional Irish attitude to science was snobbish. Jack Lynch admitted: 'We often hear it suggested that this country is spending too much money on education.'[93] An eminent schoolmaster from Newbridge College claimed that classical languages crowded out science in schools.[94]

In early 1958 the newly renovated Institute for Industrial Research and Standards opened. Its director, Donal Flood, had come home after years in the United States. Irish industrialists were wary of science, he observed, and it was difficult to hire researchers, as, paradoxically, demand for them was so high. He hoped that when the new laboratories were set up he would be able to recruit researchers from the vocational schools. Even a bishop, William Philbin, was now publicly arguing for technical education.[95] Prof. John O'Meara of UCD pointed out that there were far too many arts students in the universities, because of the heavy bias towards the humanities in secondary schools. Because of the special relationship between the Catholic Church, the state and education, 'it happens that there has been a great neglect of what one may call the secular side of education here.' Unifying the educational system in 1924 under one department had been a historical mistake, which had led to a stultifying stalemate between the church and the civil service.[96] Jack Lynch remarked in February 1958:

For too long we have been inclined to divorce education from the practical things of life. For too long we held that the farmer

needed no more than the ability to read and write. The successful farmer must be reasonably well-educated with a knowledge
of a number of the sciences which underlie modern farming.[97]

Lynch felt also that the lifting of the ban on married women
teaching would release a pool of four to five hundred extra
teachers immediately.[98] In April 1958 the *Times* argued editorially
for the reader to put the anguished and devastating protests of the
president of the INTO together with O'Meara's argument and he
would know what was wrong with Irish education: a stalemate
between Government and church that was depriving the entire
nation of a proper education.[99] Lynch commented cautiously, in
what seems to have been a rather defensive reaction, that
Government spending on secondary schools would entail
increased Government interference in the schools, thereby
evidently suggesting that a clerical veto was operating.[100]

The provost of Trinity recorded his own profound unease
about the state of the country in May 1958 in words that reflected
a near despair and a worry that the country was losing an entire
young generation.

> Some of our young people are running away from a way of life
> as well as for economic reasons. The future of any country
> depends on its young people, and this is particularly true of
> Ireland because there is not any question that this is a sick
> country. The older generation do not seem able to find a
> solution; the younger people might.[101]

The *Times* claimed that the general standard of education was
actually lower than it used to be.[102] T. J. McElligott, a veteran
teacher, agreeing with the general thrust of O'Meara's argument,
observed that the fact that 'the country has been handicapped by
an impossibly outmoded educational system has been realised for

many years . . .' In one bizarre and very revealing administrative proviso, more Leaving Certificate marks were awarded to Latin and Greek than to modern languages, and therefore the classics and the dead languages were favoured for scholarships. In 1955, 90 per cent of male candidates did Latin for the Leaving, against only 9 per cent taking French, 2 per cent doing German, fewer doing Italian and two *individuals* doing Spanish (both failing). Vocational education had been relatively successful, but there was a pronounced social prejudice against it, as O'Meara had argued.[103]

In October 1958 a bishop finally urged the raising of the school age from fourteen to fifteen or even sixteen. Things were indeed changing. What amounted to a polite outcry against the educational policies pursued since independence was going on. The *Indo* harrumphed:

Many years ago . . . the Committee [of civil servants] was against the raising of the school-leaving age on the barbaric grounds that Irish children were 'not immature for labour at the age of fourteen.' This finding was endorsed by the Government of Ireland [in 1936].

It pleaded that the Irish people had a duty to 'give the poor man's child a chance economically and intellectually.'[104] A flood of reports and letters on the persistent inadequacies of Irish technical and scientific education followed. Even the Dutch ambassador chimed in, remarking that Ireland would prosper if it invested in technical education and scientific research. The headmaster of the High School, Dublin, observed that a third of secondary schools did not teach science at all, and there were no Government grants either for the renovation of science laboratories or, incredibly, for new ones.[105] On 26 November the *Independent* warmly welcomed Whitaker's White Paper on economic development, urging investment in productive activity rather than in areas that were, in effect, merely redistributive. It was described as 'the masterly study of national development problems made by the Secretary of the Department of Finance.'

At almost the same time the *Quarterly Bulletin* of the Institute for Industrial Research and Standards, commenting on an OEEC report on the need for more scientific and technical manpower, argued that Irish people didn't understand science or the potential of scientists.

> We are short of science teachers, of industrialists who appreci-ate the value of applied science, and of university endowments for the proper equipping and staffing of science departments. We are not short of scientists relative to our present sub-standard needs; indeed, we export as many technologists as we employ at home. If the teaching of science were improved so that a growing awareness of the necessity of cultivating it were spread through the community, one might hope that, in time, our defects would be remedied, and we would employ at home most of the scientists we produce. This hope, however, does not relate to the foreseeable future.[106]

Prof. Thomas Nevin of UCD pointed out that Ireland was the only country in Europe that had not got a research nuclear reactor, even though the United States had offered 50 per cent of the cost of setting one up. A young academic and archaeologist from the same university, Liam de Paor, suggested in a public lecture that the Irish people should brood less on the past and commented darkly on the general neglect of schools and universities.[107] The headmaster of the High School, reinforc-ing de Paor's gloomy picture, complained that half of all teachers of science had no science degree.[108] The headmaster of

Masonic Boys' School noted that the five-year plan for economic expansion did not mention education at all, an extraordinary and revealing omission. 'It seems peculiar,' he remarked pungently. It certainly was peculiar. He also observed that there were few opportunities in Ireland for science graduates, the cut in the capitation grant for secondary schools was to stay, and the previous 'temporary' cut had lasted twenty-five years. Few people had any interest in education, and the much-despised and put-upon vocational education branch was easily the most successful branch of the system and generated the highest voluntary demand from the young population.[109] A similar observation was made by Donal Barrington of Tuairim.

The Whitaker report was considered to be at its weakest on education. This was in no way Mr. Whitaker's fault, but reflected the absence of original thinking on the subject of education in the whole community.[110]

In January 1959 the *Independent* was able to report that the school leaving age stayed at the archaic level of fourteen years, while in Britain it was about to be raised from fifteen to sixteen. There was even a proposal by the Conservative Party in Britain to raise it to eighteen.[111] Patrick Cannon of the Catholic Lay Schoolteachers' Association called for an overhaul of the system, pointing out that there had been no debate on education and again making the point that the Secretary of the Department of Education had, quite notoriously, been excluded from the proposed National Development Council.[112] Lynch called for the production of more technicians.

I refer to the man whose function lies somewhere between the skilled craftsman and the technologist or university graduate.

There is a dearth of technicians; modern developments in science and technology have helped to create this need. This is an educational area capable of great development in the future, and it is the task of the larger technical schools to engage in it.[113]

The Minister for Education was unwilling to continue to give grants to enable science teachers to attend refresher courses in chemistry, explaining in an almost surreal aside that this refusal was 'purely on the grounds that teachers in other subjects might look for similar facilities.'[114] In June, Father T. Molloy, president of the Vocational Education Association, reported that the increased demand for vocational education was huge.

However hopefully we look at what is being done in the vocational schools, we are appalled by the vast undone. Whether we look to Britain, Europe or to the USA we see compulsory education continued for at least a year later than the fourteen years of age, which is our upper limit.[115]

Garret FitzGerald commented in the Fine Gael party paper that for nine years all attempts at educational reform had been blocked by 'the reply that the views of the Council of Education must be awaited . . . But meanwhile the entire post-war period has passed, and the world has passed us by.'[116]

In September 1959 the *Indo* observed that there were few graduates in the civil service, most of the officers being recruited at the age of sixteen without even a Leaving Certificate to their name, much as in British times. Although the paper did not say so, it was in a way reminiscent of the civil service recruitment system of Tsarist Russia, where those who ran the empire were recruited at fourteen and kept well away from awful places like universities. The sequel is well known: Russia was taken over, and comprehensively wrecked, by an entire class of half-educated fanatics and criminals in the 1917–38 period.[117] In October 1959 the *Indo* lamented yet again the miserable numbers of county council scholarships for the universities.[118]

However, despite all this self-castigation, foreigners' negative views on Ireland were not really welcome. In October an American scientist, Dr D. M. Gates, wrote:

> Eire is an overpopulated, tragically poor agricultural country with a total lack of organisation for research. In the shadow of Great Britain it is a little surprising that more cross-fertilisation and inspiration have not taken place.[119]

Prof. T. S. Wheeler, dean of the Science Faculty of UCD, took Gates on. Ireland's GNP per head was better than those of Italy, Portugal or India, he claimed. The country had excellent research institutes and good universities.[120] Fear of being seen as a failure seems to have lain behind this reaction; Gates just might have been more right than wrong. Italy and Portugal, never mind India, were scarcely the best basis for comparison. At that time both were still very poor countries by western European standards. Being slightly better off, and slightly more literate, than Portugal, the poorest and most illiterate country west of the Iron Curtain, was nothing much to boast about. Irish emigrants, because they were relatively poorly educated, were at a huge and growing disadvantage in the British labour market.[121]

In January 1960 it reported yet again on the continuing fantastically underdeveloped state of science education.[122] Despite all this pessimism and adverse comment, Jack Lynch pronounced Ireland's future to be 'bright.'[123] The new Minister for Education, Patrick Hillery, was able to announce in February that, whereas in 1930 there were only 10,000 pupils in secondary schools, now there were 70,000.[124] Lynch felt that Irish people had been finally shaken out of 'the spirit of complacency to which they had been inclined.'[125] T. J. McElligott, a true gadfly, and a pretty well-informed one on the education issue, commented that the demand for secondary education was now (in 1959) outpacing the supply, but lay secondary schools were sprouting up in response to this demand, despite institutional resistance to such an educational springtime. The need for a variety of secondary schools 'is greatest in our small towns and villages where there is a great unused fund of unsatisfied and undeveloped intelligence.' In 1956 he said, quite shockingly, that the Minister for Education (Richard Mulcahy) had cut the secondary school capitation grant by 10 per cent, possibly in a clericalist attempt to kill off the new lay schools. The suggestion of clerical action is McElligott's. McElligott also made the fascinating and rather appalling speculation that the cut had been made in fear of a very real potential popular demand for more lay schools not controlled by the clergy. He seemed to believe that clerical forces were strangling the development of a Catholic lay cohort of schools not under the control of ecclesiastics. Another unspoken implication seemed to be that most people didn't really care whether schools taught religion or not—a very perceptive implication that was later to be thoroughly vindicated.

McElligott described the existence of national schools with a stunted secondary education stuck on top ('secondary tops') as a 'scandal'. 'Secondary tops' were evidently set up to choke off the possibility of any proper lay-run school emerging in particular localities. This mischievous tactic of using church and state resources to crowd out or stifle private enterprise in education was apparently quite common but little spoken about in the newspapers until this juncture. The following day McElligott called for mass secondary education and remarked on the 'spinelessness' of the Department of Education.[126]

In December 1959 the INTO observed: 'The expenditure on education in the Republic is the lowest, not only in these islands, but in most of the progressive countries in the world.' Teachers were paid less than anywhere else in western Europe or the British Commonwealth, and the Irish economy had been damaged by this circumstance, the organisation claimed.[127]

As late as April 1960 the *Irish Independent* commented on the utter imperviousness of the Department of Education to outside advice of any kind.[128] The vocational teachers met in the same month and argued that technical education needed to be expanded to meet the new demands of industry, that Irish pupils left school far too young, and that there was no 'follow-on' to the Intermediate (now Junior) Certificate. There was no direct route from the technical school to senior technical college or university. Vocational education should be extended to eighteen, they said, unconsciously echoing the educational programmes envisaged forty years previously by the more radical Sinn Féin, Fianna Fáil and Cumann na nGaedheal leaders of those hopeful years of the revolution. However, they wanted the ban on married women kept, arguing that the women wanted it that way.[129]

Dr Eva Philbin of UCD remarked, quite terrifyingly: 'It is difficult to believe that a boy leaving school at eighteen in the early part of this century was more likely to have a training in scientific principles than his counterpart today.'[130] The *Indo* yet again demanded that the school leaving age be raised to fifteen; in Northern Ireland it was being raised to sixteen.[131] T. J. McElligott, popping up again in typically feisty form in the pages of the Fine Gael *National Observer*, asked, 'Is education as a profession closed to laymen in the Republic?'

The number of secondary schools remains small because ecclesiastical opposition and the insistence by the [Catholic] Church that no State aid be given for the building and maintenance of secondary schools makes the establishment of such a school hazardous for a layman.[132]

In September 1960 the *Independent* felt impelled to mount a defence of the vocational schools, rebuking those who argued that we should not educate for export, as it was a waste of money; let them depart our shores ignorant ('a bitter view'). The Irish people had a duty to educate everyone, regardless of what the individual's purposes might be, the paper intoned, and the vocational schools were doing a very good job, despite all kinds of obstacles put in their way.[133] In making this claim it was apparently ratifying the suggestions contained in an article published in *Foreign Affairs* by J. V. Kelleher, a well-known Irish-American academic, on the deficiencies of Irish education.[134]

In January 1961 Miss M. Hopkins of the vocational teachers of Dublin claimed that

> tardy industrial expansion was due less than they cared to admit to limitations of capital and more to their failure to appreciate the prime necessity to learn and teach new techniques . . . the application of the clauses [of the new Apprenticeship Act] was of the utmost national and educational importance . . . Efficient production could not be realised without skilled operatives with general and specialised abilities which could be developed best by a sound system of apprenticeship training based on a liberal technical education.

She regretted that the new Vocational Guidance Service was confined to boys' schools; apparently girls were not supposed to have careers in craft or technical areas.[135]

Prof. John O'Meara, speaking to the Waterford secondary teachers in February, suggested that secondary teaching was unattractive to the average qualified graduate. The starting salary was miserly, lower than a bus conductor's wage. Also, promotion was slow and sometimes unavailable to lay persons, because the senior positions were occupied automatically by clerics. He also suspected that things were set up that way deliberately to ensure that a high proportion of the teachers would be clerics. There were many ways of preventing the future.

Professor O'Meara said it had been asserted recently that the clerical and religious owners of the majority of the secondary schools were responsible for arranging that the secondary teaching career should be unattractive in the beginning, so that lay people would be discouraged from entering and so leave the field mainly to the religious. 'One simply cannot believe that men and women making profession of Christian justice could conspire so signally for a purpose so ignoble and inhuman.' Professor O'Meara said the question had been raised: should the Church have not formal but practical control over secondary education? He would say with emphasis that if the Church was for practical purposes to have control of Irish secondary education, she must either find or be given the money to run it as a full measure of efficiency in the interest of the community as a whole. Nothing less would do.

The much-touted Council of Education was a 'farce', O'Meara said, with a savagery that was uncharacteristic of him. 'I read their report on primary schools and it was a thoroughly dishonest document the whole way through.' In reality the Department of Education gave no thought whatever to education, he felt. O'Meara advocated a measure of integration between the secondary and technical schools. Although himself a professor of classics at UCD and a brilliant lecturer, he felt that less Latin and more commerce should be taught in schools. It was pointed out by a listener that the council had sat for so long that many of its members had died before a report could be published, a scenario worthy of 'Father Ted'. In effect the council was being used as yet another means of avoiding 'certain problems'. The *Independent* almost piteously repeated the by now ancient editorial mantra that the school leaving age had remained at fourteen right through the fifties and was yet to be raised to fifteen.[136]

Several correspondents, many of them student teachers, confirmed O'Meara's general argument, and some said they were emigrating for that reason. One observed that there was actually no wage paid during the first pre-registration or apprentice year. Several other students agreed with O'Meara and with his claim that there was clerical hostility to the employment of lay teachers, including a group of student teachers from Galway. O'Meara was himself a former Jesuit cleric, therefore an in-house dissenter of sorts and much resented by many clerics for engaging in a kind of whistle-blowing. He was not alone in forming a kind of loyal opposition within the system. The students, interestingly enough, got firm public sympathy from the Connacht Provincial of the Christian Brothers.[137]

Technical education was still underdeveloped as late as 1961, despite the uphill efforts of Moylan, Lynch and Hillery. J. P. O'Donnell, professor of chemical engineering at UCD, said in June 1961 that the shortage of technicians was due to the fact that

> not enough boys were being educated to technical level and the courses available were not really suitable for training technicians . . . The present production of trained technicians was too small and this shortage was likely to prove a serious obstacle to industrial development within the next decade.[138]

He was to be proved right. However, by September the *Independent* felt able to say that the glass was half-full. It claimed that there had been a 'quite spectacular leap' in the previous ten years in the numbers of students at secondary and technical schools. Some 40 per cent now did some science, 'at least for a time.' Almost half did a foreign language, 'at least for a time.'

Things were indeed changing rapidly, in a piecemeal and spotty way, but more in response to market forces and to local isolated initiatives than to any political initiative.[139]

Tuairim, a liberal and progressive intellectual movement that had some real impact, because many younger respected intellectuals, academics, lawyers and others were behind it, commented, through a pamphlet issued by its London Branch in 1962, on what it termed 'the blackout on educational thinking.' The Irish education system, it said,

> aims at giving the hewers of wood and the drawers of water a minimum basic education. Our secondary educational system is designed to produce administrators, who are still thought of as clerks and clerics. Our universities are presumed to provide a liberal educational background for professional training for aspiring gentlefolk.

Technical education was evidently essential, but there was an obvious stalemate between church and state, a stalemate that satisfied the interests of certain sections and ignored the interests of others, never mind the general national interest. 'Irish education has remained static so long because it suits powerful sections of society, the middle class, the Churches and the politicians to keep it so.'[140] The pamphlet continued relentlessly and accurately to argue that the real problem was not so much clerical reaction as the lethal structural combination of clerical control with pitiful means.

> Most of the school buildings are owned by the churches or religious orders and they supply nearly all the school managers and a large proportion of the teachers. Their financial contribution to education is considerable and they have invested a great deal of capital in it. Therefore it is right that they should

have a considerable say in matters pertaining to educational organisation. Nonetheless, it must be accepted that what the religious organisations can do out of their own resources is limited. The state, however, cannot be expected to subsidise private institutions out of the public purse unless it has complete control over the way in which the subsidies are spent. In the past, the Department of Education appears to have found the problem of adequately financing private schools insoluble and to have assumed that any alteration of the present organisation would be detrimental to the relationship between the state and churches.[141]

Politicians feared what the pamphlet described as 'powerful sections' of the community. In particular, the churches and the middle class had conspired subconsciously to maintain a system that suited them and did not suit anyone else.

On every educational issue, whether raised behind the scenes or in public, successive Ministers of Education have played safe and this paralysis appears to have permeated the entire Department . . . Finally, we ourselves, our middle classes, religious leaders and politicians are all products of a type of education that discourages criticism, research and individual thinking. We have been trained to accept rather than to question. The fault is in ourselves . . . Nevertheless, many of our national schoolchildren, particularly those in rural areas and whose education ends on their fourteenth birthday, have poor physical coordination, bad carriage, no self-confidence or ambition, are obsequious to and fearful of authority, and have failed to assimilate, much less understand, most of what they were expected to learn. They hope only that they will be left in peace to perform some menial and ill-paid job at home or emigrate to perform some equally menial but well-paid job abroad. It has been easy for any undesirable organisation at home or abroad to channel the energies of such young people.[142]

Boys were specifically excluded from domestic science lessons, 'for no obvious educational reason . . . The reading of books, as opposed to the writing of them, is looked upon as a reprehensible habit.'[143] However, although there were many subterranean rumbles, the official intellectual climate for education seemed to be slower in changing in Dublin than among the London-Irish middle-class exiles; it was, however, changing rapidly, despite clerical minefields.

In February 1962 the occasionally persecuted and much-censored writer Frank O'Connor (Michael O'Donovan) was featured prominently in the most mainstream and popular Dublin daily newspaper, was given a sympathetic hearing and was well able to give the previous forty years of governmental educational and cultural policy a sad and terrifying epitaph. A corrosive and paralysing anti-intellectualism, allied to clerical obscurantism and cultural isolationism, had wrecked Irish intellectual culture, he asserted.

[Censorship] perpetuates the negative attitude we oppose to every manifestation of intellect and scholarship . . . We have a Censorship Board but no publishers. We have a great literature published by Englishmen and Americans, and thanks to our censors, ninety per cent of it is out of print and unobtainable, so that we have brought up a generation which knows nothing of its own country or of its own literature.[144]

The situation was even worse than O'Connor sketched it. A huge swathe of modern literature by many great writers was theoretically unavailable to the population of the Republic. A large, informal and well-organised traffic in 'banned books' existed between Belfast and Dublin. The Government's enforcement of censorship brought it into contempt among the younger and better-educated generation.

Chapter 7 ∽

DUBLIN OPINIONS:
A DISTANT MIRROR

SÉ MO THUAIRIM: IT IS MY OPINION

It is clear that the Ireland of the fifties is a foreign country but one that has strangely familiar features; half a century later it is, in Barbara Tuchman's famous phrase, a distant mirror.[1] A secrecy of political style reflected the fact that Irish politics was heavily infected with oligarchic tendencies, many of them deriving from the state and nation-building processes of the nineteenth century. It should be remembered that the older men (and they were all men) who ran the country commonly came into political life through secret societies, such as the Irish Republican Brotherhood, Ancient Order of Hibernians, or Knights of Columbanus. Even trade unions were sometimes semi-secret organisations in the early 1900s. The Catholic Church, then very much an organisation of great power and social penetration, was itself best described as a secret society in public view and in many ways was the prototype for many other public organisations.

Pressures to break down this pervasive secrecy and authoritarianism of political style in favour of a more open style of political action were relatively weak and were only beginning to assert themselves in the years 1945–60. This secrecy applied over a wide range of human life. What went on in industrial schools and the Magdalene laundries was unknown, denied, quietly approved of, secretly feared, or merely suspected. Those who raised their voices were commonly ignored, shouted down, or subjected to a peculiarly Irish mixture of intimidation and pseudo-genial ridicule. These lies of silence were legitimated by a passive popular approval that was not to be withdrawn until long after the period under discussion. A fictional character in a novel set in 1948, Mervyn Wall's *Leaves for the Burning* (1952), described the atmosphere well.

> The grotesque thing . . . is that this is the ordinary pattern of life in this country. None of us Irish sees it as in any way strange. Why, most of our public figures are straight out of comic opera—think of our politicians and even some of our prelates. You can't pick up a newspaper without finding someone in authority denouncing something which in every other country is thought to be harmless.[2]

Newspapers sometimes produced headlines of a stupefying triviality. The *Standard* produced the following in 1951: THE POPE APPROVES OF BIKES FOR NUNS. In 1958 it asked, WHAT IS THE THIRD SECRET OF FATIMA? The *Irish Independent* announced proudly in 1955: DONEGAL MAN TO APPEAR ON US TELEVISION. The *Irish Press* reported noisily in 1954: NINETY YEAR OLD MAN FOUND DEAD. Mervyn Wall parodied this trivialisation brilliantly.

However, there was also at that time a sense of underlying tectonic change, as the economic and cultural ground under people's feet was suddenly shifting, much as has been happening yet again at the end of the first decade of the twenty-first century. An essay in a political pamphlet in 1958 expressed a quiet upbeat view that became more common as the decade went on.

> Beneath the stagnant surface [of Irish life] there is much ferment; and the fifties may yet be seen, after all the disillusion, as a decade of rich growth in voluntary effort and the arts of peace.[3]

The island was partitioned, but the sense of partition's permanence was not as strong as it has since become with the passing of time and the increasing institutionalisation of the two jurisdictions. At that time, de Valera's casuistical withdrawal of recognition of Northern Ireland in 1937 was still a popular, if pseudo-legal, orthodoxy. The IRA of the fifties was a far more amateurish and less vicious creature than the monstrous IRA that was created by the Ulster crisis in the late sixties, but its semi-comic character did not prevent it raising fears of political instability and even revolution in some political leaders. Furthermore, its incompetent and aggressive activities led to the unnecessary deaths of many young men. The murder campaigns of the Provos and the loyalists had not yet awakened the South to the intrinsic cultural difference of the North. In the fifties it was still possible to think of partition as unfinished business that would eventually be sorted out in an unproblematic way; the unification of the island was seen by most people in the Republic as inevitable. It was commonly argued that partition had robbed independent Ireland of its industrial arm and could therefore be held responsible for its relative underdevelopment. The memory of the revolution was still fresh in the fifties, and partitioned independence had not yet quite become the dead and relatively undisputed fact that it has since become. Everything felt somehow provisional and changeable, and Irish reunification was very much on the cards. That is no longer the case.

Times were in some ways much simpler than they have since become. It was a far less educated, more rural and more patri-archal society than it is nowadays. The highly educated minority tended to have a classical education suitable for the religious life rather than a scientific training. Agriculture was the main eco-nomic activity, and the country saw itself as a nation of farmers, and celebrated that fact; farmers were commonly referred to as 'the backbone of the country.' Large numbers of people left school just about able to do 'arithmetic with money' and an ability to read and write. The idea that further education could be usefully seen as having something to do with one's earning capacity and therefore a source of national prosperity scarcely existed. Higher education was, on the contrary, seen as an *indicator* of great wealth and status, rather than a possible *cause* of such wealth and status. Again, a growing sense of the necessity for fairness and even equality in society was at war with the facts of Irish life. Everyone knew at some often unspoken level that Irish society was unfair and inegalitarian. Some people knew secretly that industrial schools were essentially prisons for young people, as the Magdalene laundries were sometimes lifelong and illegal prisons for women. It was sensed that the treatment of children and unmarried mothers was certainly cruel and probably illegal, but expressing one's opinion could even be penalised in the form of a trade boycott, denial of job promotion or even job loss. Honor Tracy's well-known satirical novel *Mind You, I've Said Nothing* caught the atmosphere of fifties Ireland nicely.[4]

Low-level fear encouraged silence. In the guaranteed lifelong employment world of the public service the dreaded transfer to a remote area or to a meaningless dead-end office was sufficient deterrence in many cases. Everyone had heard stories of people being committed to mental hospitals because they were unwanted by family or spouse even though perfectly sane. Everyone knew there was one law for the rich and another for the poor. Many knew that England, the old enemy, had in many ways created a fairer and gentler society than that of independent Ireland and refused to admit it, or clung to doctrines of an alleged Irish spiritual superiority.[5]

Many quietly approved of the penal treatment of unmarried mothers, homosexuals and others who defied or ignored the public orthodoxies of the time; the regime was not universally unpopular; public opinion was itself censorious, conservative and rather authoritarian in a normally easygoing way. The physical punishment of children was universal and regarded as a necessity. Animals were commonly treated with considerable cruelty. Irish people had held on to older and often harsher ways of doing things and to an increasingly archaic society under the guise of protecting national identity and tradition. Much of the welfare system was an incompletely reformed version of nineteenth-century systems left over from British times.

As we have seen, in an imperfect and disjointed way something of this sense of injustice did indeed find expression in the very middle-class national press of the time. However, the overall impression is of an inhibited attitude to discussion; there were things in Irish society which just were not talked about.

One refreshing exception to this generalisation was the organisation called Tuairim ('Opinion'), a phenomenon of the late fifties and sixties, mentioned briefly in previous chapters. By and large, there was no discussion of divorce, contraception, corruption in high places, rogue clerics or child molestation. However, economics and career choices were discussed quite freely and with some sophistication. Again, education was already a bugbear in the national papers, but reform in this area, never mind expansion, was also silently resisted.

Tuairim was quintessentially a middle-class phenomenon, set up by the sons and daughters of the new and rather raw professional strata, mainly Catholic and evidently the coming establishment of the country in the future decades. Membership was confined to those under forty years of age: when you reached forty you had to resign. The existence of an intense inter-generational conflict could not be more clearly documented. Many of these young people came of families of recent farmer origin or, in some cases, skilled working-class stock. The organisation lasted from 1954 to 1975 and faded away from the mid-sixties on as its membership became absorbed into careers and 'real work'. Also, the need for such an organisation became less obvious, as its example had been copied by the newspapers and magazines of the time. Television accelerated the transformation.

The partial liberalisation of the sixties transformed two newspapers in particular, the *Irish Times* and *Hibernia*. *Hibernia's* was the more spectacular transformation. Founded in 1935, it went from being a quiescent and pious organ of the Knights of Columbanus to being a mildly radical fortnightly paper under Basil Clancy and John Mulcahy. Eventually it became weekly. Clancy expanded its board of directors in 1959 to include a well-known trade unionist and intellectual, Charles MacCarthy, and some lecturers from UCD, including Geoffrey Hand, Jack Watt and Jack Walsh.[6] Many journalists of the next thirty years were to learn their trade by filling its pages on a penny-per-line basis.

Tuairim was a kind of political party without party politics. It worked through meetings of its branches, lectures and general meetings. It also published occasional pamphlets that had an extraordinary impact on public opinion and government, an impact that at the time seemed dramatic and innovative. From the point of view of the early twenty-first century Tuairim seems rather to represent the dusk of the pamphlet era, which, from the late Middle Ages on, had seen the expression of opinion in pamphlet form as the classic expression of individual or minority opinion in a culture dominated by the printing press. Pamphlets were published and sold on the streets for a few pence, often contained argument of a religious or political kind and sometimes collections of ballads, libels on famous people or semi-obscene verse. At a lower and cheaper level, verses in single-sheet form, often libellous or treasonable, had been hawked on the streets by itinerant balladeers up to the end of the nineteenth century. In earlier times they were often bilingual, praise being offered to a landlord or prominent person in English while vilification was supplied in Irish. Pamphlets were also used by churches to put forward points of view on moral questions or political theory.

Tuairim was therefore quite traditional in some ways. It was independent of the Catholic Church and was determinedly non-political in the narrow sense of being non-party. Two interesting features of the organisation were its explicit acceptance of the church-state relationship as laid down in articles 40 to 45 of the Constitution of Ireland, and its restriction of membership to people under the age of forty.[7] The acceptance of the constitutional articles was intended to recognise them as a reasonable compromise and to kill in advance discussion of a contentious and arguably sterile issue. Later on this condition of membership was got rid of.

The organisation had an even more outspoken and sometimes aggressive branch among expatriates in London. At its height it had over a thousand members and twelve branches. People who were to become political and cultural leaders in the following decades were commonly members as young people in the period 1954–66. People as disparate as Justin Keating, Garret FitzGerald, Barry Desmond, Donal Barrington, Ronan Keane, Miriam Hederman O'Brien, David Thornley, Michael Woods, Enda McDonagh, Margaret MacCurtain, John Whyte and Jim Kemmy were involved in their younger days. Lay people, feminists, clerics, Catholics, Protestants, Jews, would-be political leaders and future academics and journalists rubbed shoulders in a way that in its peaceable and almost comically respectable way was quietly revolutionary.[8]

Tuairim produced pamphlets on possible reforms of parliament and representative machinery, government and planning, Northern Ireland, higher education, the public care of children, censorship, and foreign affairs. It initiated an important debate on proportional representation by means of the single transferable vote in 1959, causing the Fianna Fáil political establishment a certain amount of covert and even overt irritation. Generally the organisation took a 'progressive' line on these matters, often in a way that would annoy older people but interest and even enthuse the younger generation.[9] Its style was consensual rather than confrontational, although occasionally the pamphlets showed a mild degree of directness or even righteous aggression. There seems to have been a general and rather shrewd awareness that antagonising powerful people might be counter-productive and that speaking softly and cogently from a position of sweet reasonableness would get more results in the medium run. Its irenic line was a way of coping cleverly with the obdurate authoritarianism of so many in the older generation, born, as it had been, of revolutionary violence, clerical education and pre-democratic politics. A sort of polite but determined intergenerational conflict was going on between those who remembered the British and the bitterness of the Civil War and those who were born too late to remember either and for whom independence was a dead historical given. Its irenic motto might have been 'We don't care what colour shirt you wore.'

LIMITS OF SWEET REASON

Despite a limited liberalisation, however, some subjects were impervious for some time to the blandishments of the sweetest of reasons. One of them was the institutional care of orphans and impoverished children. This huge and hideous subject is beyond the scope of this book; a case study is offered as an introduction to the magnificent work done by many scholars in the last thirty years.

Peter Tyrell (1916–67) was born into the large family of a very poor labourer in east Galway. To make a hopeless situation worse, the father was a ne'er-do-well who neglected his family. At the age of eight Peter, along with his brothers and sisters, was picked up by the Gardaí. The children were separated from each other. Peter was sent to Letterfrack Industrial School, an institution run by the

Christian Brothers and destined eventually to earn considerable notoriety. He was later to write an eminently fair-minded and devastating account of the school that destroyed him. He sent a copy of the typescript to Senator Owen Sheehy Skeffington in the sixties in the rather naïve hope of having some immediate impact on the political system by galvanising public opinion. He also contributed in 1966 to Tuairim's pamphlet on the industrial school system. A year later he burnt himself to death with petrol on Hampstead Heath in London.

On his first day in Letterfrack in 1924 Peter got a premonition of what was in store for him. Some of the boys were playing tip-and-tig in the open air.

Now all at once a Christian Brother comes running out, he is chasing the young children with a very long stick and beating them on the backs of the legs. We can now hear the screams of the little boys, some of them are only six years old. We are now frightened and struck with horror. We looked at Brother Dooley, he explained that the children get lazy and they just stand about or lean against the wall.

We are now taken down the steps to the yard or playground. I am now very lonely and frightened. Most of the children are terribly pale, and their faces are drawn and haggard. They are not like the children at home in Ahascragh school. They were always happy and smiling. The children of Letterfrack are like old men, most of their eyes are sunk in their heads and are red from crying. Their cheek-bones are sticking out. Joe now said, look at their hands. There was a boy of about my age [eight] the backs of his hands were terribly swollen, they were just a red mass of raw flesh. Brother Dooley explained that it was chilblains, which were caused by the cold, and not taking sufficient exercise.

We were reminded that we may be the same unless we played and ran about. We now came to a boy of about nine years, he was leaning against the wall, they called him 'Caleba' he was holding his hands loosely in front of the body, he was apparently asleep. There was another boy, beating him with a stick, to try and keep him awake. A boy now came running past us, he was about ten years old. He had very fair hair and was wearing glasses as he was almost blind, he was being chased by the same Christian Brother we seen earlier, beating the children. We were told his name was Brother Walsh, he was beating the fair haired boy across the back and legs with a heavy stick. Brother Dooley told us that this boy had a lazy mind and it was hoped that the beating would make him think like normal children.[10]

The book contains a relentless catalogue of beatings of small boys by the brothers, combined with isolated instances of an almost secretive kindness by more subordinate lay staff, possibly in terror of losing their jobs if they aroused the wrath of the senior brothers. Some of the brothers were themselves decent enough men but were under the domination of men who seemed to think that the main evil of childhood was laziness, and that this could be fixed by incessant and systematic thrashings. Children were beaten at random, for failure at lessons and for falling asleep during the day. Rather weirdly, instruction was good, and Peter became a pretty good tailor, although he really wanted to be a shoemaker.[11] By the time he was thirteen Peter was haunted by his ordeal, even in his sleep.

I now get bad dreams in my sleep, I was always running away, but there is a man behind me, and he is getting closer and closer. I want to scream but I can't. I now wake up and I am sweating all over. I want a drink of water but I am afraid to go in the dark. I try to keep awake because I am terrified to go asleep. I do sleep again but there is an even worse dream. I am flying over water, there is no land in sight, I am now losing height, as I touch the water I wake up again more afraid than before. It's now only a few days until the holidays commence and [Brother] Vale is standing at the organ, he appears to be looking towards our table, he is swaying slightly from side to side, like a cat about to spring at a mouse. He is swinging the rubber [truncheon] and hitting the leg of his trousers, we are well used to this, everyone knows he is about to beat someone, but who? That is the question . . . Vale becomes a savage brute during the last few days before going away on holiday, some of the lads say it's because he does not go home, but spends his holidays praying at a monastery. He now walks fairly quickly towards the kitchen. We dare not look to enquire where he is going, it would be just too bad if we did. All of a sudden there is a scream of agony as he attacks two boys. One lad we call 'Redskin' and John Kelly, they are both about twelve years old. There is no doubt as to who he is beating, I can recognise the voice of 'Redskin' and John Kelly as he cries 'please sir, forgive me sir', this is repeated every time he gets a blow. They each get about twenty blows on the back and head. Kelly is now being flogged. He is very brave and doesn't cry very much. I have seen this boy being savagely beaten on many occasions. He goes snow-white in the face. Vale always gives him several terrible blows on the backside when he is scrubbing the floor.[12]

Boys who were 'different', deformed or mentally disabled in some way were special targets of damaged men like Walsh and Vale.

They call big McLaughlin 'Kangaroo' because the day he came to the school Walsh said he looked like one. He has long legs and big ears, he is very backward at school, and has been flogged a lot more than anyone else. Boys who are not good-looking, or are in any way deformed, are laughed at, and ill-treated. Tom Thornton, a big lad for his age, has one leg, and is made to do serve duties, and washing up and scrubbing floors etc. I have seen him being beaten by Vale on the stump of his bad leg. He works in the tailor's shop and is a good tailor, he plays handball very well, and he can beat me easily.[13]

Interestingly enough, Tyrell does not mention the sexual molestation of children, which was certainly widespread in many of these schools. Possibly he was reticent, or alternatively the brothers became more adventurous later on as it dawned on them that they were invulnerable to outside attack, having the unconditional protection given to them by both major political parties. Certainly much of the aggression was driven by a repressed and inexpressible sexual frustration. Many of these young men had been dragooned into the clergy at the age of fourteen for economic reasons: to get rid of one more hungry mouth in the huge and impoverished farm families of the time. Tyrell documents the fact that some of the brothers, in defiance of the celibacy rule, had girl-friends and entertained them at the school's expense. On balance, it is to be suspected that Tyrell engaged in some self-censorship.

Tyrell just about survived Letterfrack physically, with considerable emotional stunting and with his prospects of a decent and happy life seriously damaged. Eventually he emigrated to Britain as a teenager and served in the British army. On the ship to England he encountered a young woman with her husband and a baby. As the ship pulled away from the harbour at Dún Laoghaire she looked eastwards toward Britain and said, 'I never want to see that island [of Ireland] again as long as I live.'[14] He saw military action in western Europe after D-Day and was taken prisoner in 1944 by the Germans. In the prison camps of the dying Reich he received better treatment and rations than he had done in Letterfrack. Afterwards he was so favourably impressed by the Germans that he refused point blank to believe in reports of the Nazi death camps.[15]

In his correspondence with Sheehy Skeffington in the sixties Tyrell evidently hoped that the planned publication of his memoir would cause some kind of public outcry in Ireland, even involving street demonstrations.[16] Although evidently a very intelligent and perceptive man, he probably did not fully understand the quiet and passive public consensus, reinforced by timorousness, that backed up the status quo in the Irish democracy. Apart from the Tuairim pamphlet, he wrote articles for *Hibernia*.[17] No great public outcry occurred; but in the sixties a slow but perceptible change was evolving in Irish public opinion about many officially sanctioned ideas and practices, and his contribution to the Tuairim pamphlet in 1966 may have had some small effect. However, the manuscript of Tyrell's book was lost in Sheehy Skeffington's papers because of the senator's unexpected death in 1970. In the early twenty-first century it was disinterred, edited and published by Diarmuid Whelan. It remains a classic of Irish autobiography, an extraordinary and terrifying description of the Irish children's gulag. It took until the end of the twentieth century for it to be possible to unveil the real history of what happened to the children of the poor in the tender care of the Irish Catholic Church.[18]

It was only from the late fifties onwards that the old nettle of literary and artistic censorship was finally, if timidly, grasped, partly through Tuairim and also through the efforts of independent-minded clerics such as Father Peter Connolly and Father Jack Kelly. Censorship was both strangely powerful and equally strangely restricted. Connolly argued at one stage that the censorship system was 'juvenile'.[19] It is quite clear that the Censorship Board waged a war against a range of writings that was far wider than pornography; a common remark at the time was that the list of banned books was a fairly competent digest of modern literature of any artistic or philosophical significance in the English language. Irish writers, often with a distinguished international reputation, were commonly particular targets. Films were exposed to an equally savage programme of bannings and cutting, the latter being so severe that the plots were sometimes impossible to follow.

Oddest of all was the fact that there was no censorship of theatre, despite sporadic attempts by ecclesiastics and the Government to squelch some production or other. The police, rather than the Censorship Board, were in charge of monitoring the probity of the stage and, by and large, left well enough alone unless prodded into action by clerical outrage or political circumstances. The Pike affair of 1957 was an example of one of these clumsy excursions into attempted police censorship; as we have seen, it was unsuccessful, and damaged the minister responsible. Furthermore, it was widely publicised at the time, in Ireland and elsewhere. The rather odd involvement of the police in censorship seems to have been in part a survival of the old pre-independence situation.[20] There was also the attitude that theatre-goers were likely to be more middle-class than the *hoi polloi* who went to 'the pictures' and were therefore less likely to be led into evil by advanced ideas put forward in plays by Irish Protestants such as Oscar Wilde, George Bernard Shaw or Denis Johnston. Another possible factor was a lingering fondness for the theatre of their own youth that certainly was present in the minds of some of the old leaders. Further, the cinema was regarded as something that was mainly for young people; older people went to films relatively rarely and often knew little about the medium. In the memory of this writer older people often had difficulty in following plots, time-lapse conventions and fade-ins. The cinema, therefore, was commonly regarded by older politicians and clergy as a particular 'occasion of sin' for the young. The close connection between low social class, theories of original sin and punitive policies in education and cultural policy was quite obvious. The 'submerged 30 per cent' occasionally nodded at guiltily or even fearfully by the Dublin media needed to be watched; they might yet get ideas above their station.

Behind all this was a network of lay organisations under the direct or indirect control of the Catholic bishops or, more interestingly, perhaps a cabal amongst these bishops. Chief among these was the Knights of Columbanus, which enjoyed considerable penetration of the Revenue Commissioners, the Department of Education, the Department of Health, parts of academia and much of business. There is as yet no satisfactory study of this once-powerful and much-despised organisation, whose membership and power reached a peak about 1970, experiencing a long and slow decline thereafter.

Public opinion in the Republic was also constrained by a nationalist and often sectarian orthodoxy that gripped sometimes the minds and more often the wills of the citizenry. A noisy and militaristic rhetoric about reunification and emotional reference to the tyrannical British rule of past centuries was engaged in by politicians of almost all stripes, as it distracted attention from the real and insistent social and economic problems that beset Ireland's little independent polity. As has been seen, newspapers were much inhibited by this rhetoric and in fact did much themselves to spread it around the country. However, in the fifties there could be seen in the press the germs of a more critical and free-spoken approach to the difficulties of political independence and also its potentials. Curiously, one of the sources of a new self-confidence was a hyper-nationalist documentary about the Easter Rising and the revolution in Ireland, George Morrison's *Mise Éire* (1959), its score by the up-and-coming musician Seán Ó Riada.

Independent Ireland was, then, less than totally free. Freedom of expression and of opinion was inhibited in many ways, and it took a generational change and the coming of films and television for this atmosphere of cultural fear to dissipate gradually over the following decades. Some would argue that it is still with us in 2010.

GOD WILL STILL PROVIDE

The 1950s, although the scene of a slow social and cultural upheaval, left traditional Ireland more or less intact, at least superficially. Practical problems were often still resolved by recourse to supernatural agency. A best-selling Catholic monthly, a little red-covered magazine, *Irish Messenger of the Sacred Heart,* ran a 'Thanksgiving' column throughout this entire period. Thousands of letters came in from both parts of Ireland and from Irish communities in Britain, Australia and North America, thanking God, the Blessed Virgin and various saints for relief from various worries, health scares, emotional quandaries or financial problems.[21] In January 1948 thanks were given that a daughter recovered from an illness, a daughter got a job and the wife stopped quarrelling with her husband. Another correspondent wrote in the same issue:

> Will you kindly find space in your MESSENGER to publish my grateful thanks to the Sacred Heart for the many favours I have received for the last seven years since we got married. I always get anything I pray for and during the worst years of the war I managed to get plenty of food when other people around me were always complaining. I have these healthy children and my husband is never out of work although he is only a casual labourer . . .

Another gave thanks that her daughter had been given back her health so she could stay as a novice in a convent; apparently you got thrown out if your health was dodgy—truly a Christian way of handling the problem. Other thanksgivings included passing an examination, winning a scholarship, being saved from death by drowning and having one's character cleared. One question asked in the same issue was, Could an ordinary working girl become a nun? (The reassuring answer was that certainly she could: convents always needed working girls for the kitchens.)[22]

In February 1948 thanks were offered for a conversion from Protestantism of a woman who married a Catholic son, the receipt of a satisfactory price for a house, passing an examination, a cousin's recovery from an operation, a husband's return to the sacraments after twelve years of abstention, the 'happy death' of a father, a relief from worry, a good harvest of crops and turf and the safe extraction of some teeth.[23] In March thanks were offered for averting the separation of a husband and wife.[24] In April a Protestant wrote in, having prayed, with success, for her husband's success in an examination. A teacher thanked the Sacred Heart for passing a school inspection.[25] In May thanks were given for finding a house at the right price, a Protestant proudly wrote that she was now praying like a Catholic, and thanks were given for a good crop, a death-bed conversion, a happy marriage, a job in a school, a success in an examination, peace of mind, a vocation to the priesthood, successful care of a sick animal, a successful law case and safety in a storm.[26] In June thanks were given for the finding of lost property, including the recovery of a bicycle, a watch, a garment, some money, a book, a ring and a handbag. A correspondent asked if it was licit to pray with a hat on while cycling or working. (Assurance was given that this activity was indeed pleasing to God.)[27] In August a correspondent wrote:

> Some months ago I got a spot on my lip which was very painful, and I believed myself I was getting cancer . . . my prayer was answered and the spot on my lip came to nothing, thanks to the Sacred Heart.[28]

In July 1948 a correspondent wrote gratefully: 'We leave everything to the Sacred Heart and we get what we need in His own time.'[29] It seems that while the British were building a welfare state the Irish had relied on a cheaper welfare system, supplied by the next world at a very small charge.

As late as 1962, at the end of the period under observation, things did not seem to have changed all that much. In January thanks were offered for gaining a post as schoolteacher, being successful as a soldier in the Congo, a husband passing all his examinations and a 'child obtains place in Catholic Grammar School.'[30] In February a student had not felt able to finance his own schooling but won a five-year scholarship, which solved the problem. The student did not have a high opinion of his own ability and ascribed his success gratefully to a higher power[31]; it does not seem to have occurred to him that his own efforts and intelligence might have been the explanation for his good fortune.

In April thanks were given for crops and property surviving a storm unscathed. An optical condition was cured. A dying person achieved 'resignation'. A correspondent was enabled to control his or her temper.[32] In May thanks were given for the safe return of a husband from abroad, a home saved from fire, an 'undesirable friendship broken off,' an 'undesirable engagement broken off' and the 'quiet settlement of a court case.'[33] In December the Deity and his mother were thanked for a successful Lourdes pilgrimage, 'fears of tuberculosis unfounded,' a 'Blue Card [medical card] granted' and being 'enabled to get comfortable spectacles.'[34] In November a correspondent announced happily that 'the Sacred Heart and Our Lady never fail me.'[35]

The spiritual welfare agency was apparently still working well for people who saw little relationship between their own efforts and the rewards and penalties exacted by a harsh, often unfair and somewhat incomprehensible world. The reassurance supplied by a traditional Catholicism offered a real psychological comfort that was genuinely appreciated.

Mervyn Wall described the cultural atmosphere of rural Ireland in 1948 in devastating terms.

> Even indoors he felt the heavy air and the small town lassitude, the sleepy atmosphere—eighty inches rainfall, everything damp: the fields, the roads, the exteriors and interiors of the houses. The brief spell of morning sunlight had already petered out, and the sky was grey, and charged with rain. As he gazed dully out at the sick landscape, he grew conscious of the peculiar, almost palpable, timelessness of the Irish countryside and the small town. It was as if a long time ago all the clocks had run down, and no one had since bothered to wind them up. Time simply did not exist; yet somewhere in its pocket were ten years of his life, lost irretrievably.[36]

From the viewpoint of the Ireland of 2010 fifties Ireland is indeed a distant mirror, but it is a mirror. We are not all that different from our ancestors, despite the extraordinary changes that have occurred. Magical thinking has not been abolished just because semi-pagan superstition and belief in routine divine intervention have gone into retreat. Magical thinking can survive in societies notionally inspired by rationalist and 'scientific' principles. Astrology columns are extraordinarily popular, probably more popular than they were in the fifties, because at that time they were subject to clerical denunciations, which were taken quite seriously. The church felt that if there had to be superstition in Ireland it would run it. Nowadays nobody manages superstition. It disguises itself in the fascination with UFOs, homeopathy, placebo medicines, unnecessary operations, managerial pseudo-solutions to non-problems, much of economics, quack diets, fake educational degrees, global warming, touching wood and not believing anything you read in the papers. Welcome to the nineteen-fifties.

NOTES

Chapter 1 Introduction (p. 1–16)

1. Gerard Whelan, with Carolyn Swift, *Spiked*, Dublin: New Island, 2002.
2. Brian Inglis, *West Briton*, London: Faber and Faber, 1962, 15.
3. In particular *Preventing the Future: Why Was Ireland So Poor for So Long?*, Dublin: Gill & Macmillan, 2004.
4. Terence Brown, *Ireland: A Social and Cultural History*, London: Harper Perennial, 2004, 204.
5. Terence Brown, *Ireland: A Social and Cultural History*, London: Harper Perennial, 2004, 206; see also Alexander Humphreys, *New Dubliners: Urbanisation and the Irish Family*, London: Routledge and Kegan Paul, 1966.
6. Terence Brown, *Ireland: A Social and Cultural History*, London: Harper Perennial, 2004, 214. See also Malcolm Ballin, *Irish Periodical Culture, 1937–1972: Genre in Ireland, Wales and Scotland*, New York: Palgrave Macmillan, 2008.
7. A copy of this fairest confection of the Christian Brothers survives in UCD Archives (AD UCD P150/2988, De Valera Papers).
8. 'Ireland will yet be Kate O'Dwyer's,' i.e. 'Kate' (Ireland) will get her entire land back (eighteenth-century poem).
9. *Irish Independent*, 1 July 1957.
10. *Irish Press*, 27 May 1957.
11. *Dublin Opinion*, September 1957. Ireland says to the fortune-teller, 'Get to work! They're saying I've no future.'
12. I owe this crystallisation to Frank Litton of the Institute of Public Administration, conversations, 12 February 2008.
13. Samuel P. Huntington, *Political Order in Changing Societies*, New Haven and London: Yale University Press, 1968, 433–61; Tom Garvin, *The Evolution of Irish Nationalist Politics*, Dublin: Gill & Macmillan, 1981, 1–13. Samuel Huntington, conversations,

1983–4. Huntington was particularly struck by the Indian example. For Irish and Indian parallels see Michael Silvestri, 'The Sinn Fein of India': Irish nationalism and the policing of revolutionary terrorism in Bengal,' *Journal of British Studies*, no. 39 (October 2000), 454–86. I am indebted to John O'Dowd for this last citation.

Chapter 2 Politics in the new republic, 1949–60 (p. 17–60)

1. *Irish Independent*, 17 May 1948.
2. C. S. Andrews, *A Man of No Property*, Dublin and Cork: Mercier, 1982, 85. The Furry Glen in the Phoenix Park was a legendary place for licit and illicit sex, renowned in song and story.
3. *Irish Independent*, 5 February 1951.
4. *Irish Independent*, 10 January 1949.
5. *Irish Times*, 16 April 1951.
6. *Irish Independent*, 28 February 1951.
7. *Irish Democrat*, January 1951.
8. *Irish Independent*, 11 January 1951.
9. *Leader*, 12 May 1951.
10. *Irish Press*, 18 March 1949.
11. On the Irish army in wartime see Clair Wills, *That Neutral Island*, London: Faber and Faber, 2007, 104–8 and passim.
12. *Irish Press*, 2 March 1948 (Vandenburg), 29 June 1948. See *Dublin Opinion*, September 1948, Marshall as the 'Payboy of the Western World'.
13. *Irish Democrat*, January 1951.
14. *Irish Press*, 27 April 1949.
15. R. F. Foster, *Modern Ireland, 1600–1972*, London: Allen Lane/Penguin Press, 1988, 566.
16. R. F. Foster, *Modern Ireland, 1600–1972*, London: Allen Lane/Penguin Press, 1988, 567.
17. Tom Garvin and Anthony Parker, 'Party loyalty and Irish voters: The EEC referendum as a case study,' *Economic and Social Review*, IV, 1972, 35–9.
18. Tom Garvin, 'The destiny of the soldiers: Tradition and

modernity in the politics of de Valera's Ireland,' *Political Studies*, vol. 26 (1978), 328–47.

19. Maryann Gialanella Valiulis, 'The man they could never forgive,' in J. P. O'Carroll and John A. Murphy (eds.), *De Valera and His Times*, Cork: Cork University Press, 1986, 92–100.

20. M. A. G. Ó Tuathaigh, 'De Valera and sovereignty: A note on the pedigree of an idea,' in J. P. O'Carroll and John A. Murphy, *De Valera and His Times*, Cork: Cork University Press, 1986, 63–72.

21. I am indebted to the late Liam de Paor for this insight.

22. C. S. Andrews, *Man of No Property*, Cork: Mercier, 1982.

23. C. S. Andrews, *Man of No Property*, Cork: Mercier, 1982, 346–7.

24. As quoted in R. F. Foster, *Modern Ireland, 1600–1972*, London: Allen Lane/Penguin Press, 1988, 567.

25. Tom Garvin, *Preventing the Future: Why Was Ireland So Poor for So Long?*, Dublin: Gill & Macmillan, 2004, 71–2.

26. John Whyte, *Church and State in Modern Ireland, 1923–1979* (second edition), Totowa (NJ): Barnes and Noble, 1980, 196–238.

27. *Irish Times*, 2 April 1951.

28. As quoted in Paul Blanshard, *The Irish and Catholic Power*, London: Derek Verschoyle, 1954, 81–2.

29. Seán Mac Réamoinn, conversations, 1990s.

30. Eimar O'Duffy, *Asses in Clover*, London: Putnam, 1933; *King Goshawk and the Birds*, London: Macmillan, 1926; *The Spacious Adventures of the Man in the Street*, London: Macmillan, 1928. Flann O'Brien is Brian O'Linn (hero of a nineteenth-century comic ballad) reversed.

31. Martin Quigley, *A US Spy in Ireland*, Dublin: Marino, 1999. The American images had replaced portraits of Arthur Griffith and Michael Collins in 1932 on de Valera's election to government. The fact that he had Lincoln's portrait on his wall was public knowledge; see *Dublin Opinion*, June 1953.

32. Martin Quigley, *A US Spy in Ireland*, Dublin: Marino, 1999, 97.

33. Martin Quigley, *A US Spy in Ireland*, Dublin: Marino, 1999, 103–4. On perceived analogies between the American and Irish revolutions see Kevin O'Sheil, *The Making of a Republic*,

Dublin: Talbot Press, 1920. O'Sheil was a well-known Sinn Féiner; the book is an informal and admiring history of the American revolution.

34. Charles Callan Tansill, *America and the Fight for Irish Freedom, 1866–1922*, New York: Devin-Adair, 1957.

35. *Leader*, 14 December 1946.

36. *Leader*, 10 July 1949.

37. *Bell*, vol. 16, no. 6 (March 1951), 7–18.

38. *Irish Press*, 23 January 1951.

39. 'Autoantiamericanism', 9.

40. 'Autoantiamericanism', 11.

41. 'Autoantiamericanism', 18.

42. *Bell*, vol. 17, no. 2 (May 1951), 8–28.

43. For example editorial in *Irish Independent*, 2 May 1951.

44. *Irish Democrat*, January 1951.

45. *Irish Democrat*, April 1953.

46. In March 1953, as a ten-year-old child in Ring College, Co. Waterford, I was ordered, with the rest of the class, to get down on my knees and pray for the soul of Joseph Stalin; without our prayers, we were assured, Stalin would roast in Hell for all eternity for the terrible crimes he had committed in this world. We really wanted to know what dreadful things he had done; no-one told us. Stalin's democratic claims were seen as a joke; *Dublin Opinion*, April 1950, published a cartoon portraying a worried Stalin in a dressing-gown in front of a bank of telephones as 'Stalin waiting up all night for the Russian election results.'

47. National Library of Ireland, Frank Gallagher Papers (NLI ms. 18,339); and I am again indebted to John Horgan for drawing my attention to this extraordinary document. See my *Preventing the Future: Why Was Ireland So Poor for So Long?*, Dublin: Gill & Macmillan, 2004, 45–8 and passim.

48. Tom Garvin, 'The French are on the sea,' in Rory O'Donnell (ed.), *Europe: The Irish Experience*, Dublin: Institute of European Affairs, 2000, 35–43.

49. As quoted in *Irish Times,* 10 February 1953.

50. *Irish Times,* 20 June 1953.

51. *Irish Press,* 21 May 1954.

52. *Irish Times,* 1 July 1954.

53. *Irish Times,* 7 July 1954.

54. *Standard,* 28 May 1954.

55. Al Cohan, *The Irish Political Elite,* Dublin: Gill & Macmillan, 1972.

56. *Irish Times,* 10 July 1954.

57. *Irish Times,* 25 September 1954.

58. *Irish Times,* 28 July 1955.

59. *Irish Times,* 12 October 1955.

60. *Irish Times,* 8 February 1956.

61. *Irish Times,* 27 February 1956. See also the *Statist,* as reprinted in *Irish Times,* 10 March 1956.

62. *Irish Press,* 6 June 1956.

63. *Standard,* 18 May 1956.

64. *Irish Times,* 12 June 1956.

65. *Irish Times,* 22 and 28 June 1956.

66. *Irish Times,* 23 February 1957.

67. *Irish Press,* 1 August 1956.

68. *Irish Independent,* 21 January 1957. Kelly quotation, 1980s, personal memory.

69. *Irish Independent,* 1 March 1957 (direct speech restored).

70. *Irish Independent,* 8 March 1957.

71. Tom Garvin, *Preventing the Future: Why Was Ireland So Poor for So Long?,* Dublin: Gill & Macmillan, 2004, 108–10; Charles Carter, 'The Irish economy viewed from without,' *Studies,* no. 46, 1957, 137–49. See also Charles Carter, 'The economic unity of Ireland,' *Studies,* no. 47, 1958, 379–87.

72. Charles Carter, 'The economic unity of Ireland,' *Studies,* no. 47, 1958, passim.

73. *Irish Press,* 13 January 1959.

74. *Irish Times,* 31 March and 1 and 9 April 1959. For a vivid portrait of the intimidation of teachers and civil servants by the

episcopate see T. J. McElligott, *This Teaching Life*, Mullingar: Lilliput Press, 1986, passim.

75. *Irish Independent*, 22 November 1957.

76. Albert Hirschman, *Exit, Voice and Loyalty: Responses to Decline in Firms, Organisations and States*, Cambridge (Mass.): Harvard University Press, 1970.

77. *Irish Independent*, 16 December 1957.

78. *Irish Times*, 28 November 1958. 'Gombeen' (a reduced form of 'gombeen-man') is a pejorative term that means a usurer, country-town spirit-grocer and local monopolist or, in journalism and academia, cultural faker by extension. From Irish *gaimbín*, usury.

79. *Irish Independent*, 28 August 1958.

80. Tom Garvin, 'Hogan as political scientist: Representative government in Ireland,' in Donnchadh Ó Corráin (ed.), *James Hogan: Revolutionary, Historian and Political Scientist*, Dublin: Four Courts Press, 2001, 177–84.

81. James Hogan, *Elections and Representation*, Cork: Cork University Press, 1945; Tom Garvin, 'Hogan as political scientist: Representative government in Ireland,' in Donnchadh Ó Corráin (ed.), *James Hogan: Revolutionary, Historian and Political Scientist*, Dublin: Four Courts Press, 2001, passim.

82. R. K. Carty, *Party and Parish Pump: Electoral Politics in Ireland*, Waterloo (Ont.): Wilfrid Laurier University Press, 1981.

83. *Irish Independent*, 9 January 1959.

84. *Irish Independent*, 23 January 1959.

85. John Horgan, *Seán Lemass: The Enigmatic Patriot*, Dublin: Gill & Macmillan, 1997, 182.

86. *Irish Times*, 18, 20, 23 and 24 June 1959.

87. Richard Rose and Tom Garvin, 'The public policy effects of independence: Ireland as a test case,' *European Journal of Political Research*, vol. 11 (1983), 377–97, on eras in Irish public policy.

88. *Irish Times*, 17 September 1960.

Chapter 3 Dublin newspapers and the crisis of the fifties (p. 61–77)

1. *Irish Press,* 10 January 1948.
2. *Dublin Opinion,* October 1948.
3. *Irish Independent,* 11 March 1949.
4. *Irish Independent,* 21 May 1949.
5. *Irish Times,* 23 July 1951.
6. *Irish Times,* 8 January 1952.
7. *Irish Times,* 22 January 1952.
8. *Irish Press,* 29 July 1953.
9. *Irish Times,* 10 February 1953.
10. *Irish Independent,* 13 February 1954.
11. *Irish Times,* 16 February 1953.
12. *Irish Times,* 7 July 1954.
13. *Irish Independent,* 14 May 1954.
14. *Irish Independent,* 15 June 1954.
15. *Irish Independent,* 25 and 29 June 1954.
16. *Irish Independent,* 1 October 1954.
17. *Irish Press,* 9 March 1954.
18. *Irish Press,* 27 November 1954.
19. *Irish Press,* 12 May 1955.
20. *Standard,* 31 August 1956.
21. *Hibernia,* September 1956.
22. *Irish Times,* 1 November 1956.
23. *Irish Times,* 8 November 1956.
24. *Irish Times,* 28 March 1957.
25. *Irish Independent,* 20 May 1959.
26. *Irish Independent,* 9 May 1960.
27. *Irish Independent,* 19 January 1949.
28. *Irish Democrat,* July 1951.
29. *Irish Press,* 3 September 1949.
30. *Irish Times,* 3 September 1949.
31. *Irish Press,* 31 May 1950.
32. *Irish Times,* 10 March 1950.
33. Brian Farrell, *Seán Lemass,* Dublin: Gill & Macmillan, 1991, 82–3.
34. *Irish Press,* 8 November 1952.

35. *Irish Times*, 18 January 1952.

36. *Irish Press*, 27 June 1953.

37. *Irish Press*, 27 June 1953.

38. *Irish Press*, 20 July 1953.

39. *Irish Times*, 10 October 1953.

40. *Irish Independent*, 29 June 1954.

41. *Irish Independent*, 23 July 1954.

42. *Irish Times*, 14 September 1954.

43. *Irish Independent*, 15 December 1954.

44. *Irish Press*, 3 November 1955.

45. *Irish Press*, 16 November 1955.

46. *Irish Press*, 8 February 1956.

47. *Irish Press*, 18 June 1956.

48. *Irish Press*, 18 June 1956.

49. *Irish Times*, 2 October 1956.

50. *Irish Press*, 22 February 1957.

51. *Irish Press*, 27 May 1957.

52. *Irish Press*, 27 May 1957.

53. *Irish Press*, 31 May 1957.

54. *Irish Times*, 22 August 1957.

55. *Irish Press*, 23 October 1957. See also *Irish Press*, 25 September 1957.

56. *Irish Press*, 23 December 1957.

57. *Irish Press*, 11 February 1958.

58. *Irish Press*, 14 February 1958.

59. *Irish Independent*, 24 March 1958.

60. *Irish Press*, 12 November 1958.

61. *Irish Press*, 13 July 1959 (direct speech restored).

62. *Irish Times*, 7 November 1959.

63. *Irish Independent*, 26 November 1958.

64. *Irish Independent*, 15 January 1960.

65. *Irish Independent*, 28 January 1960.

Chapter 4 From field to factory (p. 78–113)

1. Brian Farrell, *Seán Lemass,* Dublin: Gill & Macmillan, 1991, 30.
2. Brian Farrell, *Seán Lemass,* Dublin: Gill & Macmillan, 1991, 30.
3. Tom Garvin, *Judging Lemass: The Measure of the Man,* Dublin: Royal Irish Academy, 2009.
4. *Irish Times,* 18 February 1949
5. *Irish Independent,* 7 April 1949.
6. *Irish Times,* 22 March, 8 April 1949.
7. *Irish Times,* 23 April 1949.
8. *Irish Press,* 24 January 1949.
9. *Irish Press,* 23 January 1950.
10. *Irish Independent,* 3 July 1950.
11. *Irish Independent,* 11 June 1950.
12. *Irish Independent,* 30 June 1950.
13. *Irish Independent,* 22 July 1950.
14. *Irish Times,* 18 May and 26 September 1950.
15. *Irish Independent,* 23 October 1950.
16. *Irish Independent,* 11 December 1951.
17. *Irish Independent,* 21 February 1952.
18. *Irish Press,* 13 March 1953.
19. *Irish Press,* 29 July 1953.
20. *Irish Times,* 2 October 1954.
21. *Irish Independent,* 14 May 1954.
22. *Irish Press,* 27 November 1954.
23. *Irish Times,* 16 June 1954.
24. *Irish Independent,* 7 December 1954.
25. *Irish Independent,* 31 March 1955.
26. *Irish Independent,* 13 October 1955.
27. *Spectator,* 20 April 1956.
28. *Irish Press,* 27 July 1956.
29. *Irish Times,* 18 September 1956.
30. *Irish Independent,* 22 September 1957.
31. *Irish Press,* 11 February 1958
32. *Irish Independent,* 7 May 1958. On clerical fears see Tom Garvin, *Preventing the Future: Why Was Ireland So Poor for So Long?,* Dublin: Gill & Macmillan, 2004, 36–7.

33. *Irish Press,* 7 May 1958.

34. *Irish Independent,* January 1959.

35. *Irish Independent,* 24 February 1959.

36. *Irish Independent,* 20 May 1959.

37. *Irish Independent,* 1 July 1959.

38. *Irish Times,* 29 January 1959.

39. *Irish Times,* 7 October 1959.

40. *Irish Independent,* 26 September 1959.

41. *Irish Independent,* 24 and 28 November 1959.

42. *Standard,* 6 March 1959.

43. *Irish Independent,* 9 May 1960.

44. *Irish Press,* 2 March 1949 (direct speech restored).

45. *Irish Democrat,* July 1951.

46. *Irish Democrat,* July 1951.

47. *Irish Independent,* 3 March 1950.

48. *Irish Press,* 12 March 1948.

49. *Irish Press,* 12 April 1948.

50. *Irish Press,* 20 April 1948.

51. *Irish Press,* 3 June 1948.

52. *Irish Press,* 26 April 1948.

53. *Irish Press,* 14 January 1949.

54. *Irish Press,* 18 January and 5 February 1949.

55. *Irish Independent,* 13 January 1949.

56. *Irish Press,* 25 February 1949.

57. *Irish Press,* 1 March 1949.

58. *Irish Times,* 14 January 1949.

59. *Irish Times,* 14 February 1949.

60. *Irish Times,* 3 May 1949.

61. *Irish Press,* 3 September 1949.

62. *Irish Times,* 10 December 1949

63. *Irish Press,* 16 January 1950.

64. *Irish Times,* 10 March 1950.

65. Brian Farrell, *Seán Lemass,* Dublin: Gill & Macmillan, 1991, 82–3.

66. *Irish Times,* 15 April 1950.

67. *Irish Times*, 13 May 1950.

68. *Irish Times*, 20 January 1951.

69. *Irish Press*, 19 October 1950.

70. *Irish Press*, 2 February 1951.

71. *Irish Independent*, 2 February 1951.

72. *Irish Times*, 8 January 1952.

73. *Irish Times*, 18 January 1952.

74. *Irish Times*, 6 February 1952.

75. *Irish Independent*, 10 March 1952.

76. *Irish Times*, 9 and 12 February 1952.

77. *Irish Times*, 3 April 1952.

78. *Irish Times*, 21 and 22 November 1952.

79. *Irish Press*, 8 and 9 January 1953.

80. *Irish Press*, 27 June 1953.

81. *Irish Times*, 3 August 1953.

82. *Irish Times*, 3 July 1954.

83. *Irish Independent*, 23 July 1954.

84. *Irish Times*, 14 September 1954.

85. *Irish Press*, 18 March 1955.

86. *Irish Press*, 19 May 1955.

87. *Irish Times*, 13 July 1955.

88. *Irish Press*, 12 October 1955.

89. *Irish Press*, 3 November 1955.

90. *Irish Press*, 6 January 1956.

91. *Irish Times*, 10, 13 and 17 January 1956.

92. *Irish Times*, 2 October 1956.

93. *Irish Times*, 14 December 1956.

94. *Irish Press*, 29 May 1957.

95. *Irish Independent*, 29 May 1957.

96. *Irish Independent*, 29 May 1957.

97. *Irish Press*, 31 May 1957.

98. *Irish Times*, 22 August 1957.

99. *Irish Press*, 23 October 1957. See also *Irish Press*, 25 September 1957.

100. *Irish Press*, 15 November 1957.

101. *Irish Times*, 6 November 1957.

102. *Irish Press*, 15 January 1958.

103. *Irish Press*, 11 February 1958.

104. *Irish Press*, 23 September 1959.

105. *Irish Press*, 30 October and 11 November 1959.

106. *Irish Times*, 7 November 1959.

107. *Irish Times*, 7 November 1959.

108. *Irish Independent*, 2 August 1960.

Chapter 5 What we have we hold: The world of work (p. 114–55)

1. *Irish Times*, 29 January 1959.

2. Gustave de Beaumont, *Ireland: Social, Political, Religious* [1839], Cambridge (Mass.): Belknap Press of Harvard University Press, 2006, 386–8.

3. Edward Banfield, *The Moral Basis of a Backward Society*, New York: Free Press, 1958. See my *Preventing the Future: Why Was Ireland So Poor for So Long?*, Dublin: Gill & Macmillan, 2004, 101.

4. *Bell*, vol. 17, no. 9, December 1951, 7–17.

5. *Irish Independent*, 2 February 1949.

6. *Irish Independent*, 5 March 1949.

7. *Irish Independent*, 23 November 1949.

8. *Irish Press*, 9 November 1949.

9. *Irish Press*, October 1949 to March 1950. 'Borstal story,' *Irish Press*, 8 February 1950.

10. *Irish Press*, 11 May 1950.

11. *Irish Press*, 21 November 1949.

12. *Irish Press*, 28 October 1949.

13. *Irish Press*, 20 March 1950.

14. *Irish Independent*, 20 April 1950.

15. *Irish Times*, 9 June 1950.

16. *Irish Independent*, 8 November 1950.

17. *Irish Independent*, 8 November 1950.

18. *Irish Times*, 9 December 1950.

19. *Irish Independent*, 12 February 1951.

20. *Irish Independent*, 15 February 1951.

21. *Bell*, vol. 17, no. 2, May 1951, 8–28.

22. *Irish Times*, 16 November 1951.

23. *Standard*, 11 May 1951.

24. *Bell*, vol. 17, no. 9, December 1951, 7–17.

25. *Irish Independent*, 30 April 1952; *Irish Times*, 24, 26 and 30 April 1952.

26. *Irish Independent*, 2 May 1952.

27. *Irish Independent*, 2 May 1952.

28. *Irish Times*, 14 June 1952.

29. *Irish Independent*, 11 June 1952. See also *Irish Times*, 11 June 1951, for an earlier comment on dynasticism in Irish trades.

30. *Irish Independent*, 16 September 1952.

31. *Irish Independent*, 25 September 1952 (direct speech restored).

32. Gustave de Beaumont, *Ireland: Social, Political, Religious* [1839], Cambridge (Mass.): Belknap Press of Harvard University Press, 2006, 397–403.

33. *Irish Independent*, 17 October 1952.

34. *Irish Times*, 3 July 1952.

35. *Irish Times*, 17 October 1952.

36. *Irish Times*, 18 October 1952

37. *Irish Times*, 17 October 1952.

38. *Irish Independent*, 22 October 1952.

39. *Irish Independent*, 1 November 1952.

40. *Irish Independent*, 1 November 1952.

41. *Irish Independent*, 1 November 1952.

42. *Irish Independent*, 7 November 1952.

43. Michael O'Sullivan, *Seán Lemass: A Biography*, Dublin: Blackwater Press, 115–18. Morrissey quotation on Lemass, 115.

44. *Irish Times*, 28 August 1953.

45. *Irish Times*, 28 August 1953.

46. *Irish Independent*, 13 November 1952.

47. *Irish Times*, 24 and 25 February 1949.

48. *Irish Times*, 18 March 1949.

49. *Irish Times*, 15 March 1954.

50. *Irish Times,* 5 January 1954.

51. *Irish Times,* 5 January 1954.

52. *Irish Times,* 27 January 1954.

53. *Irish Times,* 10 February 1954.

54. *Irish Times,* 12 February 1954.

55. *Irish Press,* 17 July 1954.

56. *Irish Times,* 4 October 1954.

57. *Irish Times,* 3 May 1955.

58. *Irish Times,* 3 May 1955.

59. *Irish Times,* 4 May 1955.

60. Brian Farrell, *Seán Lemass,* Dublin: Gill & Macmillan, 1991, 93.

61. *Irish Times,* 24 February 1955.

62. *Irish Times,* 26 March 1955.

63. *Irish Times,* 28 January 1956.

64. *Irish Times,* 11 February 1956.

65. See *Irish Times,* 12 February 1952. M. P. Linehan, president of the Irish Conference of Professional and Service Associations: 'The Industrial Efficiency and Prices Bill of 1947 was an attempt to remedy this state of affairs. It was, however, killed by powerful influences.'

66. *Irish Times,* 19 May 1956.

67. *Irish Times,* 8 September 1956.

68. *Irish Times,* 8 October 1956.

69. *Irish Times,* 1 November 1956.

70. *Irish Times,* 5 February 1957.

71. Contrast *Irish Times,* 15 February and 1 May 1957—before and after the Fianna Fáil electoral victory.

72. *Irish Press,* 1 June 1957.

73. *Irish Times,* 23 October 1957.

74. *Irish Times,* 6 November 1957.

75. *Irish Times,* 1 January 1958.

76. *Irish Times,* 23 May 1958.

77. *Irish Times,* 7 July 1958.

78. *Irish Times,* 7 July 1958.

79. *Irish Times,* 9 December 1958.

80. *Irish Times,* 30 January 1959.
81. *Irish Times,* 23 February 1959
82. *Irish Times,* 5 March 1959.
83. *Irish Press,* 11 April 1959.
84. *Irish Times,* 16 October 1959.
85. *Irish Independent,* 23 October 1959.
86. *Irish Independent,* 9 September 1959.
87. *Irish Times,* 29 December 1959.
88. Cf. Gary Murphy, 'Towards a corporate state?: Seán Lemass and the realignment of interest groups in the policy process, 1948–1964,' *Administration,* vol. 51, no. 1–2 (spring–summer 2003), 105–18.

Chapter 6 Learning and training: The education wars (p. 156–97)

1. Dublin Diocesan Archives, McQuaid Papers, Hierarchy Minutes, 1941–9 (AB 8/XV/b/01–06), 24 April 1942. Rates were a local property tax.
2. See my *Preventing the Future: Why Was Ireland So Poor for So Long?,* Dublin: Gill & Macmillan, 2004, 125–69. See Peadar Kirby, 'Preventing the future or distorting the past?: Tom Garvin on Mancur Olson and the cause of Ireland's underdevelopment,' *Administration,* vol. 54, no. 3 (2006), 55–68, for a particularly confused and ill-informed critique. See also Kieran Allen, *Village,* 2–8 October 2004, for an unconsciously bewildered assessment.
3. Kevin O'Nolan (ed.), *The Best of Myles,* London, Picador, 1977, 93.
4. *Parliamentary Debates: Dáil Éireann: Official Report,* 23 October 1947.
5. *Irish Independent,* 19 January 1949.
6. *Irish Times,* 19 August 1949.
7. *Irish Independent,* 23 March and 11 April 1949.
8. *Irish Independent,* 22 September 1949.
9. *Irish Times,* 29 September 1949.
10. *Irish Independent,* 15 June 1950.

11. *Irish Press*, 22 June 1949.

12. *Irish Press*, 29 September 1949

13. *Irish Times*, 17 April 1950.

14. *Irish Independent*, 2 August 1950.

15. *Irish Independent*, 2 August 1950.

16. *Irish Press*, 17 April 1950,

17. *Irish Press*, 6 June 1950.

18. *Irish Independent*, 24 April 1950.

19. *Irish Independent*, 24 May 1950.

20. *Irish Times*, 30 October and 8 November 1950.

21. *Irish Times*, 28 March 1951.

22. *Irish Times*, 30 March 1951.

23. *Irish Times*, 23 July 1951.

24. *Irish Independent*, 28 September 1951.

25. *Irish Independent*, 11 December 1951.

26. *Irish Press*, 12 October 1951.

27. *Irish Press*, 12 October 1951.

28. *Irish Times*, 12 October 1951.

29. *Irish Times*, 24 January 1952.

30. *Irish Independent*, 18 January 1952.

31. *Irish Independent*, 5 January 1953.

32. *Irish Independent*, 6 June 1953.

33. *Irish Independent*, 25 July 1953.

34. *Irish Times*, 16 April 1953.

35. *Irish Independent*, 12 September 1953.

36. *Irish Press*, 8 and 9 January 1953.

37. *Irish Independent*, 29 September 1953.

38. *Irish Press*, 28 September 1953.

39. *Irish Independent*, 9 November 1953 (for Moylan), 10 and 20 November 1953.

40. *Irish Independent*, 18 January, 17 June 1954.

41. *Irish Times*, 9 June 1953.

42. *Irish Independent*, 23 July 1954 (direct speech restored).

43. *Irish Independent*, 11 October 1954.

44. *Irish Press*, 12 February 1954.

45. *Irish Press*, 15 June 1954.

46. *Irish Independent*, 13 November 1954.

47. *Irish Independent*, 9 December 1954.

48. *Irish Independent*, 1 January 1955.

49. *Irish Press*, 19 January 1955

50. *Irish Independent*, 15 April 1955.

51. *Irish Independent*, 19 and 21 April 1955.

52. *Irish Press*, 19 April 1955.

53. *Irish Press*, 2 July 1955.

54. *Irish Independent*, 17 June 1955.

55. *Irish Press*, 16 September 1955.

56. *Irish Times*, 8 September 1955.

57. *Irish Times*, 12 September 1955.

58. *Irish Independent*, 24 October 1955.

59. *Irish Press*, 20 October 1955.

60. *Irish Times*, 22 October 1955.

61. Irish Times, 20 October 1955.

62. *Irish Times*, 15, 16 and 28 November 1955.

63. *Irish Times*, 16 November 1955.

64. *Irish Independent*, 17 January 1956.

65. *Irish Independent*, 16 May 1956.

66. *Irish Independent*, 2 July 1956.

67. *Irish Times*, 16 June 1956.

68. *Irish Independent*, 20 July 1956.

69. *Irish Times*, 19 June 1956 (William Norton).

70. *Irish Independent*, 30 October 1956.

71. *Irish Press*, 20 September 1955.

72. *Irish Times*, 4 July 1956.

73. *Irish Independent*, 2 May 1957.

74. *Irish Independent*, 6 May 1957.

75. *Irish Press*, 9 March 1956.

76. *Irish Press*, 12 March 1956.

77. *Irish Press*, 5 April 1956

78. *Irish Press*, 16 July 1956; *Irish Times*, 16 July 1956. In 2008 this relatively low expenditure on third-level education still existed.

79. *Irish Times,* 19 July 1956.

80. *Irish Press,* 14 December 1956.

81. *Irish Times,* 22 September 1956.

82. *Irish Times,* 25 September 1956.

83. *Irish Times,* 6 October 1956.

84. *Irish Independent,* 9 December 1957, 21 February 1958.

85. *Irish Press,* 3 January 1957.

86. *Irish Press,* 2 May 1957; *Preventing the Future: Why Was Ireland So Poor for So Long?,* Dublin: Gill & Macmillan, 2004, 151.

87. *Irish Times,* 28 January 1957. Direct speech restored.

88. *Irish Times,* 28 February 1957.

89. *Irish Independent,* 15 March, 23 May 1958.

90. *Irish Press,* 25 April 1957.

91. *Irish Times,* 25 April 1957.

92. *Irish Press,* 7 August 1957.

93. *Irish Press,* 22 June 1957.

94. *Irish Times,* 5, 11 September 1957.

95. *Irish Press,* 4, 10 February, 11 June 1958.

96. *Irish Times,* 28 March 1958.

97. *Irish Press,* 11 February 1958, direct speech restored.

98. *Irish Press,* 23 May 1958.

99. *Irish Times,* 9 April 1958.

100. *Irish Times,* 10 April 1958.

101. *Irish Independent,* 2 May 1958, direct speech restored.

102. *Irish Times,* 23 May 1958.

103. *Irish Times,* 21 May 1958.

104. *Irish Independent,* 4 October 1958.

105. *Irish Independent,* 20, 21 October, 15 November 1958.

106. *Irish Times,* 1 November 1958.

107. *Irish Times,* 8 November 1958.

108. *Irish Times,* 15 November 1958.

109. *Irish Times,* 7 December 1958.

110. *Hibernia,* May 1959.

111. *Irish Independent,* 22 January 1959.

112. *Irish Press,* 9 January 1959.

113. *Irish Press*, 2 April 1959.

114. *Irish Times*, 7 March 1959.

115. *Irish Press*, 10 June 1959.

116. *National Observer*, July 1959.

117. *Irish Independent*, 24 September 1959.

118. *Irish Independent*, 8 October 1959.

119. *Irish Independent*, 13 October 1959.

120. *Irish Independent*, 13 October 1959.

121. *Irish Independent*, 12 December 1959.

122. *Irish Independent*, 19 February 1960.

123. *Irish Independent*, 29 February 1960.

124. *Irish Independent*, 22 February 1960.

125. *Irish Independent*, 5 March 1960.

126. *Irish Times*, 31 March, 1 April 1959.

127. *Irish Times*, 14 December 1959.

128. *Irish Independent*, 20 April 1960.

129. *Irish Independent*, 22 April 1960.

130. *Irish Times*, 21 April 1959.

131. *Irish Independent*, 27 April 1960.

132. *National Observer*, September 1960.

133. *Irish Independent*, 3 September 1960.

134. Tom Garvin, *Preventing the Future: Why Was Ireland So Poor for So Long?*, Dublin: Gill & Macmillan, 2004, 147–8.

135. *Irish Independent*, 30 January 1961.

136. *Irish Independent*, 11 February 1961 (for O'Meara), 2 February 1961 (editorial). For O'Meara see also *Hibernia*, April and July 1961.

137. *Irish Independent*, 6, 7 and 10 March 1961.

138. *Irish Independent*, 9 June 1961.

139. *Irish Independent*, 23 September 1961.

140. Tuairim, Pamphlet No. 9, London, 1962, 2–4.

141. Tuairim, Pamphlet No. 9, London, 1962, 3–4.

142. Tuairim, Pamphlet No. 9, London, 1962, 5–6.

143. Tuairim, Pamphlet No. 9, London, 1962, 7.

144. *Irish Independent*, 15 February 1962.

Chapter 7 Dublin opinions: A distant mirror (p. 198–216)

1. Barbara Tuchman, *A Distant Mirror,* New York: Alfred A. Knopf, 1978.

2. Mervyn Wall, *Leaves for the Burning,* London: Methuen, 1952, 165.

3. *National Observer,* vol. 1, no. 1, 1958, editorial. This was possibly written by Alexis Fitzgerald.

4. Honor Tracy, *Mind You, I've Said Nothing,* London: Methuen, 1953.

5. Tom Garvin, 'The quiet tragedy of Canon Sheehan,' *Studies,* summer 2009, 159–68

6. Michael Sheehy, *Is Ireland Dying?,* London: Hollis and Carter, 1968, 153.

7. Tomás Finn, 'The Influence of Tuairim on Intellectual Debate and Policy Formulation in Ireland, 1954–1975,' PhD thesis, Department of History, National University of Ireland, Galway, 2008, 1, 12–19. The articles 40–45 condition was dropped in 1966, Finn, 17–18.

8. Tomás Finn, 'The Influence of Tuairim on Intellectual Debate and Policy Formulation in Ireland, 1954–1975,' PhD thesis, Department of History, National University of Ireland, Galway, 2008, 14–17.

9. Tomás Finn, 'The Influence of Tuairim on Intellectual Debate and Policy Formulation in Ireland, 1954–1975,' PhD thesis, Department of History, National University of Ireland, Galway, 2008, passim.

10. Peter Tyrell (ed. Diarmuid Whelan), *Founded on Fear,* Dublin: Transworld Ireland, 2008, 70.

11. Peter Tyrell (ed. Diarmuid Whelan), *Founded on Fear,* Dublin: Transworld Ireland, 2008, 122.

12. Peter Tyrell (ed. Diarmuid Whelan), *Founded on Fear,* Dublin: Transworld Ireland, 2008, 160–61.

13. Peter Tyrell (ed. Diarmuid Whelan), *Founded on Fear,* Dublin: Transworld Ireland, 2008, 185.

14. Peter Tyrell (ed. Diarmuid Whelan), *Founded on Fear,* Dublin:

Transworld Ireland, 2008, 233.

15. Peter Tyrell (ed. Diarmuid Whelan), *Founded on Fear*, Dublin: Transworld Ireland, 2008, 301–11.

16. Peter Tyrell (ed. Diarmuid Whelan), *Founded on Fear*, Dublin: Transworld Ireland, 2008, 35–7.

17. Andrée Sheehy Skeffington, *Skeff: A Life of Owen Sheehy Skeffington, 1909–1970*, Dublin: Lilliput Press, 1991, 190–91. On the systematic abuse of children see in particular Mary Raftery and Eoin O'Sullivan, *Suffer the Little Children*, Dublin: New Island, 1999. On *Hibernia*, Rebecca Gageby, 'Hibernia, 1968–1980,' MA thesis, Department of Politics, University College, Dublin, 1998, 1–14.

18. Bruce Arnold, in *The Irish Gulag: How the State Betrayed Its Innocent Children*, Dublin: Gill & Macmillan, 2009, provides an authoritative and damning survey of the process by which the Irish state threw the children of the poor to clerical wolves. However, it must be remembered that the power of the church was greater than that of the state in areas of this kind; to demonise the state is to appear to exonerate, at least partially, a church that hid behind the state while forcing barbarous policies on the state apparatus. It must also be admitted that the Irish gulag was, in part, a symptom of general underdevelopment and a consequent material, moral and cultural poverty. Cf. Edward Banfield, *The Moral Basis of a Backward Society*, New York: Free Press, 1958.

19. Tomás Finn, 'The Influence of Tuairim on Intellectual Debate and Policy Formulation in Ireland, 1954–1975,' PhD thesis, Department of History, National University of Ireland, Galway, 2008, 343.

20. Andrée Sheehy Skeffington, *Skeff: A Life of Owen Sheehy Skeffington, 1909–1970*, Dublin: Lilliput Press, 1991,187–8.

21. *Irish Messenger of the Sacred Heart*, 1948–62.

22. *Irish Messenger of the Sacred Heart*, January 1948.

23. *Irish Messenger of the Sacred Heart*, February 1948.

24. *Irish Messenger of the Sacred Heart*, March 1948.

25. *Irish Messenger of the Sacred Heart*, April 1948.

26. *Irish Messenger of the Sacred Heart*, May 1948.

27. *Irish Messenger of the Sacred Heart*, June, 1948.

28. *Irish Messenger of the Sacred Heart*, August 1948.

29. *Irish Messenger of the Sacred Heart*, July 1948.

30. *Irish Messenger of the Sacred Heart*, January 1962.

31. *Irish Messenger of the Sacred Heart*, February 1962.

32. *Irish Messenger of the Sacred Heart*, April 1962.

33. *Irish Messenger of the Sacred Heart*, May 1962.

34. *Irish Messenger of the Sacred Heart*, September 1962.

35. *Irish Messenger of the Sacred Heart*, November 1962.

36. Mervyn Wall, *Leaves for the Burning*, London: Methuen, 1952, 21.

INDEX